Music, Sound and Film....

Music, Sound and Filmmakers: Sonic Style in Cinema examines the work of filmmakers whose concern is not just for the eye, but also for the ear. The bulk of the text focuses on the work of directors Wes Anderson, Ingmar Bergman, the Coen brothers, Peter Greenaway, Krzysztof Kieślowski, Stanley Kubrick, David Lynch, Quentin Tarantino, Andrey Tarkovsky and Gus Van Sant. Significantly, the anthology includes a discussion of films administratively controlled by such famously sound-conscious producers as David O. Selznick and Val Lewton. Written by the leading film music scholars from Europe, North America, and Australia, *Music, Sound and Filmmakers: Sonic Style in Cinema* will complement other volumes in Film Music coursework, or stand on its own among a body of research.

Contributors: Per F. Broman, Lisa Coulthard, Elizabeth Fairweather, Joseph G. Kickasola, Danijela Kulezic-Wilson, Michael Lee, Matthew McDonald, Kate McQuiston, Nathan Platte, Ian Sapiro, Isabella Van Elferen, James Wierzbicki, Ben Winters

James Wierzbicki teaches Musicology at the University of Sydney.

Routledge Music and Screen Media Series
Series Editor: Neil Lerner

The **Routledge Music and Screen Media Series** offers edited collections of original essays on music in particular genres of cinema, television, videogames, and new media. These edited essay collections are written for an interdisciplinary audience of students and scholars of music and film and media studies.

Music, Sound and Filmmakers: Sonic Style in Cinema
Edited by James Wierzbicki

Music in the Western: Notes from the Frontier
Edited by Kathryn Kalinak

Music in Television: Channels of Listening
Edited by James Deaville

Music in the Horror Film: Listening to Fear
Edited by Neil Lerner

Music, Sound and Filmmakers

Sonic Style in Cinema

Edited by James Wierzbicki

Routledge
Taylor & Francis Group

NEW YORK AND LONDON

First published 2012
by Routledge
711 Third Avenue, New York, NY 10017

Simultaneously published in the UK
by Routledge
2 Park Square, Milton Park, Abingdon, Oxon OX14 4RN

Routledge is an imprint of the Taylor & Francis Group, an informa business

Library of Congress Cataloging-in-Publication Data
Music, sound and filmmakers : sonic style in cinema / edited by
James Wierzbicki.
    p. cm.
Includes bibliographical references and index.
1. Motion picture music–History and criticism. 2. Sound in motion
pictures. 3. Motion picture producers and directors. I. Wierzbicki,
James Eugene, editor.
ML2075.M8797 2012
781.5'42–dc23

ISBN: 978-0-415-89893-5 (hbk)
ISBN: 978-0-415-89894-2 (pbk)
ISBN: 978-0-203-34309-8 (ebk)

Typeset in Goudy
by Cenveo Publisher Services

Senior Editor: Constance Ditzel
Senior Editorial Assistant: Mike Andrews
Production Manager: Meesha Nehru
Marketing Manager: Joon Won Moon
Copy Editor: Gail Welsh
Proofreader: Nikky Twyman
Cover Design: Salamander Hill Design

Printed and bound in the United States of America
by Edwards Brothers, Inc.

To St. John's College, Sydney,
whose motto is "Nisi Dominus Frustra"

Contents

Series Foreword

While the scholarly conversations about music in film and visual media have been expanding prodigiously since the last quarter of the twentieth century, a need remains for focused, specialized studies of particular films as they relate more broadly to genres. This series includes scholars from across the disciplines of music and film and media studies, specialists in both the audible as well as the visual, who share the goal of broadening and deepening these scholarly dialogues about music in particular genres of cinema, television, videogames, and new media. Claiming a chronological arc from the birth of cinema in the 1890s to the most recent releases, the *Routledge Music and Screen Media Series* offers collections of original essays written for an interdisciplinary audience of students and scholars of music, film and media studies in general, and interdisciplinary humanists who give strong attention to music. Driving the study of music here are the underlying assumptions that music together with screen media (understood broadly to accommodate rapidly developing new technologies) participates in important ways in the creation of meaning and that including music in an analysis opens up the possibility for interpretations that remain invisible when only using the eye.

The series was designed with the goal of providing a thematically unified group of supplemental essays in a single volume that can be assigned in a variety of undergraduate and graduate courses (including courses in film studies, in film music, and other interdisciplinary topics). We look forward to adding future volumes addressing emerging technologies and reflecting the growth of the academic study of screen media. Rather than attempting an exhaustive history or unified theory, these studies—persuasive explications supported by textual and contextual evidence—will pose questions of musical style, strategies of rhetoric, and critical cultural analysis as they help us to see, to hear, and ultimately to understand these texts in new ways.

Neil Lerner
Series Editor

Preface

The idea of the filmic *mélomane* (music lover) was addressed by Claudia Gorbman in her 2006 "Ears Wide Open: Kubrick's Music" and her 2007 "Auteur Music,"[1] the first of which dealt specifically with music in the films of Stanley Kubrick and the second of which dealt more generally with music in the films of such diverse directors as Agnes Varga, Quentin Tarantino, Wim Wenders, Jean-Luc Godard, and Tsai Ming-Liang. Aside from Gorbman's pioneering yet tentative explorations of certain filmmakers' arguably characteristic use of pre-existing music, to date relatively little about 'sonic style' in filmmaking has appeared in print.[2] This is not to say that scholars of film music/sound ignore the topic. On the contrary, some of the best-received presentations at recent conferences have focused intensely on filmmakers whose work, in one way or another, demonstrates a 'sonic style' that in many cases goes quite beyond the use of music.

Filling a sore gap in the literature, *Music, Sound and Filmmakers: Sonic Style in Cinema* brings together original chapters by scholars who at conferences and in published articles have lately demonstrated not just interest but expertise in filmmakers about whom it might be said that a significant portion of their output has a distinctive aural identity. The 'prompt' offered to potential contributors was a pair of simple questions. Can you imagine a situation in which an audience member, arriving late to a showing of a film about which he or she has no advance information, might spontaneously say: "Ah, that *sounds* like a film by so-and-so"? If such a situation could indeed be imagined, then what is it about the film's sonic content that makes the film attributable to one particular filmmaker? What is it about a filmmaker's work, as a whole, that gives it a sonic 'trademark'?

Writers who rose to the challenge took a variety of approaches, but the goal they have in common is a careful examination of how the products of certain filmmakers relate—in specific ways—to the ear. Although the work of these same filmmakers might well feature stylish language or a stylish look or a stylish dramatic 'feel,' the topic of discussion here is always the work's stylish sound.

Organization

The book begins with an introductory chapter that attempts to define cinematic sonic style and measure it against the so-called '*auteur* theory' that has long dominated film studies in the English-speaking world; importantly, the introductory chapter also defines a number of terms (source music, diegetic music, underscore, extra-diegetic music, the 'classical-style' film, *Musique concrète*) that are used not only throughout this book but throughout the broader conversation about film music and sound.

After the introduction come a dozen chapters that focus sharply on sonic style as manifest in the work not of composers or sound designers but of the people who employed them. Two of them—reflecting film studies' new interest in filmmaking as a collaborative, even corporate, process—focus on the output of sound-conscious producers who wielded tight control over their studios' activities. The rest of them—reflecting film studies' more traditional concerns—focus on the output of directors.

Choice of Chapters

As might be expected, all of the chapters deal to a certain extent with music. This includes music that the films' characters actually hear as well as music that is heard only by members of the audience. It includes music originally composed for particular films, and it includes music borrowed from a vast treasury whose inventory ranges from concert-hall masterpieces to items from the pop catalogue.

In the case of the more vintage filmmakers under discussion here, especially the producers David O. Selznick and Val Lewton, original scores come from a variety of composers (Bernard Herrmann, Alfred Newman, Miklós Rózsa, Max Steiner, Herbert Stothart, Dimitri Tiomkin, Franz Waxman, Roy Webb) who have in common both a relatively conventional approach to scoring and a solid place in the Hollywood pantheon.

In other cases original scores come from composers who are perhaps less well-known but who are nonetheless closely associated with the filmmaker whose work is the object of attention. Danny Elfman has had a long-running relationship with the films of Gus Van Sant, for example, and there are comparable relationships between Michael Nyman and the films of Peter Greenaway, between Mark Mothersbaugh and the films of Wes Anderson, between Carter Burwell and the films of the Coen brothers, between Zbigniew Preisner and the films of Krzysztof Kieślowski, between Angelo Badalamenti and the films of David Lynch. In still other cases (notably the work of Ingmar Bergman, Stanley Kubrick, Andrey Tarkovsky, and Quentin Tarantino), scores consist largely of pre-existing material that has had a healthy life of its own outside the cinema and which, because of this, likely has very different 'meanings' for different filmgoers.[3]

The chapters in this collection of course deal with music. But they also deal with sound in general, both realistic and otherwise. They deal as well with acoustic ambience, with the timbres of voices, with the fluctuating density of soundtrack content, with the pacing of sonic events and of silence, with the relationship of sonic phenomena to both dramatic effect and emotional affect. The chapters deal with how *all* of this is handled by particular filmmakers, not just in particular works but over the course of a body of work; they deal with how filmmakers use sound not just consistently but in ways that are distinctive, ways that give these filmmakers—for sonic reasons alone—a recognizable style.

In alphabetical order, the filmmakers under consideration here are Wes Anderson, Ingmar Bergman, the Coen brothers, Peter Greenaway, Krzysztof Kieślowski, Stanley Kubrick, Val Lewton, David Lynch, David O. Selznick, Quentin Tarantino, Andrey Tarkovsky, and Gus Van Sant.

But these twelve scholarly essays on sonic style in cinema represent only a first step along what surely will be a long path. Nowadays it goes without saying that film, as Michel Chion reminds us in the title of the most recent of his books to be translated into English, is indeed 'a sound art.'[4] The stylish use of all things sonic is patently evident in the work of all the filmmakers examined here, but it is evident as well in the work of such filmmakers—to name just a few—as Woody Allen, Robert Altman, Darren Aronofsky, Mel Brooks, Tim Burton, Charles Chaplin, Francis Ford Coppola, René Clair, Clint Eastwood, Federico Fellini, Michael Haneke, Akira Kurosawa, Fritz Lang, George Lucas, Martin Scorsese, Orson Welles, and Joss Whedon. For readers and scholars interested in serious discussion of the stylish use of cinematic sound, the future looks very promising.

Notes

1   These are chapters in, respectively, *Changing Tunes: The Use of Pre-existing Music in Film*, ed. Phil Powrie and Robynn J. Stilwell (Aldershot: Ashgate, 2006), and *Beyond the Soundtrack: Experiencing Music in Cinema*, ed. Daniel Goldmark, Lawrence Kramer, and Richard Leppert (Berkeley: University of California Press, 2007).

2   Two books focus on music and sound in the films of Alfred Hitchcock; these are Elisabeth Weis's *The Silent Scream: Alfred Hitchcock's Sound Track* (Rutherford: Farleigh Dickinson University Press, 1982) and Jack Sullivan's *Hitchcock's Music* (New Haven: Yale University Press, 2008). Other explorations of music/sound within the oeuvre of a single filmmaker include Katherine Spring, "Chance Encounters of the Musical Kind: Electronica and Audiovisual Synchronization in Three Films Directed by Tom Tykwer," *Music and the Moving Image* 3, no. 3 (Fall 2010); Mark Mazullo, "Remembering Pop: David Lynch and the Sound of the '60s," *American Music* 23, no. 4 (Winter 2005); David Burnand and Miguel Mera, "Fast and Cheap? The Film Music of John Carpenter," in *The Cinema of John Carpenter: The Technique of Terror*, ed. Ian Conrich and David Woods (London: Wallflower Press, 2005); and James Wierzbicki, "Sound as Music in the Films of Terrence Malick," in *Poetic Visions of America: The Cinema of Terrence Malick*, ed. Hannah Patterson (London: Wallflower Press, 2003).

3   For an in-depth study of the different effects of originally composed film scores and film scores compiled from pre-existing material, see Anahid Kassabian, *Hearing Film: Tracking Identifications in Contemporary Hollywood Film Music* (New York and London: Routledge, 2001).

4   Michel Chion, *Film, A Sound Art*, trans. Claudia Gorbman (New York: Columbia University Press, 2009).

Acknowledgments

It is impossible to say when the seeds for this collection were planted, but they first germinated in a sidewalk coversation during a coffee break at the 2008 version of New York University's "Music and the Moving Image" conference. By this time it was clear to me that it would take several lifetimes to single-handedly write about *all* the filmmakers whose sonic styles fascinated me, and exposure to MaMI presentations that year and the year before reminded me that the film music/sound community included plenty of people who could do the writing for me. Importantly, the sidewalk conversation involved K.J. Donnelly, a reader in film studies at the University of Southampton. Although Kevin is not represented by a chapter within these pages, he is every bit as much a contributor as are the authors; without his consistent encouragement, this collection never would have happened.

Obviously, this collection would not have happened without the efforts of the individual writers. Each of them is extremely well-qualified to discuss the output of the various directors and producers who count among their areas of expertise; perhaps more significant, each of them was willing to 'push the envelope' beyond traditional case studies and historiography for the sake of grappling with the tricky business of defining a filmmaker's overall 'style.' Huge thanks of course is owed to all them, but also to the universities (in Australia, Canada, England, Ireland, the Netherlands, and the United States) that supported their work, and to the archives (especially the L. Tom Perry Special Collections Library and the Harold B. Lee Library at Brigham Young University; the Fine Arts and Performing Arts Special Collections Libraries of the University of California, Los Angeles; the Harry Ransom Humanities Research Center at the University of Texas at Austin; the Ingmar Bergman Archives in Stockholm; the Audiovisual Collections at the National Library of Sweden; the Stanley Kubrick Archive at the University of the Arts, London; and the Michael Nyman Film Music Archive at the University of Leeds) that helped make their research possible.

And as always with an effort such as this, thanks is owed to the numerous persons involved in the process of publication. In the case of this book, these would include Routledge music acquisitions editor Constance Ditzell and her trusted helpers (in particular Mike Andrews and Denny Tek), the UK-based editors and proofreaders who are surely the unsung heroines and heroes of any Routledge effort, and—especially, for understanding what this project, really, was all about—the overseeing editor for Routledge's blossoming *Music and Screen Media Series*, Neil Lerner.

From the start, this was a team effort.

James Wierzbicki

Chapter 1

Sonic Style in Cinema

James Wierzbicki

The word 'sonic' is, I think, self-explanatory: it is simply an adjective that refers to sound. 'Style,' on the other hand, is a more slippery word. The large and weather-beaten *Webster's Ninth New Collegiate Dictionary* that has long been my trusted companion gives a six-point definition that runs to twenty lines; the much smaller *American Heritage Dictionary* gives only fourteen lines divided into eight definitions for nouns and three for verbs, and the *Penguin Macquarie Dictionary* that has lately helped my efforts to understand Australian English has a definition of twenty-one lines divided into no less than thirteen definitions.

Discounting those that are obviously irrelevant here (the seed-delivering part of a flower, the bit of a sundial that makes the time-telling shadow, a sharp-pointed instrument used for engraving, a bristly hair on the back of a wild boar), we are left with a large collection of definitions that all describe 'a way of doing something' but which nevertheless fall into a pair of very differently flavored groups.

On the one hand is a group of definitions that suggest a 'general' way of doing something, a way that is shared by many persons, or strata of society, or entire nations, who are somehow linked by a common locale, time period, or ideological agenda. Back in the late 1960s, bell-bottoms and beads were often ostentatiously worn by persons whom journalists dubbed hippies; even if someone were not really a hippie, he or she could nevertheless pose as one, perhaps at a costume party, by wearing hippie-style garb. In ancient Greece, monumental edifices were built according to principles espoused not just by the sculptor Phidias (who supposedly designed the Parthenon) but by numerous of his contemporaries; two and a half millennia later, we certainly recognize authentic examples of Greek-style architecture when we see them, and we likewise recognize Greek-style efforts in the facades of modern banks and town halls.

On the other hand is a group of definitions of 'style' that suggest a way of doing something that is not at all generalized but, rather, limited to a particular person or entity.

Within this second group are definitions that refer to what in effect are typographical rules. Scholars who nowadays work in music, film studies, and other areas of the humanities are typically instructed by book publishers and editors of academic journals to follow the guidelines spelled out in the aptly titled *Chicago Manual of Style*.[1] Yet individual publishers often have 'rules' of their own that differ slightly from those of the CMS. Should the second sentence of this paragraph have a comma after 'film studies' or should it not? Should the date of Christmas be offered as '25 December 2011' or as 'December 25, 2011'? In an endnote or footnote, should the second edition of a cited work be indicated as '2nd ed.' or as '2nd ed.'? Should the abbreviation of the Latin word 'ibidem' be in roman or italic type? There are no right or wrong answers to any of these questions; what matters is that different publishers have different sets of rules about such matters, and copy editors dutifully enforce their employers' rules of 'style.'

More to the point of this collection of chapters, the second group of dictionary definitions of 'style' includes a few that refer not at all to sets of rules that distinguish the products of one publisher from those of another but, rather, to sets of characteristics unique to the output of creative individuals. "A distinctive manner of expression" is the first definition offered by *Webster's Ninth New Collegiate Dictionary*; "individuality expressed in one's actions and tastes" is the third definition (after "the way in which something is said, done, expressed, or performed" and "sort; type") in the *American Heritage Dictionary*; "a particular, distinctive, or characteristic mode of action" is the second definition (after "a particular kind, sort, or type, as with reference to form, appearance, or character") in the *Penguin Macquarie Dictionary*. It is in the sense of these last-cited definitions—which focus on "distinctive manner[s]" and expressions of "individuality" and "characteristic mode[s] of action"—that the word 'style' figures into this book.

Scholars of literature would likely agree that there is indeed such a thing as 'Elizabethan-style' drama, but probably they would be quick to point out the differences between the literary-theatrical styles of such Elizabethan playwrights as, say, William Shakespeare and Ben Jonson. Art historians might well concur on the overall style of painters who nowadays are lumped together in the category of French Impressionism, but many of them have staked entire careers on demonstrating precisely the ways in which the 'Impressionistic' style of Édouard Manet, for example, differs from the equally 'Impressionistic' style of Claude Monet. Indeed, some scholars have dug deeply into the matter of style, identifying and analyzing not just Shakespeare's and Jonson's literary style in general, for example, but in particular their stylish uses of iambic pentameter.

It is in this last-mentioned sense that the word 'style' is employed throughout this book. Broadly speaking, all the filmmakers under consideration have 'a way of doing something'—that is, a way of making films— that is distinctly their own. But the deliberately narrow focus here is on the filmmakers' stylish use of sound.

Filmmakers

Film production is a collective exercise, not necessarily a collaboration in the most idealistic sense of that word but certainly a joint effort whose final result involves the input of numerous creative minds. The obviousness of this fact has long been apparent to persons even tangentially involved with the film industry, and probably it did not go unnoticed by the serious thinkers who fifty years ago laid the foundations for what in anglophone academia is now known as 'film studies.'[2] Only in recent years, however, has the idea of film as the product of teamwork emerged from the background and come to the fore of film scholarship, and thus only in recent years has there been a generally accepted debunking of what British writer Richard Dyer in 1998 dubbed "film studies' greatest hit."[3] Dyer was referring, of course, to the pretentiously misnamed '*auteur* theory.'

The seeds for what in the English-speaking world has come to be known as '*auteur* theory' were planted, innocently enough, by the critics who in the 1950s wrote for the monthly Paris-based magazine *Cahiers du Cinéma*. For these film critics, the word '*auteur*' was nothing more than the French equivalent of the English 'author,' and they meant it precisely that way when they announced their group decision to shift the focus of their writing. Whereas their commentaries since the magazine's founding in 1951 had centered for the most part on the authors of screenplays, after the 1954 publication of François Truffaut's landmark essay "Un certaine tendence du cinéma Français" their commentaries tended to center on those French filmmakers "who often write their dialogue and [in some cases] invent themselves the stories that they direct."[4]

Filmmakers who exemplified this "certain tendency in French cinema," Truffaut wrote, included such directors as Jacques Becker, Robert Bresson, Jean Cocteau, Abel Gance, Max Ophüls, Jean Renoir, and Jacques Tati. Because they actually penned so much of their films' content, Truffaut suggested, these filmmakers were in certain ways comparable to playwrights and the authors of novels. And thus *Cahiers du Cinéma*'s boldly proclaimed new policy—to take seriously the contributions of such filmmakers—was called the "Politique des auteurs."

André Bazin, one of the founders of *Cahiers du Cinéma*, expanded on the policy in a 1957 article titled "De la politique des auteurs." Paying close attention to a film director who might also be the author—literally speaking—of the film's screenplay and dialogue, Bazin wrote, was just a logical application to the cinema of an idea that had long been applied in serious criticism of literature, music, and painting. *Cahiers du Cinéma*'s new "politique des auteurs," he wrote, behooved critics to take notice of whatever elements a number of films 'authored' by a particular filmmaker might have in common. The *Cahiers'* new author-based policy fairly mandated that film critics adopt as a "criterion of reference" what Bazin called a filmmaker's "personal factor." The policy also mandated, Bazin strongly suggested, that critics seeking to identify whatever "personal factor" marks the work of an arguably 'authorial' filmmaker should engage not just in "postulating [the] permanence" of this "personal factor" from one film to another but also in exploring the "progress [of this factor] from one work to the following."[5]

As articulated by Bazin, in other words, the French critics' author-based policy called not only for attention to be paid to a filmmaker's style as demonstrated in a particular film; it also called for identification of that style, and for comparisons of evidence of that style as exhibited in any number of films. To act on the policy indeed required close observation of a film's content, but it did not require making value judgments. The "politique des auteurs" simply outlined an approach to film criticism that focused on a certain filmmaker's characteristic traits; aptly named, it was a policy, and there was nothing theoretical about it.

The policy morphed into something *called* a 'theory' in the early 1960s, when critics in England and the United States self-consciously began writing about film as an art form. The theory's main champion, expressing his opinions in *Film Culture*, the *New York Film Bulletin*, and the UK-based journal *Movie*, was Andrew Sarris; its chief opponent was Pauline Kael, at that time (that is, before the 1968 start of her long tenure as film critic for *The New Yorker*) a writer for such publications as *City Lights*, *McCall's*, and *The New Republic*. In 1963 Kael and Sarris squared off famously in the pages of *Film Quarterly*. Kael struck the first blow, in particular targeting the second of three premises that Sarris had spelled out the year before in an article in *Film Culture*. The first premise of what Sarris clearly labeled "the *auteur* theory" involved consideration of a director's technical competence, and the third premise involved consideration of a film's "interior meaning"; the second premise— the one that Kael found so galling—involved consideration of "the distinguishable personality of the director as a *criterion of value*."[6]

"The smell of a skunk is more distinguishable than the perfume of a rose," Kael noted, and then she asked: "Does that make it better?"[7] Sarris hit back by arguing that his 1962 article had been grossly misread by Kael; he insisted that the *auteur* theory—as formulated by him, not by the French writers of the 1950s—was "never intended as an occult ritual" for determining the artistic worth of a film product, and he reminded readers that "without the necessary research and analysis" the *auteur* theory can easily "degenerate into the kind of snobbish rubbish which is associated with the merchandising of paintings."[8]

Over the next several decades English-language journals regularly hosted debates of considerable intensity, usually with the pro-Sarris participants continuing to fetishize the apparently misunderstood French word and in the process introducing such polyglot terms as 'auterism,' 'auteurship,' and 'auteurists.' Lately, however, the discussion has cooled down. To judge from recent synoptic accounts,[9] the ideology offered by Sarris and others—to the effect that a film could be considered to be art only if "it was demonstrably the work of a highly individual artist"[10]—is largely a thing of the past.

What is very much a thing of the present is the simple fact that certain filmmakers *are* highly individualistic. Film studies in the twenty-first century clearly recognizes, and even celebrates, the collaborative nature of filmmaking. Still, it remains that there *are* filmmakers—not just directors but also producers and studios—whose work somehow stands apart from the crowd, filmmakers whose work resonates with what Bazin called a "personal factor," whose work demonstrates a recognizable style.

As with the French directors who prompted the writers for *Cahiers du Cinéma* to declare their "politique des auteurs," the filmmakers who nowadays are considered to be especially stylish for the most part demonstrate their 'authorial' individuality through the dramatic structure and verbal content of their screenplays. But often filmic style is demonstrated as well through such purely visual elements as costume and set design, lighting, pace of cutting, and overall cinematography. And sometimes the trademarks of cinematic style involve what transpires on the music and sound-effects tracks.

Music

Many films made over the past seventy-five years can be said to be in all ways, including their use of music, expertly made. Many films that are perhaps not so expertly made nevertheless feature good film music, that is to say, music that very ably serves films' needs. Many films feature music that posterity has deemed worthy of being removed from its original context and showcased in the concert hall. Many films feature music by composers whose approach to harmony or melody is easily recognizable, and some of these are films whose directors in various ways demonstrate 'authorial' individuality.

But relatively few films demonstrate, through music or anything else, their makers' sonic style. This is because very few filmmakers, past or present, *have* a sonic style. One of them who did was Alfred Hitchcock, a director long revered by proponents of the '*auteur* theory' even though he authored neither screenplays nor dialogue for his films.[11] Shedding a little light first on Hitchcock's treatment of music, and then on his treatment of sound effects, will, one hopes, illuminate this book's theme.

It is difficult to think of Hitchcock's films from the late 1950s and early 1960s and not hear, in one's mind, the music of Bernard Herrmann. Herrmann provided music for seven Hitchcock films: *The Trouble with Harry* (1955), *The Man Who Knew Too Much* (1956), *The Wrong Man* (1957), *Vertigo* (1958),

North by Northwest (1959), *Psycho* (1960), and *Marnie* (1964).[12] Although the scores for these films are of course different from one another, they do have in common certain elements of gesture and voicing, and three of them (*Vertigo, North by Northwest, Psycho*) draw from the same rich but limited harmonic vocabulary.[13] Especially in these three last-named films, the blend of propulsive and unsettled orchestral music with heart-racing dramatic content is so distinctive that it can be easily parodied. Indeed, parody of this musico-dramatic combination is at the very heart of Mel Brooks's 1977 comic yet respectful homage to Hitchcock, *High Anxiety*.[14]

For all that, Hitchcock's sonic style is related only superficially to the memorable 'Herrmannesque' sound that permeates *Vertigo* et al. From his arrival in the United States in 1940 until his death forty years later, Hitchcock worked with numerous of Hollywood's A-list composers, including not only Herrmann but also Miklós Rózsa, Dimitri Tiomkin, and Franz Waxman.[15] These composers had distinctive voices, and as time allowed they made efforts to express their unique artistic personalities in works designed for the concert hall. When they wrote for films, however, they functioned as chameleons, adapting readily to whatever conditions were warranted by a particular project. Rózsa's psychologically dark score for Hitchcock's 1945 *Spellbound* perhaps has something in common with the music that around the same time he wrote for Billy Wilder's *Double Indemnity* (1944) and *The Lost Weekend* (1945), but it hardly resembles his music for sword-and-sandals epics along the lines of William Wyler's *Ben-Hur* (1959) and Robert Aldrich's *Sodom and Gomorrah* (1962). Similarly, Tiomkin's scores for Hitchcock thrillers bear little resemblance to the music he provided for such Westerns as *High Noon* (1952) and *The Alamo* (1960) or such war films as *The Guns of Navarone* (1961) and *36 Hours* (1965). All these composers, and others, gave Hitchcock what he wanted for the sake of whatever film was at hand, but their music in itself has little to do with Hitchcock's sonic style.

Like most filmmakers, Hitchcock specified that his films include both music that is apparently heard by the fictional characters and music that is actually heard but only by the real-life members of the audience. Music of the former sort has long been described by participants in the film industry as 'source music' (because its source is visible, or at least implied, in the filmic image), and in academic writing it often is called 'diegetic music' (because it seems to exist within the filmic narrative, or diegesis). In the film industry, music of the latter sort since the early 1930s has been known as 'underscore' (because it involves a recorded score mixed under a film's dialogue and sound effects); because such music does not belong to, or is extraneous to, the film's narrative/diegesis, in academic writing such music is often called 'non-diegetic' or 'extra-diegetic' music. Whether source music or underscore, whether diegetic or extra-diegetic, the content of the music in Hitchcock's films is not especially relevant to Hitchcock's sonic style; what matters, in terms of sonic style, is what Hitchcock *did* with this music.

Hitchcock's use of (underscore) derived from decisions about when to apply it and when not to, and in these decisions Hitchcock for the last thirty-five years of his career was arguably not much different from the typical Hollywood filmmaker. To this generalization, of course, there are striking exceptions; both *Lifeboat* (1944) and *The Birds* (1962) daringly feature no underscore at all,[16] and memorable segments in various of his other films— for example, the prolonged exploration of the ominous windmill in *Foreign Correspondent* (1940), the crop duster scene in *North by Northwest*, the climactic police raid in *Family Plot* (1976)—are oddly devoid of the mood-enhancing, action-illustrating, drama-propelling music that represents the norm for the so-called 'classical-style' film.[17] For the most part, though, Hitchcock's use of underscore during his long and productive Hollywood period holds closely—and thus unremarkably—to the classical-style film's conventions.[18]

Hitchcock's use of (source music, on the other hand, was unconventional and canny—and thus stylish—to the extreme. Along with *Blackmail* (1929), the best-known of his pre-Hollywood films are likely those of the 'thriller' sextet produced by British-Gaumont between 1934 and 1938; of these six films, no less than four of them—*The Man Who Knew Too Much* (1934), *The 39 Steps* (1935), *Young and Innocent* (1937), *The Lady Vanishes* (1938)— feature source music that not only pertains directly to the plots but also provides the audience with clues as to how the plots might unfold. Probably nowhere in Hitchcock's films is source music so integral to the plot as in *The Man Who Knew Too Much*, in which a climactic moment of a large-scale cantata (both in the original version and in the 1956 Hollywood remake) serves as the cue for an assassination attempt.[19] But Hitchcock throughout his career wove source music tellingly into his plots. One thinks, for example, of the persistent iterations of Johann Strauss's *Wiener Blut* waltz in *Suspicion* (1941), of the nervous playing of Poulenc's "Mouvement perpétuale no. 1" by one of the murderers in *Rope* (1948), of the song "Lisa" whose diegetic creation fairly permeates *Rear Window* (1954), of the arguably symbolic performances of "And the Band Played On" in *Strangers on a Train* (1951) and the "Merry Widow Waltz" in *Shadow of a Doubt* (1943), of the balletic interpretation of Tchaikovsky's *Francesca da Rimini* that triggers the escape sequence in *Torn Curtain* (1966). One thinks, too, of the fact that so many of Hitchcock's main characters—Gilbert in *The Lady Vanishes*, Charlotte in *Stage Fright* (1950), Jo in the 1956 version of *The Man Who Knew Too Much*, Manny Balestrero in *The Wrong Man*—are professional musicians. And one thinks of Hitchcock's cameo appearances as a musician, carrying a violin in *Spellbound*, a cello in *The Paradine Case* (1947), a double bass in *Strangers on a Train*, always looking awkward, yet at the same time always looking intensely serious.

Music was obviously important to Hitchcock. As early as 1934, in the wake of *Waltzes from Vienna*, his music-filled lightweight biography of Johann

Strauss, Jr., the director discussed filmic music with an interviewer. Amongst other things, he said:

> The arrival of the talkies, as you know, temporarily killed action in pictures, but it did just as much damage to music. Producers and directors were obsessed by words. They forgot that one of the greatest emotional factors in the silent cinema was the musical accompaniment. They have gradually realized that action should still come first—that, talkies or not, they are still making motion pictures. But music as an artistic asset of the film is still sadly neglected.[20]

Asked if he felt that films should be fitted with complete musical scores before they go into production, Hitchcock replied:

> I do. Though by "complete" I do not mean continuous. That would be monotonous. Silence is often very effective and its effect is heightened by the proper handling of the music before and after.
>
> There is, somewhere, the correct musical accompaniment for almost any scene—music which will improve the scene. But none at all is better than the wrong music.[21]

Hitchcock, of course, never made a film whose conventional score was composed before shooting commenced. But arguably he made many films that involve *un*conventional scores completed not before production began but certainly before post-production was finished. In his book-length interview with François Truffaut, Hitchcock said that "after a picture is cut, I dictate what amounts to a real sound script to a secretary. We run every reel off and I indicate all the places where sounds should be heard."[22] Many of Hitchcock's 'sound scripts' are archived at the Academy of Motion Picture Arts and Sciences' Margaret Herrick Library in Beverly Hills; these are extraordinarily thorough, and—if one takes a very broad view of music—arguably they *do* amount to 'complete scores.'

Sound

Hitchcock certainly took a broad view of music. In his book *Hitchcock's Music*, Jack Sullivan states that Hitchcock's definition of music "encompassed street noise, dialogue (especially voice-over), sounds of the natural world ... sonic effects of all sorts ... [and] silence, the sudden, awesome absence of music, capable of delivering the most powerful musical frisson of all."[23] Probably Hitchcock would have agreed with this. Shortly before his death in 1980, he suggested to an interviewer that he had long thought of music as just one more sonic element whose placement in a film demanded careful consideration. "After all," he said, "when you put music to film, it's really sound; it isn't music *per se*."[24]

Some filmmakers (or the critics who analyze their work) might be inclined to reverse that statement and suggest that when one puts sound to film it becomes music; it is no longer sound per se. And this prompts a digression into a genre of music that for more than sixty years has been insistently described in English-speaking countries by the French term 'musique concrète.'

As first theorized by the French audio technician Pierre Schaeffer in the aftermath of World War II, musique concrète was a radically new form of music that used a collection of 'concrete' sonic objects as the starting point for 'abstract' musical compositions. Whereas traditional music begins with an abstract idea in the mind of its composer and becomes concrete sound only when its carefully worked-out notational instructions are executed by performers, the music proposed by Schaeffer follows the opposite path; the process begins not with abstract ideas but with the survey of an array of concrete sounds collected by the composer, and the music takes shape only after these concrete sounds are sorted out and purposefully arranged.

Although some of the concrete materials that Schaeffer used for his eventually abstract compositions were recordings of conventional voices or musical instruments, a great many more were recordings—sometimes electronically manipulated—of everyday noises. Modern parlance has lost sight of Schaeffer's seminal ideas and has concentrated on this last-mentioned aspect of Schaeffer's work. Nowadays the label 'musique concrète' is applied almost exclusively to electroacoustic music that somehow makes use of collected bits of sound drawn not from the rarefied atmosphere of the concert hall but from the real, or 'concrete,' world.

Was Hitchcock anticipating musique concrète when, in the breakfast scene of his 1929 Blackmail, he had reverberant extra-diegetic iterations of the word 'knife' "hammer on the consciousness of the girl" who, the night before, had used a knife to kill her assailant?[25] Was he anticipating musique concrète when, near the end of his 1930 Murder!, he mixed voice-over speech fragments with a radio broadcast of the Prelude from Wagner's Tristan und Isolde, or when, near the end of his 1936 Secret Agent, he had his sound engineers deftly morph the normal racket of a railroad train rolling over its tracks into a quite abnormal incantation whose insistent whispers press the main female character to save the man she loved?

Probably not, yet it seems clear enough that Hitchcock in these and other scenes from his early films was utilizing sound quite deliberately in what Elisabeth Weis, in her 1982 The Silent Scream: Alfred Hitchcock's Sound Track, calls "expressionistic" ways.[26] Hitchcock in the late 1920s and early 1930s, of course, was not alone in his "expressionistic" application of filmic sound. Other films of the period that feature bold engagements with sound for expressive purposes include Walter Ruttmann's Melodie der Welt (1930), Lewis Milestone's All Quiet on the Western Front (1930), Josef von Sternberg's Der Blaue Engel (1930), Fritz Lang's M (1931), Georg Wilhelm Pabst's Kameradschaft (1931), and Carl Theodor Dreyer's Vampyr (1932).[27] They include as well a number of films by René Clair—for example, *Sous les toits de Paris* (1931), *Le Million* (1931), *À nous la liberté!* (1931)—who pioneered the distinction between the mere talkie (*film parlant*) and the 'true' sound film (*film sonore*) that made creative use of sound effects not for the sake of realism but for the sake of adding extra layers of meaning to a film's narrative. In a 1929 letter that was later published as an essay titled "The Art of Sound," Clair wrote:

> We must draw a distinction here between those sound effects which are amusing only by virtue of the novelty (which soon wears off) and those that help one to understand the action, and which excite emotions which could not have been roused by the sight of the pictures alone. The visual world at the birth of the cinema seemed to hold immeasurably richer promise. ... However, if *imitation* of real noises seems limited and disappointing, it is possible that an *interpretation* of noises may have more of a future in it.[28]

After the full blossoming of the narratively straightforward classical-style film in the late 1930s, most filmmakers with their sound effects tracks did in fact opt for the "limited" imitation of real noises. This generalization includes Hitchcock, whose Hollywood films in most ways indeed epitomize the classical-style norms. But Hitchcock, for all his post-1940 interest in filmic realism, still knew the value of the deftly placed sound effect.

The above-mentioned book by Elisabeth Weis ostensibly owes its title to the famous sequence, early in Hitchcock's 1935 *The 39 Steps*, when the proprietress of a rooming house stumbles across the body of a murder victim; the landlady opens her mouth, but instead of the expected scream the audience hears the shriek of a train whistle that propels the story into its next arena of action. Two years later Hitchcock applied a similar conceit in *Young and Innocent*, in the opening scene of which he replaced the scream of a woman about to be strangled to death with a cacophonic chorus of seagulls. But Hitchcock's concept of the 'silent scream' was perhaps most fully realized, almost three decades after his 'impressionistic' experiments, in *The Birds*.

In his book-length interview, Truffaut asked: "When Jessica Tandy discovers the farmer's body, she opens her mouth as if to scream, but we hear nothing. Wasn't that done to emphasize the sound track at this point?" Hitchcock's response is revealing. Tellingly, he said:

> The sound track was vital just there; we had the sound of her footsteps, running down the passage, with almost an echo. The interesting thing in the sound is the difference between the footsteps inside the house and on the outside. Did you notice that I had her run from the distance and then went to a close-up when she's paralyzed with fear and inarticulate?

There's silence at that point. Then, as she goes off again, the sound of the steps will match the size of the image. It grows louder right up to the moment she gets into the truck, and then the screech of the truck engine starting off conveys her anguish. We were really experimenting there by taking real sounds and then stylizing them so that we derived more drama from them than we normally would.[29]

It was only in his conversation with Truffaut in regards to *The Birds* that Hitchcock fully articulated his idea that highlighted sound effects should be the equivalent of dialogue, that they should 'say' something relevant to the drama.[30] But such highlighted sound effects, used not for realistic but for expressive purposes, were a part of Hitchcock's filmmaking right from the start. Like his decisions to use underscore and source music, and his decisions to *not* use music of any sort at key moments in his films, the meaning-laden sound effect was integral to Hitchcock's sonic style.

As early as 1937 the French art critic Louis le Sidaner suggested that "the true cinematographic music of the future" might well contain

the noise of flowing water; the grinding of carriage wheels, the stridency of a policeman's whistle; the languorous voice of a "vamp"; the chug-chug of a motor; the irregular tic-tac of a typewriter; the barking of a dog; even silence; a man sneezing; church bells; the caustic laugh of a "boulevardier"; the cry of a child who suffers or is frightened; the song of the nightingale; the grunts of a pig or the tender murmur of happy lovers.[31]

Almost forty years later theorist Raymond Bellour observed that a film's deliberate and "arbitrary" noises, noises that involve much more than what is simply "motivated" by a scene's need for realism, "can go so far as to serve as a [musical] score" that fairly escapes the limits of "translatability," because noise "is much less easy to reduce … to the signified" than are words, and it is not "codified as the [conventional] musical score is."[32] And not too long ago the Venezualan-British composer Julio d'Escriván reminded us that

music has gradually been subsumed into the soundtrack as another element of the film sound world and sound design is often on an equal footing with it. Sound designers are increasingly entrusted with complex non-diegetic tasks that were formerly only performed by film music, thus exploring the more psychological dimensions of sound.[33]

D'Escriván's optimistic assessment does not apply, of course, to all films being made today. But it does seem to apply to the work of filmmakers who over the years have taken a stylish approach to both music and sound effects, filmmakers whose work vis-à-vis sound in general exhibits an individualist approach, filmmakers who doubtless would agree with Hitchcock's statement, in the 1934 interview, that "words and incidental noise and 'song numbers' are surely *not all* the sound track was invented for."[34]

Notes

1   Now in its sixteenth edition, the *Chicago Manual of Style* began in 1906 as a set of guidelines for spelling, punctuation, and other typographical matters both in manuscripts submitted to the University of Chicago Press and in the final versions of theses and dissertations submitted to the University of Chicago's library.

2   For recent accounts of the field's origins, see Dana Polan, *Scenes of Instruction: The Beginnings of the U.S. Study of Film* (Berkeley: University of California Press, 2007), and the essays by Polan and others in *Inventing Film Studies*, ed. Lee Grievson and Haidee Wasson (Durham, NC, and London: Duke University Press, 2008).

3   Richard Dyer, "Introduction to Film Studies," in *The Oxford Guide to Film Studies*, ed. John Hill and Pamela Church Gibson (Oxford: Oxford University Press, 1998), 5.

4   François Truffaut, "Un certaine tendence du cinéma français," *Cahiers du Cinéma* 31 (January 1954): 29. Quoted, in a translation by Diane Staples, in Donald E. Staples, "The Auteur Theory Reexamined," *Cinema Journal* 6 (1966–7): 2.

5   André Bazin, "De la politique des auteurs," *Cahiers du Cinéma* 70 (April 1957): 10. Quoted, in a translation by Diane Staples, in Donald E. Staples, ibid., 4.

6   Emphasis added. The quoted material is from Andrew Sarris, "Notes on the Auteur Theory in 1962," *Film Culture* 27 (Winter 1962–3).

7   Pauline Kael, "Circles and Squares," *Film Quarterly* 16, no. 3 (Spring 1963): 15.

8   Andrew Sarris, "The Auteur Theory and the Perils of Pauline," *Film Quarterly* 16, no. 4 (Summer 1963): 28.

9   See, for example, the entry by James Naremore on "Authorship" in *A Companion to Film Theory*, ed. Toby Miller and Robert Stam (Oxford: Wiley-Blackwell, 1999); Pam Cook's "Authorship and Cinema" chapter in *The Cinema Book*, ed. Pam Cook and Mieke Bernink (London: British Film Institute, 2007); and the various essays in David A. Gerstner and Janet Staiger, eds., *Authorship and Film* (New York and London: Routledge, 2003), Virginia Wright Wexman, ed., *Film and Authorship* (New York: Rutgers University Press, 2002), and Barry Keith Grant, ed., *Auteurs and Authorship: A Film Reader* (Oxford: Wiley-Blackwell, 2008).

10   Dyer, "Introduction to Film Studies," 5.

11   Two books that deal with Hitchcock's sonic style are Jack Sullivan, *Hitchcock's Music* (New Haven: Yale University Press, 2006) and Elisabeth Weis, *The Silent Scream: Alfred Hitchcock's Sound Track* (Rutherford: Farleigh Dickinson University Press, 1982). Smaller publications that deal specifically with Hitchcock's use of music are Nathan Fink, "The Sound of Suspense: An Analysis of Music in Alfred Hitchcock's Films" (Barcelona: International Society for Music Perception and Cognition, 2006): 193–8; and Kevin J. Donnelly, "Hitchcock's Music Lesson," *Film International* 122, no. 4 (2002): 1–7. As one might expect, the literature teems with scholarly articles that focus on the music in one or another of Hitchcock's films.

12   Herrmann served as musical consultant for Hitchcock's 1962 *The Birds* (see note 16 below); he was contracted to write the music for Hitchcock's 1966 *Torn Curtain* but was dismissed and replaced by John Addison.

13   For details on the shared harmonic language of *Vertigo*, *North by Northwest*, and *Psycho*, see Royal S. Brown, "Herrmann, Hitchcock, and the Music of the

Irrational," *Cinema Journal* 21, no. 2 (Spring 1982): 14–49. The article is reprinted in Brown's *Overtones and Undertones: Reading Film Music* (Berkeley: University of California Press, 1994), 148–74.

14 The composer for *High Anxiety* was John Morris; the film's title song, the melody of which figures prominently in the underscore for the main titles and the opening sequence, is by Brooks.

15 Rózsa scored Hitchcock's *Spellbound* (1945); Tiomkin scored *Shadow of a Doubt* (1943), *Strangers on a Train* (1951), *I Confess* (1953), and *Dial M for Murder* (1954); Waxman scored *Rebecca* (1940), *Suspicion* (1941), *The Paradine Case* (1947), and *Rear Window* (1954).

16 *Lifeboat* features music, by Hugo Friedhofer, in its title sequence; aside from several bits of diegetic music, the 'score' for *The Birds* consists entirely of quasi-realistic avian sounds generated electronically by the German composer Oskar Sala on an instrument called the Trautonium. For a full account of the the the 'score' for *The Birds*, see James Wierzbicki, "Shrieks, Flutters, and Vocal Curtains: Electronic Sound/Electronic Music in Hitchcock's *The Birds*," *Music and the Moving Image*, vol. 1, no. 2 (Summer 2008).

17 The term 'classical-style' film apparently owes to comments made throughout the 1950s and 1960s by French critic André Bazin, collected in the first volume of his *What Is Cinema?*, trans. Hugh Gray (Berkeley: University of California Press, 1967); it was formalized by film historians David Bordwell, Janet Staiger, and Kristin Thompson in their 1985 *The Classical Hollywood Cinema: Film Style and Production to 1960* (London: Routledge & Kegan Paul, 1985). In essence, the 'classical-style' film is a film whose story-telling is "excessively obvious" (ibid., 1), a film whose various technical devices are used in tandem "to explain, and not obscure, the narrative" (Susan Hayward, *Cinema Studies: The Key Concepts* [London: Routledge, 2000], 64).

18 These conventions, the result not of fiat but of trial and error, began to be manifest ca. 1933 with Max Steiner's score for *King Kong* and had become more or less established ca. 1938 with the same composer's score for *Gone with the Wind*. For itemizations of the musical conventions of the classical-style film, see Claudia Gorbman, *Unheard Melodies: Narrative Film Music* (Bloomington: Indiana University Press, 1987), 73–91, and Kathryn Kalinak, *Settling the Score: Music and the Classical Hollywood Film* (Madison: University of Wisconsin Press, 1992), 66–134.

19 The 1956 version of *The Man Who Knew Too Much* used in its Albert Hall scene a much-expanded version of the "Storm Clouds Cantata" that Arthur Benjamin composed for the 1934 film; for details on how Bernard Herrmann adapted this music for the later film, see James Wierzbicki, "Grand Illusion: Arthur Benjamin's 'Storm Cloud' Music and *The Man Who Knew Too Much*," *Journal of Film Music* 1, nos. 2–3 (Fall–Winter 2004): 217–38.

20 Alfred Hitchcock, quoted in Stephen Watts, "On Music in Films," in *Hitchcock on Hitchcock: Selected Writings and Interviews*, ed. Sidney Gottlieb (Berkeley: University of California Press, 1995), 241–2. The interview originally appeared in *Cinema Quarterly* 2, no. 2 (Winter 1933–4): 80–83.

21 Ibid., 242.

22 Alfred Hitchcock, in François Truffaut, *Hitchcock* (New York: Simon & Schuster, 1984), 297. The original edition was published, in French, in 1983 by Éditions Ramsay.

23 Sullivan, *Hitchcock's Music*, xv.

24 Kyle B. Counts, "The Making of Alfred Hitchcock's *The Birds*: The Complete Story behind the Precursor of Modern Horror Films," *Cinefantastique* 12, no. 2 (Fall 1980): 29.

25 Alfred Hitchcock, "My Own Methods," *Sight and Sound* 6, no. 22 (Summer 1937): 62. The article is an abridged version of Hitchcock's contribution to the book *Footnotes to the Film*, ed. Charles Davy (London: Lovat Dickson, 1937), 61–3.

26 Weis, *The Silent Scream*, 19–20.

27 For more on these films, and on the considerable amount of serious attention they have attracted from film scholars, see James Wierzbicki, *Film Music: A History* (New York and London: Routledge, 2009), 100–2, 256–7.

28 René Clair, "The Art of Sound," trans. Vera Traill, in *Film Sound: Theory and Practice*, ed. Elisabeth Weis and John Belton (New York: Columbia University Press, 1985), 93. Emphases original.

29 Truffaut, *Hitchcock*, 295–6.

30 Ibid., 297.

31 Louis le Sidander, "l'Importance de Cinématographe," *Mercure de France* (n.d.), quoted by Arthur Benjamin in "Film Music," *The Musical Times* 78, no. 1133 (July 1937): 595.

32 Raymond Bellour, "The Unattainable Text," *Screen* 16, no. 3 (Autumn, 1975): 23–4.

33 Julio d'Escriván, "Sound Art (?) on/in Film," *Organised Sound* 14, no. 1 (2009): 72.

34 Hitchcock, in Watts, "On Music in Films," 245. Emphasis added.

Chapter 2

Music, Sound, and Silence in the Films of Ingmar Bergman*

Per F. Broman

The *auteur*—in the lore of the medium—has been seen as the director/creator mastermind who puts his or her unique stamp on the work. This is an unreasonable idea, of course: The creation of a film is a gigantic group project, and the director is far from being the sole creator. But auteur theory, nevertheless, holds a firm grip on Ingmar Bergman scholarship, and not without reason: *auteurism* must include, as Janet Staiger points out, a unified personal vision across an entire oeuvre, which is easily observed in Bergman's output.[1] Bergman's recycling of tropes, actors and other collaborators, and character names across a career that spanned fifty-seven years and included some fifty authored and/or directed feature films draws us to coherences in his work, and weaving a web of these threads is a gratifying task. Combine this with the mystic, often dark, metaphysical character of his dramas and a personal life that was often closely mirrored in his work, and one can scarcely fault attempts to create a coherent life-achievement-as-one-single-work. Director Oliver Assayas, who always considered artists he admired (such as Vermeer, Pierre Bonnard, and Bergman) in their entirety, expressed it beautifully: "The most apparent, the most insignificant, the most alien, is what appears as the most valuable, since it exists in a context, in a totality."[2]

Nevertheless, Maaret Koskinen has recently drawn attention to the fact that the auteur-focused approach to Bergman has its pitfalls.[3] Not only are there similarities between Bergman's works and those of his contemporaries: Michelangelo Antonioni's work has long been compared to Bergman's, for example, and the comparisons regained traction when both directors died on July 30, 2007. Idiosyncratic Swedish circumstances, typically absent in non-Swedish analyses, also curtail the auteur reading of Bergman. So do cinematic features resulting from technological changes and innovations in the movie industry and from a general *Zeitgeist*—or in Koskinen's words, "intertextual patterns conducive to modernist sensibilities in contemporary European culture."[4]

In terms of sound and music in Bergman's films, there is an even greater temptation to create an all-encompassing, chronological and analytical narrative. Musically, Bergman certainly differs from most of his contemporaries, including Antonioni, although he does seem to connect with Pier Paolo

Pasolini and Andrey Tarkovsky, directors who, like Bergman, utilized Bach in several films, albeit after Bergman's first unequivocal use of Bach in *Through a Glass Darkly* (1961).

Bergman's use of Bach constitutes one example of a life-long obsession, evident beginning with *Prison* (1947)[5] and on through to his last film, *Saraband* (2003). His fondness for the art music repertoire, from Bach to Wagner,[6] and including Stravinsky, is well-known, as is made clear in many interviews and by his frequent attendance of concerts in the Oscar Church, his home parish in Stockholm, as well as by the large record collection in his *Nachlass*.[7] Furthermore, music appears not only in his films' diegetic and extra-diegetic domains; his characters also *talk* about music, and many of them are either musicians or non-musicians who interact with music. Bergman's sonic world, then, has to be put in a comprehensive context that includes sound as well as narrative.

Is there such a thing as a Bergmanian sonic world, and can we indeed distinguish a soundtrack of Bergman's from one by any other filmmaker? The short answer is "yes": With few exceptions, since 1960 Bergman has preferred to use pre-existing music rather than original scores, both diegetically and extra-diegetically; most often he has chosen works from historic art-music composers, including Bach, Beethoven, Bruckner, Chopin, Mozart, Scarlatti, Schubert, Schumann, and Britten. But non-musical sounds and silence also play a significant role in his soundtracks.

When asked in 2005 if he believed in God, Bergman replied: "I believe in other worlds, other realities. But my prophets are Bach and Beethoven; they definitely show another world."[8] A post-rationalization, perhaps, but with the addition of Chopin and Mozart, nothing in his oeuvre contradicts this statement, which underscores the power of music as a fundament of his aesthetic vision. When Bergman uses music, he often lets it completely dominate the narrative as well as the diegetic and extra-diegetic domains. For extra-diegetic music in his early films, Bergman relied on the studios' staff composers; most notable among these was Erik Nordgren (1913–92), music director at Svensk Filmindustri, who produced many conventional scores but also some highly original music, of which his solo-guitar score for Bergman's *The Magician* (1958) is an outstanding example. Sofia Jönsson convincingly showed that the several-decades-long collaboration between Nordgren and Bergman was essential for Bergman's approach to sound in general.[9]

Music, Sound, and the Artist

In Vilgot Sjöman's 1962 documentary *Ingmar Bergman Makes a Movie*,[10] Bergman offers uncompromising arguments against using music in film:

> If one departs from the principle that film is rhythm and that it in that regard is similar to music, it is almost always wrong to use music in films.

That would be like adding music to music. Therefore one must search for other acoustic accompaniments. There is one principle that has to be the deciding one: one should, in all circumstances, be sparse. The sounds one chooses have to be evocative: They should convey to the audience an unconscious feeling that surrounds the main feeling created by the images.

This rather perplexing statement can be seen as a reaction to the excessive underscoring of the Hollywood tradition, but it is also a reflection of the film on which Bergman was working on at the time. *Winter Light* (1963) is a film with no music other than hymn singing, paced almost in real time and with suggestive sound effects.[11] Filmed right after the script of *Winter Light* was completed, but before the filming had begun, *Ingmar Bergman Makes a Movie* gives fascinating insights into how sound and silence, the "other acoustic accompaniments," interact even before a single frame has been shot. Bergman describes the dialogue between Tomas, a minister who lost his faith, and the clinically depressed Jonas, a fisherman and father who is reaching out for help. When asked to explain details of the camera positioning, Bergman instead turns to his approach to sound. He describes how, after Jonas's departure, the background noise completely disappears. The absolute silence is supposed to *hit* the audience, as they are not used to it. The silence is interrupted by Tomas uttering: "God, why have you deserted me?" Although the final result differed in many ways from the script, Bergman's sonic conception remained the same. Bergman used traditional musical stingers in many films, sometimes to a perhaps unintended comic effect, as for example the timpani stinger in *The Passion of Anna* (1969) or the piano stinger in *Face to Face* (1976). But this stinger of silence is, by comparison, deeply arresting.

Bergman's music-negating statement from 1962 was contradicted in virtually all of his films both before and after *Winter Light*.[12] Music was too important to him personally and fit into his predominant narrative themes: The search for God and the silence of God; death; struggles in the hetero-sexual relationship; childhood struggles; and not least, art making, whether theater, literature, poetry, music, or the visual arts. These themes recur again and again, from his earliest film, *Crisis* (1946), to *Saraband*. They are realized less through action than through dialogue and iconic, breathtaking images, often close-ups. And they dominated Ingmar Bergman's own life, as is documented in numerous articles and interviews.[13]

Journalist Camilla Lundberg pointed out to Bergman in 2000 that many of the main characters in his films are musicians. Bergman appeared surprised and responded: "Really? I haven't thought about that." But surely Lundberg's observation could not have come as a surprise. Even in *The Shame* (1968), a film that has virtually nothing to do with art, the main protagonists are violinists. The artists portrayed in Bergman's films are nothing special, though. They are often vain, living through a mythological notion of the power of artistic creation, and often their artistic occupations are represented as just nine-to-five jobs. In *To Joy* (1950), the quite accomplished orchestral violinist Stig wants to escape the collective and play the Mendelssohn concerto with the orchestra; when he gets the chance, his inabilities show and he fails miserably. In *Sawdust and Tinsel* (1953), the theater actors display their contempt for the circus artists, whose pursuit is not art but cheap tricks; in the end, both actors and circus performers reveal their human flaws and limited talents. Even *The Magic Flute* (1975) portrays the singers as humans with imperfections, sleeping and reading comic books behind stage, rather than as divine artists. In *Fanny and Alexander* (1982) the theater company is depicted merely as a group for communal support, not as a professional ensemble that aspires to real art; instead, the narrative's real artistic experience is shown in the asceticism and discipline of the sadistic bishop, who plays Bach on the flute in the stern, warrior-like tradition of Frederick the Great. Indeed, for the serious artist in Bergman's films, maintaining high artistic standards has consequences.

At the same time, though, Bergman's films suggest that art, if performed with conviction and skill, can have an immense impact. In the TV drama *The Rite* (1969), the three beleaguered actors perform a Dionysian ritual before a judge, and the performance's awesome power kills him; in another TV drama, *In the Presence of a Clown* (1997), the play-within-the-play about the dying Franz Schubert's "sinking world" deeply moves the audience in a small Swedish village. But there are also early Bergman films in which music is simply overwhelming: one example is the scene in *Music in Darkness* (1948) that involves the blind children gathering in an assembly hall to the accompaniment of Chopin's D-minor Prelude, and another is the scene in *To Joy* (1950) that features a cathartic rehearsal of Beethoven's Ninth Symphony and ends the entire film with a close-up of the boy who just lost his mother. It's an easy trick, no doubt, and Bergman himself has mocked it, but the *Wozzeck*-like ending of *To Joy* is nevertheless incredibly effective. Even *High Tension* (1950), arguably the worst film Bergman ever made and the only one he forbade to be shown in public, has interesting musical moments when the Eastern European refugees gather together in what they believe to be their safe new homeland.

The Unmusical Musician

Bergman referred to himself as having very modest musical abilities. He claimed to have a complete inability to remember or to reproduce a melody.[14] To him it was an immense effort to learn a piece of music; to make any sense of it he had to spend hours upon hours listening while following along in the score. Considering his three successful opera productions—along with *The Magic Flute* film, these are Stravinsky's *Rake's Progress* in 1961 and Daniel Börtz's *Bacchae* in 1996, both at the Royal Opera in Stockholm—this may seem perplexing; after all, these opera productions are tremendous statements that present Bergman as one of the most musical "unmusical" geniuses of cinematic history.[15]

Yet Bergman is not widely recognized as such; rather, he has been seen mainly as the ultimate inventor of breathtaking images and deformed mirrors of human anxiety. Indeed, in his original conception of one of his most successful films, *Cries and Whispers* (1972), there were only images, no narrative or music. "I see a road, and a girl on her way to a large house, a manor house, perhaps," he said. "She has a little dog with her. Inside the house there's a large red room where three sisters dressed in white are sitting and whispering together." Turning to Sven Nykvist, he asked: "Do you think it could turn into a film?"[16] Whether or not this recollection is true, Bergman spent a great amount of time dealing with the imagery before shooting, and the deep red color scheme of *Cries and Whispers* is what many remember most about the film. From Bergman's perspective, an ideal watcher would be Roger Ebert, for he appreciated the film's ability to reach directly to the emotional center:

> These two scenes—of Anna, embracing Agnes, and of Karin and Maria touching like frightened kittens—are two of the greatest Bergman has ever created. The feeling in these scenes—I should say, the way they force us to feel—constitutes the meaning of this film. It has no abstract message; it communicates with us on a level of human feeling so deep that we are afraid to invent words for the things found there. The camera is as uneasy as we are. It stays at rest mostly, but when it moves it doesn't always follow smooth, symmetrical progressions. It darts, it falls back, is stunned. … The movie is drenched in red. Bergman has written in his screenplay that he thinks of the inside of the human soul as a membranous red.[17]

So successful was Bergman at communicating on a direct emotional level that Ebert did not even mention the music that is so essential to the second of these scenes (although it was an afterthought, as Bergman initially had planned it to be without music).[18] The Sarabande from Bach's Fifth Suite for Solo Cello accompanies this central redemptive scene, the sole expression of emotional intimacy between the two characters. The mostly dialogue-free scene follows Karin's expression of hate toward her sister shortly after the flashback to Karin's genital self-mutilation as an act of desperation in a loveless marriage. In seconds the scene moves from absolute anguish to redemption: Karin cries out and asks her sister to forgive her; the music takes over completely and contradicts everything from Bergman's 1962 statement, and then the sisters are back to being on unfriendly terms.

In his existential dramas from the 1960s and 1970s, Bergman had moved far from the more or less conventional[19] use of music in his early films, which were scored by Nordgren and also by Dag Wirén, Erland von Koch, and Karl-Birger Blomdahl. The Swedish-Estonian pianist Käbi Laretei (b. 1922), who in 1959 became Bergman's fourth wife, was decisive in this change of approach. An accomplished concert pianist who later would give recitals in Carnegie Hall and other major venues, work directly with Stravinsky and Hindemith, and host her own show on Swedish television, Laretei introduced Bergman to lots of music, including the Chopin mazurkas, one of which—Op. 17, No. 4—was featured in *Cries and Whispers*. More important, Laretei constantly exposed Bergman to music through her practicing. Bergman claimed that Laretei was instrumental in his aesthetic change toward what he called chamber dramas, that is, films with few characters that were to a certain extent inspired by chamber music.

In his autobiography *Laeterna Magica*, Bergman explained in detail his fascination with the discipline and rigorous methods of music-making. He attended sessions in Stuttgart with Laretei's teacher, Maria-Luisa Strub-Moresco—in his book he gives her the Bergmanesque name Andrea Vogler-Corelli—and he described the lesson: "A phrase was broken up into its smallest parts, was practiced with pedantic fingering for hours, and assembled again when time was ready." In an extensive paragraph filled with Strub-Moresco quotations, he noted that her pedagogic personality seemed as "merciless as a lawn mower"; as he listened to Strub-Moresco, he concluded, he "thought about theater, myself, the actors. Our sloppiness, our ignorance. Our damned everyday matters that we presented for money."[20] Bergman claimed to have learned more about film work from Strub-Moresco than from anyone else; in particular, she made him conscious of the approach of perfecting the small parts before assembling them into a whole.[21] In a Swedish television documentary on Laretei that features a lesson in Stuttgart, there is nothing in the footage of Laretei's interaction with Strub-Moresco that contradicts Bergman's account.[22] Strub-Moresco seems to have been an extraordinary pedagogue with an intense personality.

Laretei has provided an account of Bergman that describes him as having quite unexpected musical abilities. During a concert she had a slight memory lapse of the kind that hardly anyone would notice.[23] But Bergman, who was in the audience, knew the piece well and almost had a heart attack. In Laretei's opinion, Bergman was in fact quite musical, although he lacked the ability to reproduce pitch with his voice. Laretei recalled another episode during which Bergman heard her practice the last movement of Beethoven's Piano Sonata No. 23 ("Appassionata"); finding that the movement contained a few "ugly chords," he convinced her to bring these to the foreground. And this added an interesting twist to their relationship, with the "unmusical" Bergman being the provider of a key to the musical interpretation.

The Musician as a Model

For Bergman, the musical process was the ideal working method for the performing artist. It was disciplined and hard, just like Bergman's approach to directing, where there is no room for improvisations or vagueness, where everything must be planned in advance and tightly controlled. Bergman even believed that music notation was superior to written language in that it was more exact.[24]

His most noteworthy depiction of music-making occurs in *Autumn Sonata* (1978), when the concert pianist Charlotte (played by Ingrid Bergman) gives her amateur daughter Eva (Liv Ullmann) a piano lesson during which they both perform Chopin's Prelude in A Minor. Käbi Laretei recorded the prelude in two versions, one for each character, and coached the actresses in their pretend performances.

The Op. 28, No. 2, Prelude in A Minor is a significant piece, one of Chopin's most enigmatic compositions, and one that has been the subject of numerous studies. As early as 1883 the pianist and author Jan Kleczynski (1837–95) suggested that the piece was too "bizarre," and in his performances of the Op. 28 cycle he skipped it and played the first prelude twice. Bergman recalled that he had heard Anton Rubinstein perform the A Minor Prelude on the radio and was fascinated because it differed so much from the others in the set. During the shooting of *Autumn Sonata*, actress Ingrid Bergman noticed strange qualities in the music. "My god," she exclaimed. "Will this boring piece of music be performed twice? But Ingmar, this is insane; the audience will fall asleep. You could at least have chosen a more beautiful and shorter one. This one is too gloomy. I'm yawning myself to death."[25] But herein lies the strength of using this piece. At first glance it seems like a typical Chopin composition, with a steady accompaniment in the left hand and a melody in the right. But the harmony is quite eccentric, and the final cadence arrives as somewhat of a surprise. It is an ideal piece in that it invites many different interpretations, and it opens itself to interesting analytical narratives.

After many years apart, the mother and daughter of *Autumn Sonata* have met again. There is tension in the air, but nothing serious. After dinner, they approach Charlotte's turf. Charlotte warms up with the beginning of the third movement of Schumann's Piano Concerto, an excerpt that Laretei suggested for the scene and a work that she had performed with orchestra. The piano is decent and in tune; Charlotte is in a good mood. Then, as Eva hesitantly plays the Chopin Prelude, the camera focuses on Charlotte, who seems impatient yet nevertheless shows tenderness toward her daughter. Eva's interpretation is somewhat naïve, technically imperfect, of course, but not unacceptable. It is somewhat reminiscent of Rubinstein's early recording of the piece, quite fast and with an emphasis on the right hand.

In the behind-the-camera documentation of the filming process,[26] Laretei complains that pianists in movies typically move too much. Only their eyes should be moving, she says, and this is a piece of advice that Bergman took to heart, for the actual filmed scene consists mostly of close-ups of Charlotte's and Eva's faces. Later in the documentation footage, Bergman and Laretei have a lighthearted argument about whether or not it would be realistic if Charlotte gave her monologue while playing. They reach a compromise in which at first most of Charlotte's talking occurs *between* the first two musical phrases. In the final edit, Charlotte's initially condescending tone gives way to the mode of a neutral lecture:

> We disregard the purely technical, which wasn't that bad, although you could have paid attention to Cortot's fingerings since they assist interpretation. But never mind.
>
> Chopin was strong in emotion, but not emotional. There is a gorge between emotion and sentimentality. The prelude you're playing speaks about restrained pain, not reverie. You have to be calm, clear, and arduous. See the first measures—it hurts, but he doesn't show it. Then a brief relief. But it disappears almost immediately. Then the pain is the same—neither more, nor less.
>
> The control is complete the entire time. Chopin was proud, sarcastic, intense, anguished, and very masculine. Thus, he wasn't an emotional old bag. This second prelude has to be played almost ugly. It must never become flattering. It should sound wrong, with effort or successfully fought. Like this.

Charlotte then performs the entire piece. When asked by Laretei how he came up with this narrative, Bergman simply explained that this kind of musical interpretation is not much different from interpreting a text for a play, rather like one does with a text by Strindberg.

Music plays a very complex role in the scene. Charlotte's narrative and interpretation are metaphors for her approach to life and motherhood. Between daughter and mother, music is a source of alienation. Music-making requires great self-sacrifices in terms of weeks away from home; Charlotte's career was the reason why she couldn't see her grandchild—she was recording all the Mozart sonatas and concertos. But serious music-making also results in physical pain—back pain, in particular. The musical outcome *should* reflect this discipline. During the performance, Eva stares at her mother, and there is no doubt that this is a pivotal scene. Eva realizes, through the music, who her celebrated mother really is, a professional (a heartless professional in my reading, a dedicated one in Laretei's), and she knows that this was the reason why Charlotte gave up on her family. "I see," Eva says when her mother is finished. This is the seed of her tirade later in the film and of the accusations that culminate in her charge: "People like you are lethal: They should be locked up and terminated."

"Almost ugly" is an apt description of Charlotte's interpretation, one in which she dwells on the dissonances and makes the left-hand accompaniment as important as the right-hand melody. Laretei told me that neither Charlotte's nor Eva's version was really hers, but that she was very impressed with

Bergman's script for the scene as an antithesis of the over-romanticized Chopin.[27]

The comments Charlotte makes about Chopin resemble Bergman's description of Strub-Moresco and her understanding of Beethoven, which may be another reason the script resonated so well with Laretei. "There are no instruments, and there will never be, that will be able to reproduce the dynamics that Beethoven imagined in his deaf world," Bergman wrote in his autobiography. "In Beethoven, there are no fillers. He speaks persuasively, furiously, sadly, joyfully; he never mumbles."[28] In a 2004 Swedish radio program Bergman described an image of Chopin. It was not the typical youthful portrait but, rather, the only known photograph of Chopin taken by Louis-Auguste Bisson in London in 1849, shortly before Chopin's death. This was an image Bergman could not escape, and he observed that Chopin's hands were not as graceful as one might have thought. The composer

> sits there and has lost a lot of weight. His costume is too large for him. He looks into the camera …. The most interesting thing is that he put his hands on his knees and crossed them …; they are a pair of large meat mallets. They lay there inactive, large and clumsy, and do not fit with the sunken skinny body and the eternally sad face.[29]

This description sheds a different light on Charlotte's monologue, and it helps explain how sound and image interact and complement one another. The extra-musical connotation relating to a performance or a composer becomes important in yet another of Bergman's films, *Hour of the Wolf* (1968).

A Message from Beyond

Hour of the Wolf does not belong among Bergman's most celebrated works; even Bergman himself realized that in its central conception it was unsuccessful:

> To see a man who is already mad become crazier is boring. What would have been interesting would have been to see an absolutely sane woman go crazy because she loves the madman she married. She enters his world of unreality, and that infects her. Suddenly, she finds out that she is lost. I understood this only when the picture was finished.[30]

Despite what he saw as its flaws, Bergman acknowledged that he liked *Hour of the Wolf*, and he hoped that it eventually might gain recognition.[31] Following as it does Bergman's nervous breakdown in 1965, the film's nightmarish sequences experienced through the eyes and writings of the delusional painter Johan Borg (Max von Sydow) have often been understood in an autobiographic light. One year before *Hour of the Wolf*, Bergman released *Persona*, a modernistic masterwork not tied to conventional film genres, and one of the most analyzed movies in cinematic history.[32] Bergman commented on the differences between the two movies, and he called *Hour of the Wolf* not a regression but an uneasy step in the right direction. Two of the film's most fascinating scenes are musically imperative; one of them features an excerpt from *The Magic Flute*, and the other is set to music by the Swedish composer Lars Johan Werle.

Painter Johan and his wife Alma (Liv Ullmann) have settled on a remote island. Soon after their arrival, people on the island begin to appear and interact with the couple. It is certainly not clear from the beginning, but it turns out that these people are daemons. As noted by Philip Strick and Ellen Burns,[33] and others, the entire film borrows an important storyline from *The Magic Flute*. Through the twisted paths of his disturbed mind, Johan is on a search for Veronica Vogler, his former mistress. A deformed Papageno figure occurs in the form of the "birdman" Lindhorst, played by Bela Lugosi lookalike George Rydeberg, who displays his wings toward the end of the film. Following dinner at the daemons' castle, Lindhorst presents a puppet show, with a live puppet performing the recitative "O ew'ge Nacht" from *The Magic Flute*. The topics of this recitative—questions about the afterlife, eternal life, and love—have been featured over and over again in Bergman's oeuvre, but surely this is one of their most significant treatments. Tamino's questions and the answers given by the chorus (see below) become an incantation, a voice from the other side, brought forward through music.

TAMINO:
O ew'ge Nacht, wann wirst du schwinden?   O eternal night, when will you disappear?
Wann wird das Licht mein Auge finden?   When will the light find my eye?
CHORUS:
Bald, bald, Jüngling, oder nie.   Soon, soon, young one, or never.
TAMINO:
Bald, bald, bald, sagt ihr, oder nie?   Soon, soon, soon, you say, or never?
Ihr unsichtbaren, saget mir,   You invisible ones, tell me,
Lebt denn Pamina noch?   Lives then Pamina still?
CHORUS:
Pamina, Pamina, ja sie lebt!   Pamina Pamina, yes she lives.

After the death of his fifth and last wife, Bergman confessed that he found it unimaginable that he would not meet her again. Growing up in a religious home—his father was a minister, a quite prominent one, the minister of the Royal Court—Bergman struggled to come to terms with Christianity; his level of faith seemed to oscillate between religiosity, agnosticism, and doubt. Using almost the same language as Lindhorst does in the film, Bergman described how important the Mozart recitative was to him. But he went further, noting that these particular measures touched him more deeply than did any of the music he carried with him through life.[34] They represent a calling from an afterlife, he said, and they provide two answers: to the question of when he should find light, the dying Mozart receives the response "Soon, soon or never more," and the syllabic singing of the name "Pa-mi-na" becomes an incantation that represents hope of an existing love.[35] But not only does the performance give answers, albeit vague ones; it also provides a respite for the tortured daemons.

The character Lindhorst says that the recitative's text is naïve, which underscores Bergman's Schopenhauerian understanding of music as the elevated art that can raise even the naïve to the sublime. Indeed, the importance of this scene is confirmed by the script's various drafts. While the script in general underwent many changes,[36] Lindhorst's monologue remained virtually unchanged from 1964, when the movie was called "The Daemons," through a typed draft from 1964–6, when it was called "The Cannibals," through the finished script from 1968. In Bergman's mind, the questions raised in the recitative represent not just the suffering that Mozart experienced at the end of his life but also the suffering of the recorded performance's conductor, Ferenc Fricsay (1914–63). Fricsay's interpretation, which Bergman felt was marked by his disease (Fricsay would suffer and die from cancer at the age of forty-eight) led Bergman to compare Fricsay to the sick Adrian Leverkühn character in Thomas Mann's novel *Dr. Faustus*, and to argue that interpretive geniality could result from disease—in this case, a simplicity and a calmness.[37] Bergman admitted that, despite having access to wonderful musicians in his own *Magic Flute* production, he could not achieve the same emotional level that Fricsay had reached.[38] In fact, the two versions of the recitative do not differ that much, although the chorus in the opera film lacks the distant-sounding quality—as if coming from a different world—that characterizes the *Hour of the Wolf* performance.

During the performance, Johan and Alma, as well as the ghosts, halt their conversations and listen, mesmerized. In terms of narrative, the scene parallels Karin's and Maria's brief moment of reconciliation in *Cries and Whispers*. But the musical message in *Hour of the Wolf* seems more powerful; it can control even ghosts.

Although there are several scenes featuring music in *Hour of the Wolf*, one more is worth mentioning here, one that involves extra-diegetic music by Lars Johan Werle, probably the most important Swedish opera composer during the mid-1960s through the early 1980s. Several of Werle's works belong to the Swedish opera canon, although they are rarely performed abroad. Nicolas Slonimsky described Werle's "amiably modern idiom" as "stimulating to the untutored ear while retaining the specific gravity of triadic tonal constructions."[39] While this description certainly resonates with several of Werle's works, it is far from the modernist sonic world of *Hour of the Wolf* or of *Persona* (1966), the other Bergman film for which he wrote. The confusing written score for *Hour of the Wolf* lies far from what is heard on the completed soundtrack: the score was altered both during the recording session and in the editing room, and several sections consist of free improvisation.[40]

By the light of matches, Johan tells Alma about the "Hour of the Wolf," the hours between 3 a.m. and 5 a.m. during which, according to Swedish folklore, most people die and most children are born, and when nightmares appear. Then he tells how as a child his parents punished him by repeatedly locking him in a closet and then spanking him. Johan's description is reproduced almost verbatim in Bergman's autobiography *Laterna Magica* from two decades later, and a similar incident—obviously based on Bergman's own experiences—occurs in *Fanny and Alexander* (1982). In confidence, Johan offers what he thinks to be the truth about why he came home earlier with a wound on his face. The reason was not a snakebite, he says, but a disturbing incident featuring a young boy: Johan was standing alone, fishing, when the boy appeared and watched him; after examining his possessions. Johan grabbed the boy, shook him, killed him with a rock, then threw the body into the sea. In the film, the boy does not appear to have done anything to provoke this, but the script explains that Johan believed the boy stole his watch. Bergman described the boy as a small daemon, and added: "The problem was just that the daemon should have been naked! And if one takes this one step further, Johan should also have been naked."[41]

Musically the scene is remarkable, with a combination of conventional Hollywood suspense clichés, mickey-mousing, and stingers. The insertion of the boy's screams, in a scene devoid of natural sounds, is very effective and adds a layer of almost comical absurdity. Importantly, the music challenges the images by renouncing and contradicting them. The overexposed footage calls to mind another striking episode in a Bergman film that is told through image and music alone; this is in *Sawdust and Tinsel* (1953) when Alma, the wife of Frost the Clown, is bathing naked in the sea with soldiers from the regiment, set to music by another then-living Swedish art-music composer, Karl-Birger Blomdahl.

Utilizing two so contrasting musical styles—Werle and Mozart—in a single film is unusual for Bergman, and so is the use of modernist music in conventional ways. The Mozart scene, on the other hand, is typical of Bergman's oeuvre: it involves a standard-repertoire piece that to Bergman has high emotional value, and it is not just performed but discussed by the film's characters.

Sarabande(s)

Chadwick Jenkins gives a beautiful interpretation of the historical, pre-Bach Sarabande. "Originating as a salacious entanglement of two sexualized bodies," he writes, "the dance became the embodiment of balance and reserve." He makes the analogy to Bergman's chamber films, in which the Sarabande "mirrors the director's tendency to construct a film out of a series of duets,

[of] searching dialogues between characters that greatly need to communicate with each other but only manage to engage in a hopelessly desperate dance."[42] Jenkins puts the finger exactly on Bergman's two-person interactions that are accompanied by the Sarabande movements from Bach's second and fifth suites for solo cello. Despite the differences between these two Sarabandes, they share the same function: they interrupt the narrative and elevate their scenes to a purely emotional realm in which the only time is musical.

Through a Glass Darkly (1961) features the Sarabande from the second suite as its sole music, apart from diegetic guitar music during the "play-within-the-play" scene. The Sarabande dwells in the cello's lower register, and its minor mode and slow rhythmic motion give it a severe mood; its key is D, and this is also the pitch of the foghorn that is heard in several of the film's scenes. Along with serving as the music for the main title sequence, the Sarabande is heard three times in the course of the film, during the most dramatic moments. Each usage of the Sarabande features a different version recorded by cellist Erling Blöndal Bengtsson. The version used for the main titles has the slowest tempo and the most expressive dynamics; after Karin reads in her father's diary that her disease is incurable and that he is tempted to study her decline for artistic purposes, the Sarabande is heard faster and lighter; after the incest between Karin and her brother the Sarabande slows down; at the end of the film, when the ambulance helicopter carries Karin away, the dynamic expressiveness is back but the tempo is faster. The differences between the versions are not obvious, because they are so spaced out in time. But they follow the dramaturgy of the plot, and they illustrate Bergman's attention to the most minute sonic details. Blöndal Bengtsson recalled that he made the recordings during a single studio session, and that he was asked by the producer (Bergman was not present) to make several versions.[43] He was not informed how the music would be used in the film, and he was not asked to synchronize his performances with any footage.

Bergman's last film was *Saraband* (2003), the epilogue to the 1973 *Scenes from a Marriage*; it sums up many of the artist-related issues raised during Bergman's career, and it is also his most elaborate and most musically complex film. Throughout the movie the Sarabande from Bach's fifth cello suite runs like a refrain, and it stands at the center of the incestuous relationship between father Henrik (Börje Ahlstedt) and daughter Karin (Julia Dufvenius), both of whom are cellists.

Other bits of diegetic music in *Saraband* are associated with various secondary characters; Bruckner's Ninth Symphony is linked with Henrik's authoritarian and severe father (Erland Josephson), for example, and Brahms's String Quartet in A Minor, as heard on the radio, is linked with Henrik's former wife, the mellow Marianne (Liv Ullmann). Some music in the film is not performed but only discussed, again illustrating how in Bergman's world musical compositions often transfer into real-life experiences. For example, Karin channels her anger toward her father as both teacher and human being through an outburst over the performance instructions—"Lebhafte Viertel (ohne jeden Ausdruck und stets Pianissimo)"—for the fourth movement of Hindemith's Sonata for Cello, Op. 25, No. 3, and this culminates in a flashback of an actual fight between father and daughter.

The use of Bach in *Saraband* resembles the use of the same composer's music in *Through a Glass Darkly*. The piece is iterated numerous times, but typically only in short phrases; it is heard in the main title sequence and in the epilogue, in transitions between various scenes, and—significantly—in the central scene when Karin plays the piece and breaks up with her father, which results in Henrik's attempted suicide. Bergman used one commercially available recording of the piece, by Thorleif Thedéen, with added reverb; for the diegetic performance by Karin he used a version recorded in the studio by Åsa Forsberg-Lindgren. In both recordings the entire A-section is played only twice, and never with repeats. The most stunning usage comes at the end of scene five of the film, when Henrik articulates his vision of death: "We walk through our entire life and wonder about death and what does and does not follow, and then it is this easy: Through music I can sometimes get a hint, just a hint, as in Bach." This was also Bergman's own vision of death, as expressed in a 2000 interview, before making the film.[44]

The cello's register may be the reason why Bergman used Sarabandes for that instrument rather than for violin or keyboard.[45] That the cello is the instrument that most closely resembles the human voice seems a cliché, but it is a useful one: In *Faithless* (2000), for which Bergman wrote the script, he has the young conductor Markus ask a cellist to sing her line in the slow movement of Brahms's C Minor Piano Quartet.

Saraband offers a take on the musician's role as a mirror of society that is different from the one represented by the orchestral musician who wants to break out, as in *To Joy*, or by the pianist who sacrifices everything for the sake of her career, as in *Autumn Sonata*. Indeed, it is quite the opposite. Bergman has Karin say:

> I do not believe in myself as a soloist. I want to become an orchestral musician. I want to be surrounded by a sea of sound, in that enormous common effort. Not sit on a podium alone and exposed. I want to live a regular life. I want to belong.

Twenty-five years after *Autumn Sonata* and fifty-three years after *To Joy*, in *Saraband* Bergman had found yet another musical metaphor for life.

Notes

*   I am grateful for assistance from several friends and colleagues: the Bergman Archives, in particular Margareta Nordström and Hélène Dahl, Torbjörn Ehrnvall, assistant director of *Saraband*, the Audiovisual Collections at the National Library of Sweden, in particular Ann-Charlotte Gyllner-Noonan, Erling Blöndal

Bengtsson, and Swedish Music Information Center. Joakim Tillman and Nora Engebretsen provided valuable comments on the entire text. In this chapter, all quotes have been taken from the Swedish original and translated by the author.

1   Staiger writes: "Authorship-as-personality analysis, and its variant auteurism, continue unabated today, with scholars usually attempting to avoid some of the fallacies—such as doing a much better job placing the director within historical circumstances, not elevating directors to romantic geniuses, and judging films on grounds other than who the director is." Janet Staiger, "Authorship Approaches," in *Authorship and Film*, ed. David A. Gestner and Janet Staiger (New York and London: Routledge, 2003), 39.

2   In Stig Björkman's documentary ... *But Film Is My Mistress* (2010).

3   Maaret Koskinen, *Ingmar Bergman's The Silence: Pictures in the Typewriter, Writings on the Screen* (Seattle: University of Washington Press, 2010).

4   Ibid., 31.

5   If one is willing to attribute the church-bells hymn to Bach's Cantata No. 137 rather than to its composer, Joachim Neander. See Charlotte Renaud's groundbreaking study, "La citation musicale dans les films d'Ingmar Bergman" (unpublished thesis, Université de La Sorbonne Paris III-Censier, 2007).

6   His attraction to Wagner changed, however, from early devotion to a more critical stance.

7   Louise Eulau assembled a list of his entire collection. It is available at the Bergman Archives.

8   Jannike Åhlund, "Gud och kannibalism fick fart på Bergman och Koskinen," *Svenska Dagbladet*, July 1, 2005.

9   Sofia Lilly Jönsson, "Ljudestetik i spelfilm: Om sju minuter i Bergmans *Fanny och Alexander*" (unpublished master's thesis, Department of Musicology and Theater, Stockholm University, 2011), 23.

10   Available in the Criterion DVD set "A Film Trilogy by Ingmar Bergman". Sjöman (1924–2006) also wrote a book documenting Bergman's process, *L 136: dagbok med Ingmar Bergman* (Stockholm: Norstedt, 1963).

11   The statement was not a one-time event; he expressed a similar opinion more than twenty years later, phrased slightly differently: "Both music and film strike the emotional center of our consciousness and music to film would be too much of a good thing." In the TV program "Kväll med Käbi," Swedish Television, January 1, 1985.

12   Two exceptions are *Face to Face* (1976), which features only three instances of diegetic music and one brief stinger, and no music for the beginning and end credits, and the rarely discussed *Brink of Life* (1958), which has absolutely no music.

13   The most comprehensive source of reference is Birgitta Steene's monumental *Ingmar Bergman: A Reference Guide* (Amsterdam: Amsterdam University Press, 2006).

14   This is a topic that Bergman discussed in the documentary "Kväll med Käbi" and Camilla Lundberg's interview "Ingmar Bergman och musiken," Swedish Television, December 25, 2000.

15   Bergman also staged three operettas, *The Three penny Opera* (1950), *The Merry Widow* (1954), and *Värmlänningarna* (1951, 1958).

16   "Cries and Whispers," available at: www.ingmarbergman.se/page.asp?guid= 62F04380-F5E6-42B6-87F3-0A807B627DAE.

17   Roger Ebert, "Cries and Whispers," *Chicago Sun-Times*, February 12, 1973, available at: http://rogerebert.suntimes.com/apps/pbcs.dll/article?AID=/19730212/REVIEWS/302120301/1023.

18   "Gäst hos Käbi."
19   I say more or less, since there are extraordinary examples of innovative use of both diegetic and extra-diegetic scores in the early films, in particular, perhaps, in *Crisis*, *The Magician*, and *Sawdust and Tinsel*.
20   Ingmar Bergman, *Laterna Magica* (Stockholm: Norstedt, 1987), 261.
21   Käbi Laretei, *Såsom i en översättning: teman med variationer* (Stockholm: Bonnier, 2004), 128, and "Ingmar Bergman och musiken."
22   TV documentary "Känner du Käbi Laretei?" Swedish Television, December 27, 1976.
23   In a conversation with the author, 2008.
24   "Musikalisk salong," Swedish Television, March 10, 1966.
25   *Laterna Magica*, 214.
26   The complete behind-the-camera footage of Laretei's coaching session is available in the Bergman Archives. An abridged version was included with the monumental volume *The Ingmar Bergman Archives*, ed. Paul Duncan and Bengt Wanselius (Hong Kong and Los Angeles: Taschen, 2008).
27   For a contrasting overview of the image of the piano, see Ivan Kaykoff, "Hollywood's Embattled Icon," in *Piano Roles: 300 Years of Life with the Piano* (New Haven: Yale University Press, 2000), 329–57.
28   *Laterna Magica*, 261.
29   "Sommar," Swedish Radio, July 18, 2004.
30   "Hour of the Wolf," available at: http://bergmanorama.webs.com/films/hour_of_ the_wolf_commentary.htm.
31   "Kväll med Käbi."
32   Not least sonically, see Michel Chion, *Audio-Vision: Sound on Screen*, ed. and trans. Claudia Gorbman (New York: Columbia University Press, 1994), which includes a "model analysis" of the introduction of the film.
33   Philip Strick, "Hour of the Wolf," *Sight and Sound* 37, no. 4 (Autumn 1968): 203–4, and Ellen Burns, "Ingmar Bergman's Projected Self: From W.A. Mozart's *Die Zauberflöte* to *Vargtimmen*," *Analecta Husserliana* 94 (2007): 459–68.
34   "Kväll med Käbi."
35   As Sofia Lilly Jönsson (2011) points out, Lindhorst's monologue is alluded to in Bille August's *A Song for Martin* (2001), when the Alzheimer's-stricken conductor and composer Martin has gathered with his family in the garden.
36   For example, the latter part of the final script differs drastically from the early versions; most significantly, it includes an extensive and bizarre episode in which Alma has an affair with Fredrik Egerman (a character in *Smiles of a Summer Night*), gets pregnant, loses the child, and then seeks punishment by the police.
37   "Gäst hos Käbi." There is a short documentary on YouTube following Fricsay's death, www.youtube.com/watch?v=0oE6V1pwQPg&feature=related, along with a documentary, "Classic Archive—Music Transfigured: Remembering Ferenc Fricsay Euroarts Catalog # 3078528," 2009.
38   "Ingmar Bergman och musiken."
39   Martin Anderson, obituary "Lars Johan Werle," *The Independent*, 29 September 2001, available at: www.independent.co.uk/news/obituaries/lars-johan-werle-729452.html.
40   The scores for both *Persona* and *Hour of the Wolf* are available at the Swedish Music Information Center in Stockholm.
41   Ingmar Bergman, *Bilder* (Stockholm: Norstedt, 1990), 35.
42   Chadwick Jenkins, "The Profound Consolation: The Use of Bach's Music in the Films of Ingmar Bergman (Part 1)," October 13, 2006, available at: www. popmatters.com/pm/column/the-profound-consolation-the-use-of-bachs-music-in-the-films-of-ingmar-berg/.

43 In an interview with the author on January 13, 2011.
44 "Ingmar Bergman och musiken." See also Torbjörn Ehrnvall's video diary from the making of *Saraband*, included in *The Ingmar Bergman Archives*.
45 One exception is the Sarabande from Bach's Keyboard Partita No. 3, BWV 827, which is used in *Hour of the Wolf*. Solo cello pieces were, however, featured in another film; these are Benjamin Britten's Solo Suites Nos. 2 and 3, used in *Fanny and Alexander*.

Chapter 3

Andrey Tarkovsky

The Refrain of the Sonic Fingerprint

Elizabeth Fairweather

Richard Dyer noted of auteurship that it "made the case for taking film seriously by seeking to show that a film could be just as profound, beautiful and important as any other kind of art, provided … it was demonstrably the work of an highly individual artist."[1] There is no doubt that Andrey Tarkovsky is such an artist, or that his use of sound is not only profound and beautiful but also wholly unique and distinctive. Identification and analysis of Tarkovsky's 'sonic fingerprints' are useful tools for establishing how his films work overall, for Tarkovsky considered sound to be as important a vehicle for the communication of specific meaning as any other cinematographic element. But what, exactly, are his characteristic and recognizable uses of sound? What are the 'sonic fingerprints' that recur throughout Tarkovsky's films?

Tarkovsky's Cinematic Style

Tarkovsky made seven feature films: *Ivan's Childhood* (1962), *Andrei Rublev* (1966), *Solaris* (1972), *Mirror* (1974), *Stalker* (1979), *Nostalghia* (1983), and *The Sacrifice* (1986). They share general characteristics, such as metaphysical or transcendental themes that often seem to be of an autobiographical nature, themes of the sort that Bhaskar Sarkar described as "intimations of an enigmatic inner life."[2] Memory, reflections, dreams, and flashbacks, sometimes to childhood, feature regularly. Scenes are often structured around long takes in which images and sounds of natural beauty are given the breathing space they need in order to register with the audience.

One of Tarkovsky's contributions to film scholarship was his development of a structuralizing theory of cinema that he called 'sculpting in time.' This refers to the idea that the audience's sense of time and place is subject to manipulation, and the resulting illusion in a way amounts to a means of artistic expression in and of itself. The theory of 'sculpting in time' acknowledges that human feeling and emotion are timeless and, ultimately, transcendental. Tarkovsky writes:

> I find poetic links, the logic of poetry in the cinema, extraordinarily pleasing. … I am more at home with them than with traditional

theatrical writing which links images through the linear, rigidly logical development of the plot …. [I]n my view poetic reasoning is closer to the laws by which thought develops, and thus to life itself.[3]

All unedited shooting of course records real time. By using long takes with relatively few cuts, Tarkovsky achieved both a heightened sense of time and a temporal blurring; he experimented with time's passing, loss, and chronological place, and this enabled him to approximate a representation of human thought as it actually transpires. Tarkovsky explored this concept in his works up to and including *Mirror*. After this, he changed his working philosophy and explored the dramatic possibilities afforded by concentrating the action in a single location and within a short span of fictional time. In *The Sacrifice*, for example, the main character and his family experience what seems to be a nuclear holocaust. In despair, he vows to give up all he loves in exchange for salvation, and to seal his promise he sleeps with a woman rumored to be a witch. When he awakes everything appears to be normal, but the audience begins to wonder if perhaps it was all a dream. In any case, the character makes his sacrifice by burning down his house before being taken away in a little white van.

In his efforts to create temporal blurring, Tarkovsky's use of color is allied with his shooting techniques. Several films have sequences in which the coloring is unusual: the black-and-white *Andrei Rublev*, for example, features an epilogue in full color, and *Solaris*, *Mirror*, and *Stalker*—all shot in color—contain scenes in monochrome or sepia. Writing about film in general but making a point about Tarkovsky, Robert Bird notes that "black and white images free the cinema artist from the illusion of realism and allow for the manipulation of scale and perspective."[4] Always careful in his use of color, Tarkovsky observed that

in everyday life we seldom pay any special attention to colour …. [O]n the screen colour imposes itself on you, whereas in real life that only happens at odd moments, so it's not right for the audience to be constantly aware of colour. Isolated details can be in colour if that is what corresponds to the state of the character on the screen … [but] as soon as you have a coloured picture in the frame it becomes a moving painting. It's all too beautiful, and unlike life.[5]

Tarkovsky believed that in life only "transitional states of nature,"[6] such as sunsets, were actually perceived as colorful. Robert Bird's interpretation is that forcing color upon the spectator conveyed a "transition within the represented object, corresponding to a change in texture."[7] In his films, Tarkovsky achieved changes in texture by skillfully manipulating elements of nature, but his use of the pictorial was not confined to the purely natural. Julia Shpinitskaya suggests that Tarkovsky typically "cod[ed] the narration with [an] inter-circulation of texts" that belonged to such "diverse, non-cinematic art-realities" as "music and painting."[8] Indeed, Tarkovsky's 'sonic style' involved the use of fragments of pre-existing music that in some films are situated alongside images of certain paintings; by matching images from Bruegel's *The Hunters in the Snow* with the music of J.S. Bach in *Solaris*, for example, Tarkovsky used different forms of media to fully encompass different versions of the same narrative meaning.

Natural elements feature prominently in Tarkovsky's films. Earth, water, wind, and fire—in a variety of forms, situations, quantities, and, most importantly, media—are used metaphorically. Sarkar describes Tarkovsky's technique as "eschew[ing] a narrowly construed narratological rationalism,"[9] and this seems to apply especially to Tarkovsky's treatment of water. In Tarkovsky's films, water crosses the entire spectrum of possibilities, from torrential rain to a single, amplified drip from a tap. Often the depiction of water creates an irritating and intrusive effect, and sometimes it seems as though Tarkovsky's world is perpetually damp. Occasionally, as in *Stalker* and *Ivan's Childhood*, water is used to set an especially miserable scene, such as when the 'stalker' rests on a small patch of damp ground amid an otherwise waterlogged area, or when Ivan crawls miserably through a bare, waterlogged forest. The use of water in this manner is entirely intentional. "Water is a mysterious element," Tarkovsky has said; "it can convey movement and a sense of change and flux. ... [M]aybe it has subconscious echoes— perhaps my love of water arises from some atavistic memory of some ancestral transmigration."[10]

Tarkovsky's admission of the influence of his subconscious upon his works, Sarkar argues, combines with a "striving for transcendence" to produce a "simultaneous stress on the factual and the inscrutable: all the world's mysteries inhere in its mundane facticity."[11] But however it is described, it is this obsession with the natural and normal, and the insistence on its prominence as a means to a higher plane of expression, that sets Tarkovsky apart from most other directors. Tatiana Egorova compares Tarkovsky to another Russian director, Georgy Sviridov, whom she describes as "a destroyer of stereotypes,"[12] and she notes that both Tarkovsky and Sviridov "achieved the modulated transition from metaphor to [the] reality of everyday life."[13] In the case of Tarkovsky, the modulated transitions owe a great deal to the director's use of sound.

Tarkovsky's Sonic Fingerprints

One very quickly becomes aware of the sound in a Tarkovsky film. Often the sound is of everyday reality, where it would be considered insignificant or unnoticeable, but Tarkovsky makes it lend meaning to the narrative. Andrea Truppin argues that the privileging of ordinary sound in Tarkovsky's films operates on a transcendental level in which it surpasses logic and reason and speaks with unspoken intuition and immediacy. Meaning is generated from these sonic fingerprints not just in individual films but across the totality of Tarkovsky's output. The recurring use of a certain sound in a variety of different situations causes that sound to act as a refrain. A particular sonic element might be varied only slightly—for example, a bird call might come first from a crow and later from a cuckoo—but this recognizable similarity will in itself generate meaning, and the differences in sound will be crucial.

At times, Tarkovsky subjugates the use of dialogue in favor of this heightened level of wordless communication. His versatile use of sound can invite both structuralist comparisons and independence from such parameters. A sonic element can emphasize and auralize reality, and it can highlight the otherworldly. Sound can function independently from the accompanying visuals to aid with the process of temporal blurring, and it can also fuse closely with the visuals to clarify a sense of the present. Tarkovsky wrote that

> music is not just an appendage to the visual image. It must be an essential element of the realization of the concept as a whole. Properly used, music has the capacity to change the whole emotional tone of a filmed sequence.[14]

Sound is an equal partner; it has parity within the integrated whole, and it can contribute as much meaning as any other cinematic feature. Rather than automatically regarding sound as an accompaniment to the usually dominant visuals, the director must not only consider this but must work it to his advantage.

Tarkovsky often used both acoustic and manipulated natural sounds as a powerful means of expression. But he was not as interested in sound per se as in achieving a meaningful result with it; for Tarkovsky, the very same sound could be diegetic in one scene and extra-diegetic in another. While it is indeed possible to generalize for ease of categorization, it remains that Tarkovsky's cinematic process involves so many different factors that no two of his uses of any type of sound are exactly alike. Nor are they predictable. Each individual use of sound strives to communicate with a nuance at least slightly different from every similar example, bearing out Tarkovsky's idea that music and sound have a 'refrain' element.

Tarkovsky used both pre-composed and original music, but sparingly and only at pertinent moments. He was very clear as to the role he expected music to play in his films:

> I find music in film most acceptable when it is used like a refrain .... Music does more than intensify the impression of the visual image by providing a parallel illustration of the same idea; it opens up the possibility of a *new*, transfigured impression of the same material: something different in kind.[15]

In this statement, Tarkovsky in effect explained why his use of sound is so unique. His comment reveals a synecdoche in which his sense of 'refrain' applies to sonic elements both within individual films and with regard to the whole of his output. Interestingly, Tarkovsky's diegetic sounds are just as effective and revealing (if not more so) as the music in his underscores. In all seven of his full-length films, diegetic sound is indeed closely aligned with Tarkovsky's idea of music allowing a "transfigured impression of the same material."

Ivan's Childhood features an example. The film's protagonist is a twelve-year-old war orphan whose parents have been killed by the Nazis. To help overcome his grief, Ivan volunteers as a scout for the Russians; the narrative sometimes focuses on his yearning for his lost childhood and his dreaming of happier times with his mother. The opening credit sequence is underscored by a cuckoo call (perhaps an overt political protest against the Soviet government's repression of free speech, and possibly a reference to the alleged first words ever uttered by Tarkovsky himself: "Mama, a cuckoo"[16]). Later, an insistent woodpecker punctuates Masha's and Leonid's walk through the forest, and seagulls cry near the river as Kholin and Galtsev undertake their mission at the German Front. Throughout the film, the changing details of birdsong metaphorically suggest narratives of human expression, location, emotion, liberty, and oppression.

The Sacrifice also opens with the natural sounds of birdsong and lapping water. *Andrei Rublev*, too, uses birdsong, along with the sounds of a canoe paddling and of fire crackling, another of Tarkovsky's sonic refrains. Elsewhere in *Andrei Rublev*, the recurring sound of a bell is an example of the synecdoche: bells are connotative signs for calling to prayer and for sounding both warnings and celebrations, but for the title character they have a personal significance. The very idea of the bell here is metaphorical in several ways. It is an expression of absolute faith as Rublev's pursuit of truth leads him, after witnessing an attempted rape, to take a vow of silence. But it is also an expression of artistic resurrection; acting secretly on his own initiative, a young boy casts a bell with know-how he claims to have been passed to him by his dead father, and this 'magical' casting causes Rublev to break his vow of silence and return to his life as a painter of religious icons.

The prelude of *Mirror* fades beneath birdsong and the sound of a train as the scene shifts to show a contemplative woman sitting, smoking, on a rural fence. In the opening dialogue between the woman and a passer-by, the birdsong is privileged in the mix and augmented by the sound of unseen migrating geese. After breaking the fence by sitting on it, the stranger, now identified as The Doctor, lies down in the grass and contemplates aloud as to whether or not plants can think; at this moment there is an insect hum, apparently near him in the film's diegetic space; as he leaves, the wind rustles through the trees and strengthens to a gale. What of all these sounds and their metaphorical implications? The implications are two-fold: the sounds of nature auralize and highlight ordinary life and its passing time, but they also call attention to human frailty, to how quickly others can turn against us, to how easily equilibrium can be upset. Tarkovsky's establishing of this 'refrain' so early in the film not only draws attention to the natural sounds as potential leitmotifs but also emphasizes the possibility that transfiguration of these sounds will later be a structuralizing mechanism.

The Recurrence of Pre-existing Music

Mirror is also significant for its use of J.S. Bach's Chorale Prelude in D minor, "Das alte Jahr vergangen ist,"[17] heard first just after a speech therapist attempts to cure a young man of the debilitating effects of a stammer. The metaphorical effect here is on a higher spiritual plane, negating the need for dialogue as the young man at last—figuratively as well as literally—masters the phrase "I can speak." In Mirror, Tarkovsky takes the idea of 'refrain,' initially expressed by means of birdsong, and expands it with transcendental effect through his use of pre-existing music.

Egorova writes that Tarkovsky has a "great predilection for music and art, and in each of his films there are episodes where the canvases of great artists appear, which supply clues to the understanding of the author's conception."[18] The purpose in this chapter is not to present an analysis of Tarkovsky's use of specific paintings in combination with pre-existing music, for this has been done before.[19] Rather, the purpose here is to consider the recurrence of bits of pre-existing music, and of paintings, as yet another example of 'refrain.' Throughout his films Tarkovsky uses such cultural artifacts purposefully, to communicate unspoken emotions that circulate through his narratives in an almost subliminal way.

Solaris makes use of Bach's Chorale Prelude in F Minor, "Ich ruf zu Dir, Herr Jesu Christ,"[20] in four scenes, and in all of them the music is matched with Pieter Bruegel's 1565 landscape painting The Hunters in the Snow. The planet named in the film's title is a sentient 'thing' with the ability to penetrate the thoughts of its visitors. Guests on the earth-based space station that orbits around Solaris see significant figures from their past, and this triggers from them all manner of personal reflection. The psychologist Kelvin, sent to the space station to investigate a variety of strange on-board happenings, lost his wife to suicide and is desperate to return to all that had been dear to him, namely the earth and his family. As Kelvin nostalgically views old film footage of his time on earth, both the Bruegel painting and the Bach music serve as metaphors that instantly summarize and encapsulate his memories. Especially noteworthy is the scene during which the Bach music accompanies Kelvin's recollections—apparently triggered by the sentient planet—of images of his parents' dacha. Rain falls throughout this possibly hallucinatory scene, and perhaps this is a metaphor both for the dissipation of Kelvin's past and for the emotions Kelvin experiences as he tries to come to terms with his current situation. In any case, the 'numinous' use of Bach's music in this scene, in combination with the persistent sound of rain, helps Tarkovsky blur both the temporal and the psychological parameters of Kelvin's despair.

This wordless form of expression also occurs at the beginning and end of *The Sacrifice*, with the inclusion of the aria "Erbaume dich, mein Gott" from Bach's *St. Mathew Passion*, in which St. Peter begs God for forgiveness for his betrayal of Christ.[21] The opening credits roll over a still image of Leonardo Da Vinci's painting *The Adoration of the Magi*; as the Bach aria plays, the camera focuses on the kneeling Magi. This gives way to sounds of the seaside as the camera moves upward over a shot of Alexander planting a dead branch and recounting a parable to his son: if you repeat the same action in a dedicated way each day, then your hard work will eventually pay dividends and you will succeed, even given a seemingly hopeless cause. At the end of the film, as Alexander is taken away to an asylum, having set fire to the family home, his son is shown continuing to water the tree.[22] The uses of this piece of Bach are now clear; the music suggests Alexander's desire for retrospective forgiveness and his regret, the inevitability of fate, and the human need to have faith in a higher authority. The dichotomy of Tarkovsky's method can be expressed almost as a ratio, as the need for transcendence versus the desire for the expression of reality; in many cases, the link between the two is sound.

Temporal Blurring

Tarkovsky's wish to convey absolute reality resulted in his "flouting the standard conventions of time-space,"[23] or what has come to be understood as temporal blurring. His notion of chronology was a fluid concept and, as we have seen in *Solaris*, for example, he used this to suggest those thoughts, feelings, and levels of understanding that often remain unspoken but with which we can all identify. This unspoken thought generally occurs independently from time, giving a sensation of 'everything' going on around us. Tarkovsky realized that recreating this sensation filmically required an all-encompassing approach that would immerse the audience totally. Watching pictures on our own heightens the sense of "being a spectator," thus leading to greater emotional disengagement. Sound, even if divorced from its accompanying visuals, envelops us immediately and places us at the epicenter of the action. It somehow has the ability to get 'inside our heads' more easily, inducing strong feelings that may override our registering some of the more mundane aspects of our current situation. This facility of sound can then be used to blur some of the structuralist comparisons that occur naturally in life, such as comparisons of subject and object, of deliberate and intuitive, of rational and emotional. These comparisons often feature in his cinematic narratives—how did Tarkovsky use sound to help him express them?

In *Solaris*, the journey to the planet is represented metaphorically; there is no overt reference to space travel, only footage of a lengthy car drive through a network of urban road systems at different times of day and night. The car journey focuses on Berton, a survivor of the Solaris space station, returning home after briefing Kelvin, who is about to visit the space station as an investigator. Eduard Artemyev's score uses synthetic rather than acoustic sounds, with individual, filtered timbres counterpointed to create a variety of tone-colors active within the soundscape. One of the sounds results from sawtooth waves; it has a harsh, brittle effect and is perhaps indicative of a meta-diegesis, as Berton's forward movement is shown from a point of view behind his head. Another sound, heard whenever Berton is filmed from the front, involves an intrusive, high frequency and an ear-piercing timbre. Still other sounds—all of them suggesting Berton's lack of control and self-awareness—include sets of ascending arpeggios, descending glissandi that call to mind sci-fi laser-guns, a 'solar wind' effect, and clouds of indistinguishable 'cocktail party' chatter. Under all of this there is a permanent drone of traffic noise, implying that life goes on even though time, for Berton, seems to be standing still. Berton in this sequence is driving on autopilot, considering the events of a different time continuum; for the audience, this is conveyed not by the repetitious visuals but, rather, by the sounds.

As Truppin has noted, Tarkovsky played upon the ability of a sound to function ambiguously and independently, thus intentionally obscuring its obvious meaning. This is especially true when the sound does not automatically accompany an image. An example can be found in a scene from *The Sacrifice*, after Otto the mailman has told Alexander that he must visit the house of Maria, the local witch, if he wants to save his family. In this scene, temporal blurring is combined with a blurring of dream and reality, enhanced by two additional strands of music: a melody played on a Japanese flute and chants traidionally used by Swedish farmers to call their livestock. There is also the sound of a ticking clock, and of a flock of sheep, with dogs barking in the distance (clocks and dogs are among Tarkovsky's refrain elements). Alexander sits on a creaking chair as he plays the organ. He asks Maria to save him, and offers sex in return. Distressed, he shoots himself in the head. Instead of hearing a gunshot, the audience hears fighter jets pass overhead, shattering the ambience created thus far by the array of naturalistic sounds. As the shepherds' chant and the Japanese flute music return, the scene jumps to black and white footage of crowds in a city, running, panic-stricken after an unspecified disaster; the crowds' footsteps remain audible while the shepherds' chant grows louder.

How is this scene connected with the previous one? A bicycle bell rings and Alexander is now outside, sitting on the grass with Maria. After another close-up of the Da Vinci painting, the scene's final shot is of the now empty couch where Alexander earlier had reclined. Which sound goes with which visual? Without resorting to a dual screen or disjointed cuts, images can only be presented in a sequential order; it is sound—asynchronous, deliberately positioned *not* to coincide with any change of image—that here achieves the effect of temporal ambiguity.

The refrains in Tarkovsky's films involve not just sounds but also images, especially images of things that behave in unpredictable ways, such as dripping water, rustling foliage, glassware, or clothing material. Sarkar writes about how sound is often used to heighten changing emotion suggested by these seemingly innocuous visual elements. In *The Sacrifice*, sound creates a sense of all-encompassing and unknown terror as a low-pitched, loud rumbling pans across the audio track. The accompanying images are not of destruction but of furniture and wine glasses shaking while the characters look skywards. The rumbling reaches a peak when a jug of milk moves to the edge of its shelf and crashes to the floor. Intuition informs the audience that the sound comes from fighter jets flying over the house. But the characters in the diegetic space know before the audience does that the vibrations are being caused by something else.

Tarkovsky has allowed the audience to be misled by certain ambiguous sounds, all the more effective because they are placed in the context of other ambiguous sounds. The scene as Tarkovsky made it surely is more sinister than one that would have concluded with the image of the jets actually causing destruction. The sight and sound of bombs falling, and the ensuing apocalyptic vision, would have provided a sense of the finite; in such a scene, the 'World' would have a clear end. But Tarkovsky's use of sound—with the glass vibrations and the intrusive noise of shattering glass—allows the emotion contained in the scene to remain unresolved; the emotion 'hangs' over the characters, and thus it continues to impinge upon both them and the audience.

The Recurring 'Sensorium'

The scene from *The Sacrifice* described above fully involves the audience in the world of the film; with such a scene, it is easy to believe that you are enclosed as a virtual observer within the film's diegetic space, and across his output Tarkovsky makes this effect repeatedly by careful selection and placement of sound.

Consider his use of water. In *Nostalghia*, Andrei Gorchakov (a Russian writer) travels to Italy to research the life of an eighteenth-century composer, Pavel Sosnovsky. He meets the troubled Domenico, who some years earlier had imprisoned his family in a barn in order to save them from all evil (an idea similar in sentiment to Alexander's in *The Sacrifice*). There is a scene in which Andrei enters Domenico's old house and finds the floor covered in puddles, with rain pouring outside and water dripping everywhere. The presence of the water in so many forms is overbearing. Also overbearing is the water's sound, which includes drips and splashes that echo across the bare room and a high-pitched whistling caused by water falling into empty bottles. The sensation of cold and wet, of desolation and misery, is palpable. Viewed in silence, the scene is unequivocally dismal; viewed with the sound, the scene forces the audience to 'feel' the sensations of the dismal world. Sarkar described Tarkovsky as "embed[ding] his characters in a unifying sensorium."[24] Indeed, Tarkovsky embeds his audience as well.

This idea recurs in *Ivan's Childhood*, which also makes extensive use of water, the sound of which invokes contrasting moods and emotions. After Ivan's misery in the waterlogged forest, there is the nostalgic warmth implied after his capture when he is given a hot bath in an old fashioned metal tub near a crackling fire. Water drips relentlessly as Ivan eats and is carried to bed, and this sound gives the sequence both a disquieting sense of momentum and some narrative continuity. The camera traces the sound to the bath and to a close-up of Ivan's hand; when the camera pans out, Ivan is shown to be down a well, still with water running over his hand and with his mother above him. Tarkovsky then reveals that Ivan's mother had been shot but Ivan had been saved because he was down the well, with her bucket falling on top of him.

In both *Nostalghia* and *Ivan's Childhood* water is used as a refrain. The insistence of water's sound prompts the audience member to make structuralist comparisons between misery and comfort, between rest and agitation, and, ultimately, between life and death.

Electronic Manipulation of Sound

In the 1970s, Tarkovsky met a young composer, Eduard Artemyev, who in turn had met Yevgeniy Murzin, the inventor of a photoelectric synthesizer called the ANS (named after the initials of Alexander Nikolayevich Scriabin). This instrument inspired Artemyev to further develop his interest in electronic music. Artemyev had been influenced by the compositional possibilities of the avant-garde, and his innovative ideas, combined with the timbral possibilities afforded by the ANS, enabled him to effectively auralize Tarkovsky's concepts about expression through the medium of sound. Thus began a collaboration that resulted in the filmscores for *Stalker*, *Mirror*, and *Solaris*.

Tarkovsky said that "electronic music to me seems to have enormously rich possibilities for the cinema."[25] He believed that filtered sound achieved a better effect than a sound's 'dry' version, and he sought sounds that somehow communicated the idea that "reality is conditional."[26] Electronic music, he said, should be free of what he called "its chemical origins."[27] An example of all these ideas can be found in one of the refrain-filled seminal scenes from *Mirror*.

Mirror depicts the thoughts of Alexei, possibly Tarkovsky's alter ego, across three different times: the period before World War II, the wartime itself, and the postwar 1960s. In a pre-war scene, near the film's beginning, Alexei's mother is conversing with a passing doctor. Dialogue is limited, but all the sounds are prominent. There is a prolonged section with a ticking clock and an unseen mewing cat. More intrusive are the sounds of barking dogs, filtered with a slight reverb so that they seem to resonate through the sparsely furnished house in a way that suggests to the audience that something 'more' is happening. As the children move away from the table, a cuckoo calls and a bottle rolls off the table, seemingly on its own, tinkling across the floor without breaking. The camera pans slowly to the open door and torrential rain is heard, coupled with ambiguous sounds that possibly could be produced by extreme weather but which prove to result from the crackling fire of a burning barn. A whistling sound occurs; it is not human-like whistling but, rather, something that occasionally gives the impression of breathy panpipes. The scene cuts to a sleeping Alexei, and Artemyev seamlessly introduces music from a wordless choir, very low in the mix, and at first atonal; the sleeping child is thus given a mysterious, sinister quality.

Later, Alexei's mother is shown washing her hair, but the sound of the water does not match the accompanying visuals. The water sounds as though it were in a cave, dripping for much longer and reverberating much more fully than the natural action would suggest. As Alexei's mother stands up, an electronically produced sound akin to a metallic train or a jet engine rumbles into the mix, punctuated by a clanging, bell-like sound as the ceiling collapses under the weight of the water above. The audience does not hear the entire collapse, only the noise of debris lightly hitting the floor. The manipulation of sound here causes a quite intentional disengagement from the action; it shifts attention to the mother, who seems to be screaming in a void, much like Berton does in *Solaris*.

In *Solaris*, water sounds are comparably filtered. Tarkovsky asked Artemyev to orchestrate natural, ambient sounds, and in response Artemyev created a collage that depends strongly on the multi-timbral combination of acoustic and synthetic sounds. Used in this manner, sound suggests the sense of 'otherness' that surrounds the titular planet, but the idea is set up at the very start of the film by the foregrounding of such 'earthly' sounds as the trickle of a brook, the songs of birds, the whinnies of a horse, and the barking of a dog. This emphasis on the sounds of both worlds is, in itself, suggestive of the numinous. Even in the film's opening sequence there is a suggestion of 'otherness' in the filtered sounds of raindrops edited so that their echoes resemble a continuous pitch sung with shifting vowels. The timbre of the raindrop sounds changes; by implication, the nature of the Earth as we know it also changes.

Conclusion

A study of these films reveals that Tarkovsky's sounds, diegetic and otherwise, do achieve his ideal status of 'refrain.' For Tarkovsky, the refrain is never simply a leitmotif; it is a structurally significant event, and this is what distinguishes Tarkovsky, in his use of sound, from most other directors.

What is so important to Tarkovsky is not the nature of a sound but, rather, the manner in which a sound is used to personify and define an extra dimension of expression that is not immediately apparent. Rarely do Tarkovsky's refrains recur without there being a difference or a development. But Tarkovsky hardly makes sonic changes just for the sake of change.

The repetition of any sound, of course, reaffirms whatever emotional connection was established with the sound's first use, and thus it re-communicates an associated emotion. A subsequent development of that sound, logically, communicates a heightening of the emotion. During any Tarkovsky film, audience members will have a number of different emotional 'compartments' auralized for them, sometimes in tandem with the visuals but often in opposition. Perhaps more than any other director, Tarkovsky consistently uses sound in this way, as a means of transcending whatever mundane reality is suggested by his visual imagery.

Notes

1 Richard Dyer, *Stars* (London: British Film Instititue, 1998), 5.
2 Bhaskar Sarkar, "Threnody for Modernity," in *Tarkovsky*, ed. Nathan Dunne (London: Black Dog Publishing, 2008), 236.
3 Andrey Tarkovsky, *Sculpting in Time: Reflections on the Cinema*, trans. Kitty Hunter-Blair (Austin: University of Texas Press, 1986), 20.
4 Robert Bird, *Andrei Tarkovsky: Elements of Cinema* (London: Reaktion Books, 2008), 16.
5 Maria Chugunova, interview with Tarkovsky, published as an appendix in *Time Within Time: The Diaries 1970–1986*, trans. Kitty Hunter-Blair (Calcutta: Faber, 1991), 356–8.
6 Leonid Kozlov, "Beseda O Tsvete," *Proizvedenie Vo Vremeni* (Moscow, 2005), 430–6, cited in Bird, *Andrei Tarkovsky: Elements of Cinema*, 156.
7 Bird, *Andrei Tarkovsky: Elements of Cinema*, 156.
8 Julia Shpinitskaya, "*Solaris* by A. Tarkovsky: Music-Visual Troping, Paradigmatism, Cognitive Stereoscopy," *Transcultural Music Review*, No. 10 (December 2006), available at: www.sibetrans.com/trans/index.htm.
9 Sarkar, "Threnody for Modernity," 241.
10 Tony Mitchell, "Tarkovsky in Italy," *Sight and Sound* 52, no. 1 (Winter 1982), 54–6.
11 Sarkar, "Threnody for Modernity," 237.
12 Tatiana Egorova, *Soviet Film Music: An Historical Survey* (New York and London: Routledge, 1997), 157.
13 Ibid., 158.
14 Tarkovsky, *Sculpting in Time: Reflections on the Cinema*, 158.
15 Ibid.
16 Donato Totaro, "Nature as 'Comfort Zone' in the Films of Andrei Tarkovsky," *Offscreen* 14, no. 12 (December 2010), available at: www.offscreen.com/index.php/pages/essays/nature as comfort zone/.
17 BWV 614, from the *Orgelbüchlein* (1708–14).
18 Egorova, *Soviet Film Music: An Historical Survey*, 234.

19 See texts such as Shpinitskaya, "*Solaris* by A. Tarkovsky: Music-Visual Troping, Paradigmatism, Cognitive Stereoscopy," and Egorova, *Soviet Film Music: An Historical Survey*.
20 BWV 639, from the *Orgelbüchlein* (1708–14).
21 The text translates as: "Have mercy Lord, My God, because of this my weeping! Look thou here, Heart and eyes now weep for thee Bitterly."
22 The metaphorical 'palm' tree has a biblical significance. In Christianity, the palm tree is a representation of martyrdom, or triumph over death. For further information, see www.biblestudytools.com/dictionaries/smiths-bible-dictionary/palm-tree.html.
23 Sarkar, "Threnody for Modernity," 238.
24 Ibid., 250.
25 Tarkovsky, *Sculpting in Time: Reflections on the Cinema*, 162.
26 Ibid.
27 Ibid.

Chapter 4

"It's All Really Happening"

Sonic Shaping in the Films of Wes Anderson

Ben Winters

> Anderson ... projects a carefully authored public image of himself as author, and his largely DVD-mediated image shares many qualities with its fictive counterparts, who, like him, arise as redeemed or redeemable, largely sympathetic authors, functioning, in the end, in the name of the community.
>
> Devin Orgeron[1]

Wes Anderson is that rarity of contemporary cinema, the quintessential quirky director with enough mainstream appeal to be of interest to major Hollywood distributors. As someone who is committed to writing in addition to directing his films—*Bottle Rocket* (1996), *Rushmore* (1998), *The Royal Tenenbaums* (2001), *The Life Aquatic with Steve Zissou* (2004), *The Darjeeling Limited* (2007), and *Fantastic Mr. Fox* (2009)—he might also be considered a prime candidate for inclusion in an updated version of that now somewhat discredited list of 'auteur' directors that Andrew Sarris proposed in the late 1960s.[2]

It is perhaps unsurprising, then, that in a recent article for *Cinema Journal* Devin Orgeron suggested that both Wes Anderson's films and the director himself engage overtly with authorship debates in ways that reflect the impact of DVD technology; moreover, Orgeron did so in a way that aligned Anderson's work, albeit trepidatiously, with what he called the "'director as auteur' hardliners."[3] In short, Orgeron argues that DVD technology has inaugurated a new age of the cinematic author, and Anderson not only engages with the technology in order to mediate his own self-image but also creates film characters who—in addition to often literally being authors as playwrights, novelists, and academics—are in a sense 'authors' of the stories of which they are a part. As such, these characters might be seen as reflections of the director himself; they offer a means to acknowledge the centrality of Wes Anderson as an 'auteur,' complicated as that might be both by the charged debates surrounding authorship discourse in film studies and Anderson's desire to 'deauthorize' himself by situating his creative contributions in a more collaborative framework.

While Orgeron's close reading of the films' characters and their motivations are persuasive, he almost entirely neglects to comment on what might be considered an intrinsic part of Anderson's style: namely, the very careful selection and treatment of music, another aspect about which Anderson has often commented in DVD extras or other supporting material. In many of Anderson's films, characters take great care in selecting music to play and, as such, can be seen as corollaries of Anderson himself. They—and, by extension, he—use music not to reveal narrative information (perhaps the most common way in which criticism engages with film music) but to shape the narrative space around them, as a "technology of self," to use Tia de Nora's phrase.[4] Moreover, Anderson's concern with blurring boundaries between the diegetic and extra-diegetic in his film worlds (particularly in *The Life Aquatic with Steve Zissou*) might also suggest a similar blurring should be the norm when considering his characters' interaction with the films' scores (usually composed by Mark Mothersbaugh). In the same way that characters may choose particular pieces of diegetic music, they might shape the score that surrounds them. In that sense, what we might have assumed to be music emanating from an extra-diegetic source—representing the voice of a separated narrator figure, perhaps even the filmmaker himself—might be productively thought of as a musical landscape that is very much within the world inhabited by the characters. As such, these characters become composers of their own scores, concerned less with narrative explication and more with expressing their own aesthetic choices. In doing so, they reveal their indebtedness to, and their mirroring of, Anderson's creative persona.

In order to explore this idea, I want to examine the ways in which characters in Wes Anderson's films foreground the selection of music and then look at several sequences—from *The Royal Tenenbaums* and *The Life Aquatic*—in which characters appear to shape the scores that surround them. This has implications for the way in which we might view the scores' functions, and it is arguably a consequence of the self-reflexive style that is most noticeable in *The Life Aquatic*. First, however, I want to briefly examine Anderson's self-image where music is concerned, since it is one area of his filmmaking that is often commented upon in promotional material.

Music and Wes Anderson's Filmmaking

The centrality of music to the quirky, near-reality worlds that Anderson creates is certainly recognized by his collaborators, who have commented on the early attention he affords music in the screenwriting process. Barry Mendel, his co-producer on *The Royal Tenenbaums*, observed: "It's very fun to have him very early in the first draft of the script play you a song and explain each moment of what's happening."[5] Randall Poster, music editor on most of Anderson's films, traces back the concern with music even further:

Wes and I first started working on [*The Royal Tenenbaums*] when the movie was a one-sentence idea. … We just go back and forth with songs, listening to them, and discuss them back and forth with each other. It's a very organic process, and I would say we had seventy-five percent of the songs picked out and licensed before we even started shooting the movie.[6]

Poster describes Anderson's interest in the songs for *Rushmore* as dating back "a couple of years" before shooting. Even regular score composer Mark Mothersbaugh appears to get in on the act at an unusually early stage. For *The Royal Tenenbaums*, Mothersbaugh recalls, Anderson "called me to discuss music as he was putting the script together"[7]; this practice was to continue in *The Life Aquatic*, with the composer "working on the music in my studio while Wes was sitting behind me, still writing the script."[8] Mothersbaugh's music is often included on the soundtrack records, something that the composer attributes to the director: "With my pieces on *Tenenbaums*, it's Wes's call. He was very adamant about the score being on the soundtrack. That's the only reason it's there."[9]

Music, then, appears to be central to the director's creative personality, and his love of it is frequently emphasized in the media produced to accompany his movies. *Bottle Rocket*'s press kit describes Anderson as "an avid fan of all kinds of music" and "a confessed jazz fan,"[10] while the kit for *The Royal Tenenbaums* talks of music being a passion[11]—something evident from the eclecticism of Anderson's taste, which ranges from The Rolling Stones to David Bowie via the film scores of Satyajit Ray. At the time of *Rushmore*'s release, Poster said that "I think that the music will help stamp [Wes's] identity on the brow of filmgoers throughout the world,"[12] while *Bottle Rocket* producer Polly Platt observed in connection with Anderson's directing style that "I think he has music in his head."[13] Anderson, then, not only takes great care in selecting music (whether original score or pre-existing songs) but is also keen to highlight his interests through the promotional material attached to his films.

Character Shaping: Song Selection in *Rushmore* and *Fantastic Mr. Fox*

As a director, Anderson is by no means unique in the close attention paid to music, as this volume makes clear.[14] Nor is it surprising that his characters seem to echo his concern with the careful selection of music, since many of them also appear to reflect aspects of the director's personality (despite his disavowals that the family of dysfunctional geniuses in *The Royal Tenenbaums*, for example, are based on his own).[15] His second movie, *Rushmore*, was filmed at Anderson's school in Houston,[16] and the character of precocious fifteen-year-old playwright and theater director Max Fischer (Jason Schwartzman) is certainly close to Anderson's self-image, at least as he presents himself (in jest) in his American Express commercial "My Life, My Card."[17]

The fictional Fischer's careful control over all the aspects of his "hit plays" spills over into his life as he attempts to orchestrate the events of the film: perceiving himself as the victim of a terrible injustice, he tells his erstwhile friend and love rival Mr. Bloom (Bill Murray): "I was going to try and have that tree over there fall on you." Fischer, however, sometimes uses music as part of this attempt to control his surroundings. His frustrated romance with elementary school teacher Miss Cross (Olivia Williams), for example, almost achieves success when he fakes a bicycle accident and turns up at her bedroom window armed with a cassette of Yves Montand singing "Rue St. Vincent." Shaping his sonic world to set the appropriate atmosphere for his imagined romantic liaison, his fakery is, however, exposed ("is this fake blood?"), and the intimacy of his encounter with Miss Cross is broken. Fischer leaves through the window, not forgetting to take his Yves Montand tape with him. Similarly, in the film's final scene—a typically Andersonian gathering of the main principals in a communal affirmation of the inherent goodness of Fischer's plans to put on a new hit play and resolve the tensions he has helped create—the characters are all dancing to Django Reinhardt's and Stéphane Grappelli's version of "Manoir des mes Rêves." Miss Cross asks Fischer if he'd like to dance, but he decides the music isn't quite right. Calling out to the DJ, he indicates a pre-planned choice: the hot-club jazz is silenced, to the confusion of the other dancers, and "Ooh La La" by The Faces begins. Another moment of unmistakable intimacy occurs between Fischer and Miss Cross as she removes his glasses, and as the metaphorical (and literal) curtain comes down they are framed in the center of the shot in a dancer's embrace (Figure 4.1): Max's musical choice appears finally to have had the desired effect.

Music, for Max Fischer, appears to be about setting the mood and creating the right sonic environment for his romantic fantasies, something to which he appears to attend with the same care that he lavishes on the sound design of his plays. Similarly, in the short film that precedes *The Darjeeling Limited*, Jack (a novelist played by Jason Schwartzman, who in another parallel to Anderson's life continually denies that his characters are based on his family) is shown selecting music—Peter Sarstedt's "Where Do You Go To (My Lovely)"—on his iPod to set the atmosphere for a Parisian encounter with his ex-girlfriend (Natalie Portman). In the main feature that follows, Jack carries this iPod and its speakers across India on the train ride he takes with his brothers, selecting Sarstedt's song again as the background for an intimate post-coital scene with the train's stewardess, Rita (Amara Karan). He even takes the iPod and speakers with him into the desert, selecting a performance of Debussy's *Clair de lune* to provide the aural backdrop for the brothers' campfire attempt to get high on cough syrup. It is a moment that in the language of cinema perhaps seems to

Figure 4.1 The closing curtain in *Rushmore*

be artificially contrived. Nevertheless, it is true both to this character's need to control his surroundings and to the realities of everyday life (in which we, too, are often required to make musical choices if we want to shape our sonic environments). I will return to this artificial or constructed aspect of Anderson's films and its implications for music later.

In Anderson's most recent film, *Fantastic Mr. Fox*, the animated character's musical choices and the nostalgic technology on which they are played are clearly important, if the camera work is anything to go by.[18] Mr. Fox (voiced by George Clooney) has a "walk-sonic" portable radio, and the camera lingers lovingly on his manipulation of its controls (see Figure 4.2). We are first introduced to him listening to "The Ballad of Davy Crockett," but equally significant is his choice later in the film to underscore the speech that outlines his "go-for-broke rescue mission." Once again, the camera lingers on Fox's manipulation of his "walk-sonic," a piece of technology whose antiquated status is highlighted at the end of the film by his son's use of his "walk-sonic (digital)"; with the opening pseudo-Baroque gestures of Georges Delerue's *Le Grand Choral* from the film *La Nuit Américaine* (François Truffaut, 1973) sounding through the tinny radio, Fox feels able to make his 'grand' speech, calling upon the talents of his animal friends to help him save his nephew.

With his walk-sonic attached to his jacket pocket, Fox carries around his music, and shapes his sonic environment, just as surely as do Jack in

Figure 4.2 Mr. Fox's radio

The Darjeeling Limited or Max in *Rushmore*. *La Nuit Américaine*, known in English as *Day for Night*, is one of Anderson's aesthetic influences—his American Express commercial not only appears to reference it in what Orgeron calls its "barely controlled chaos'"[19] but is underscored with the same music by Delerue—and this suggests that Fox's aesthetic choices can be seen as reflections of Anderson's own. But Anderson responds more overtly with his own choice: as the other animals agree to help Fox, we hear The Beach Boys singing "I Get Around." The contrast in levels of audio fidelity (tinny radio versus full stereo soundtrack) perhaps masks the idea that both of these choices are at once Anderson's and Fox's. As with *Rushmore*, the final track of *Fantastic Mr. Fox* (in this case, "Let Her Dance" by the Bobby Fuller Four) is selected by a character (Fox's son) for the sake of encouraging the principal characters to dance.

These and other examples (the pivotal record-playing scene in *The Royal Tenenbaums*, the scenes in *The Life Aquatic* where Steve Zissou pipes music into his divers' suits or selects music to be played in his submarine) suggest that not only the characters but also Anderson himself may be choosing music for reasons that are not principally narrative-driven. Whereas a great deal of film music criticism is concerned with tracing the effect of music on the audience's narrative comprehension, the actions of Anderson's characters (who we might logically assume are not concerned with aiding explication of the narrative of which they are a part) suggest that Anderson may be choosing pieces of music because they provide an appropriate 'register' (to use the sociolinguistic concept) with which to characterize the events occurring on screen.

The temptation for scholars to look for narrative meaning in film music is, of course, all the more alluring when words are involved,[20] but this has recently been questioned by Michael Long.[21] For Long, language-based modes of criticism that neglect the vernacular operation of 'register' are in danger of homogenizing their subjects; in being in thrall to ideas derived from Gérard Genette's narratology (via Claudia Gorbman)—most obviously, distinctions between diegetic and extra-diegetic narrative levels—they may limit the range of potential approaches possible. This is an idea I recently explored in the context of what might be termed traditional underscore,[22] but it might apply just as well to Anderson's use of songs. Rather than examining them for the narrative implications of their 'texts' (taken literally or in the Barthesian sense), Anderson's musical choices might be more fruitfully examined for their registral content, for the easily understood vernacular stylistic or generic markers that indicate the appropriateness of their sound for the scenes.

Certainly that is how Mr. Fox selects the music to accompany his grand speech. The fact that many of the instances of music selection by characters in Anderson's films are concerned with functionality—whether it be in providing music to dance to, make a speech to, aid romantic seduction, or to act therapeutically (as with Margot's playing of Richie's records in *The Royal Tenenbaums*)—points to the importance of music in shaping both the characters' sense of self and their environments. Given, too, the importance of music to Anderson's own self-image (at least as reported), we may also wonder about the director's selection of music. Are *his* choices not also shaped primarily by function and the registral appropriateness to the scene, rather than with the aim of communicating information of narrative importance? That is not to say that such information cannot be found, but I suspect that for most viewers the 'appropriateness' of Anderson's aesthetic preferences plays a far greater role than do subtle intertextual interplays with narrative content.

Scoring Musical Environments: *The Royal Tenenbaums* and *The Life Aquatic*

That characters explicitly shape their musical environments is also apparent when considering Mark Mothersbaugh's scores. Mothersbaugh has, to date, contributed to four of Anderson's films (*Bottle Rocket*, *Rushmore*, *The Royal Tenenbaums*, and *The Life Aquatic*) and, as noted above, the collaboration has been a particularly close one. In two of those scores, there are sequences that suggest characters may be shaping the score to better reflect their sense of self. In *The Royal Tenenbaums*, the opening segment, which introduces the pre-history of the Tenenbaum family, is scored with an instrumental version of

The Beatles' "Hey Jude." As the press kit proudly announced, "during this sequence specific instruments become associated with individual characters, and this continues throughout the rest of the film. Anderson says that it is 'the most complex, ambitious musical piece I've ever worked on.'"[23] That the creation is attributed to both "Anderson and Mothersbaugh" is in itself telling, but the principle of associating particular instrumental timbres with characters subtly introduced in the "Hey Jude" sequence is given a virtuoso treatment in the film's first major narrative section (titled "Chapter One" in a typically Andersonian referencing of existing narrative structures).[24]

Slightly anticipating the entrance of Alec Baldwin's narration—which seemingly follows the imagined narrative voice of the novel *The Royal Tenenbaums* (whose opening lines are displayed at the beginning of each chapter in the DVD presentation of the film; see Figure 4.3)—a version of the *Allegro molto moderato* from George Enescu's Cello Sonata No. 1 in F minor begins. Aside from the fact that the piece starts after Enescu's opening octave piano and cello gestures, this appears at first to be a straightforward use of a pre-existing piece of classical music, its ostinato-like spiky cello line and piano chordal accompaniment providing a background for Baldwin's narration. Soon, however, we become aware that Enescu's original is simply a starting point for Mothersbaugh's cue.

Baldwin's narration initially deals with Royal Tenenbaum (Gene Hackman); as we learn about his financial troubles we hear a snarling trombone, an

Figure 4.3 "Chapter One" of *The Royal Tenenbaums*

instrument that throughout the film becomes increasingly associated with Royal. We next see the character framed in a window with a snowy ledge, and sleigh bells enter the accompaniment. As the scene shifts to Richie Tenenbaum (Luke Wilson) on board the ocean liner the *Cote d'Ivoire*, the spiky cello sonority is replaced by something all together softer (organ); although the piano chords of the original Enescu are retained, by the time the scene shifts to Eli Cash (Owen Wilson) in his cowboy hat and fringed buckskin jacket, the course of the Enescu original has been forever altered. Cash's version of the music re-introduces the ostinato-like cello, while over the top a combination of classical guitar, castanets, and trilling strings suggests something of the pulp fiction Western novel *Old Custer* he is reading aloud to his audience.[25] Still, however, the Enescu is present, albeit altered. This subtle re-arrangement and re-composition of the Enescu original continues with Alec Baldwin's introduction of the other characters: Margot (Gwyneth Paltrow) is underscored with harp, antique cymbals, and piano; the "writer and neurologist" Raleigh St. Clair (Bill Murray) is associated with the harpsichord (an instrument that dominates Mothersbaugh's score for the similarly academic environment of *Rushmore*); the introduction for Chas (Ben Stiller) seems to abandon temporarily the Enescu as it launches into elaborate drum fills, but as Baldwin's narration re-enters the pizzicato chords that concluded Raleigh's section return, signaling a return to the Enescu cello and piano music, this time with subtle drum accompaniment. This process continues until all the major characters have been introduced. The Enescu music is ever present, but it is altered anew by each character.

How, then, might we read this music? Might we not see it as interacting with the characters themselves, who subtly (or not so subtly in the case of Chas) shape the Enescu to better suit their often remarkably dysfunctional and idiosyncratic personalities? That Alec Baldwin's presence always seems to pull us back to something approaching the Enescu original might suggest that the music is partly functioning as an extra-diegetic narrative voice to partner Baldwin's narration, but the way in which the diegetic characters could be said to wrestle control of the music away from Baldwin certainly suggests a permeable boundary between the diegetic and the extra-diegetic; or, more precisely, it renders the distinction somewhat irrelevant. These are all characters in Anderson's film, and all of them (including Baldwin) appear to have the ability to shape the underscore to suit themselves.

A similar process occurs in Mothersbaugh's score to *The Life Aquatic*, where the first movement of Bach's Cantata BWV 140, "Wachet auf, ruft uns die Stimme," is subjected to re-arrangement in line with the characters on screen, although without the presence of the voice-over narration heard in *The Royal Tenenbaums*. The fictional character Steve Zissou (Bill Murray) presents his latest documentary film, *The Life Aquatic, Adventure No 12: "The Jaguar Shark"* (*Part 1*),[26] which includes footage of Zissou's friend Esteban being eaten by the eponymous beast; this prompts a decidedly awkward Q&A session after the screening, and then Zissou meets with his public at a drinks reception. With each encounter, the Bach ritornello is subtly rearranged: as Zissou converses with his producer (Michael Gambon) and is introduced by him to a wealthy backer, the instrumentation suddenly changes to pizzicato strings and harp, with chamber organ. When Zissou is asked to pose with fellow explorer and oceanographer Alistair Hennessey (Jeff Goldblum), the score is overtaken by pompous-sounding Baroque trumpet figurations. Zissou seems to match Hennessey's pomposity with his own, though, and the two trumpets (read: competing explorers and rivals for the attentions of Zissou's wife, Eleanor) engage in a duet. The entrance of Eleanor herself (Anjelica Huston) is characterized by soft classical guitar and flute sonorities, abandoning the dotted French overture rhythms of the ritornello and altering its harmonic trajectory. When Zissou's colleague Klaus (Willem Dafoe) introduces his young nephew, the Bach-derived material instantly takes on timbres associated with evocations of childhood (celesta, marimba, and glockenspiel, with a harpsichord bass); when Zissou is accosted by an elderly Italian gentleman seeking his autograph, the score is overtaken by a mandolin-dominated version of the ritornello, with the original first oboe line also returning.

After its first few iterations, which stick to the harmonic sequence of the ritornello, "Wachet auf" emerges sometimes only indistinctly (mostly through the dotted rhythm, Baroque-like gestures, and occasional harmonic nods to the sequences of the ritornello). But the cue nonetheless starts off identifiably as an arrangement of the Bach and gradually transforms as more and more characters begin to shape it to suit themselves. Since the Bach would also be appropriate source music at such a reception, trying to identify this as diegetic or extra-diegetic music seems an exercise in futility. Regardless of who can or cannot hear it, it is music that seems to be shaped by the characters themselves, not for the purpose of revealing narrative truths (that is, unlocking secrets, the love of which Carolyn Abbate has christened "the cryptographic sublime"[27]) but because it helps make the space around the characters more personal and reflects who they are. As such the accompanying music might be seen as part of the same process as characters' selection of music to play on record players, iPods, "walk-sonics," or whatever other technology Anderson chooses to employ, and it can also be seen as a reflection of Anderson's own selection of music for his films.

It should by now be apparent that this interaction between characters and all the music of a film (not just the music that they obviously hear) suggests a blurring of film musicology's traditionally held distinction between diegetic and extra- or non-diegetic music. Although as an interpretive strategy it has relevance beyond the present discussion, the fact is that Anderson's narrative style *often* blurs this distinction. At the same time, Anderson's style typically makes apparent the mechanisms of filmmaking, and it is this playful interaction with the nature of cinema that is one of the most charming aspects of Anderson's films.

Conclusion: Anderson's Filmmaking and *The Life Aquatic*

Although *Rushmore*'s stage metaphors and *The Royal Tenenbaums*' nod to literary models of narrative involve substantial extra-diegetic inserts, *The Life Aquatic* takes this to another level. In being concerned with a failed filmmaker, *The Life Aquatic* offers Anderson the opportunity to reveal and celebrate the filmmaking process. That much of the movie was filmed at Rome's Cinecittà studios, a studio particularly associated with the films of Federico Fellini, makes a comparison with Fellini's paean to the filmmaking process 8½ (1963) especially pertinent.[28]

In perhaps his most celebratory exposure of the filmmaking process, Anderson reveals Zissou's research vessel, the Belafonte, to be a huge movie set; as Zissou and his (possible) son Ned (Owen Wilson) move throughout the ship's interior while arguing, Anderson takes us through walls and shows us the edge of the set (see Figure 4.4) in a way that recalls the ending of Fellini's *E la nave va* (1983) and looks forward to Anderson's own later film, *The Darjeeling Limited*.[29] Moreover, we also see crew member Vikram (Waris Ahluwalia) point his camera through one of the ship's windows. Although throughout much of the film a cameraman and soundman are visible, this is partially explained by the fact that Zissou and his crew are making a documentary film, recording their mission to chase down the Jaguar Shark that ate Esteban in Part 1 of their film ("it's a cliff-hanger," as Zissou puts it). This scene, however, blurs the distinction between what is 'real' and what is part of this interior film. Indeed, as Jane Winslett-Richardson (Cate Blanchett) had suggested in response to the showing of Part 1 of Zissou's film, "aspects of it seemed slightly fake."

This is a comment that applies as much to the characters' relationships as to the narrative style of Anderson's film. As Ned and Zissou argue, Ned notes: "You don't know me. You never wanted to know me. I'm just a character in your film." Zissou responds: "It's a documentary, it's all really happening." By revealing the movie's set, Anderson shows us what is 'really' happening, namely the filming of *his* movie, and the effect is to cause us to question the way in which the rest of the film is presented to us: is it the tale of a bad filmmaker making a film, or is some of *The Life Aquatic* the actual documentary film itself? Although Anderson normally 'frames' portions of his film that should be seen as Zissou's film (see Figure 4.5), there are moments that challenge this simple distinction. James Mottram notes: "The invasion of the pirates aboard the Belafonte and the subsequent rescue of the kidnapped bail bondsman Bill Ubell (Bud Cort) from Ping Island are so ham-fisted in their

Figure 4.4 Revealing the set in *The Life Aquatic*

execution, you almost suspect Anderson is doing it deliberately."[30] Indeed, consideration of how the music functions in the rescue of the "Bond company stooge" is vital to seeing this deliberately ham-fisted sequence as an example of Zissou's staged filmmaking.

The rescue scene is preceded by a music discussion between Zissou and Vladimir Wolodarsky (Noah Taylor)—a character introduced earlier by Steve as "physicist and original score composer." They try Wolodarsky's latest electronic composition, designed by Mark Mothersbaugh to sound like "cheap synth sounds,"[31] against picture. "Not bad," Zissou remarks. "We'll tamper with that anyway." The "ham-fisted" rescue scene follows with an acoustic version of Wolodarsky's music track, suggesting that what we are watching is a strange mixture of Zissou's filmmaking and Anderson's more polished version of the same.[32] Mothersbaugh asked his musicians "to sound like Casio instruments";[33] the music thus plays a key role in blurring distinctions between these different narrative worlds, and thus between notions of diegetic and extra-diegetic sources of music. Likewise, the film ends with a curtain call, in which all the principal characters come together to the backing of David Bowie's "Queen Bitch."[34] This gathering of the principals, in a nod to the theater, might be labeled as 'extra-diegetic' (it includes the deceased Ned standing at the top of the ship: see Figure 4.6), but it should be clear by now that in this film the distinction between the diegetic and extra-diegetic is so fluid that it makes little sense to attempt to define the boundary.

Anderson's films problematize consistently the assumptions we might make concerning the narrative role of music. Whether its source is shown

Figure 4.5 Framing Zissou's films in *The Life Aquatic*

Figure 4.6 Curtain call for *The Life Aquatic*

within the diegesis or not, music is seemingly both potentially accessible to the characters to shape and reflective of Anderson and Mothersbaugh's aesthetic choices. As such, its role is perhaps less that of an extra-diegetic voice—the carrier of narrative information that it is the critic's role to decode—and more a reflection of the subjectivity of the characters and, by extension, the director himself; it is a reflection of the ways in which, as Tia de Nora put it, "music is appropriated by individuals as a resource for the ongoing constitution of themselves and their social psychological, physiological and emotional states."[35]

Perhaps, then, we should turn to a comment of Anderson's to conclude. When commenting on Seu Jorge's Portuguese versions of David Bowie's songs for *The Life Aquatic*, Anderson admitted: "I never was certain if they were completely accurate translations … but I became convinced that Pele's words—and, unquestionably, his beautiful performance—captured the spirit of Bowie and of the film."[36] It is this "spirit" rather than any narrative content that seems important to Anderson's use of music, and it is this "spirit" that ultimately contributes to our impression of his films as particularly strong statements of personal expression.

Notes

1   Devin Orgeron, "La Camera-Crayola: Authorship Comes of Age in the Cinema of Wes Anderson," *Cinema Journal* 46, no. 2 (Winter 2007): 43.
2   Andrew Sarris, *The American Cinema: Directors and Directions 1928–1968* (New York: E.P. Dutton, 1968). Sarris's project has generally been blamed for turning what had been a method of classification in the hands of the auteurist critics of *Cahiers du Cinéma* into an evaluative theory of directorial ability, used specifically to culturally elevate the American cinema. That it should appear at roughly the same time as Roland Barthes's essay "The Death of the Author"—the single piece of writing that arguably did more than any other to challenge the basis of Sarris's brand of *auteur* theory—is ironic, indeed (Barthes's essay first appeared in the Fall–Winter 1967 issue of *Aspen*).
3   Orgeron, "La Camera-Crayola," 41.
4   This is the title of the third chapter in Tia de Nora, *Music in Everyday Life* (Cambridge: Cambridge University Press, 2000).
5   *The Royal Tenenbaums* press kit, 19. All press kits were downloaded from http://rushmoreacademy.com/.
6   Harvey Kubernik, *Hollywood Shack Job: Rock Music in Film and on Your Screen* (Albuquerque: University of New Mexico Press, 2006), 112–13.
7   Ibid., 196.
8   *The Life Aquatic* press kit, 40.
9   Kubernik, *Hollywood Shack Job*, 195.
10 *Bottle Rocket* press kit, 7.
11 *The Royal Tenenbaums* press kit, 19.
12 *Rushmore* press kit, 11.
13 *Bottle Rocket* press kit, 7.
14 As with many of Quentin Tarantino's characters, the act of selecting music is also explicitly celebrated. See, for instance, Ken Garner's essay "'Would You Like to Hear Some Music?' Music in-and-out-of-Control in the Films of Quentin

Tarantino," in *Film Music: Critical Approaches*, ed. K. J. Donnelly (Edinburgh: Edinburgh University Press, 2001), 188–205.

15 Anderson has talked about the resemblance of Etheline Tenenbaum to his mother: "Her approach to raising the children, and the household that that character runs, are connected to my mother. My father was worried because the mother is so much like my mother that he felt this was my take on him." Quoted in James Mottram, *The Sundance Kids: How the Mavericks Took Back Hollywood* (New York: Faber & Faber, 2006), 346.

16 Ibid., 217. Mottram also notes that until Anderson changed his appearance during the shooting of *The Life Aquatic*, he "even looked like one of his creations" (136).

17 See www.youtube.com/watch?v=UAKwITTMCxI.

18 Indeed, many of Anderson's films emphasize in their near-reality worlds the somewhat anachronistic analogue technology of tape and record (*The Royal Tenenbaums*, *Rushmore*, *The Life Aquatic*) over the digital medium that is ubiquitous in our everyday reality. *The Darjeeling Limited* is an exception to this, however.

19 Orgeron, "La Camera-Crayola," 61.

20 Elena Boschi, for instance, places great emphasis on the narrative implications of songs' words. See "'Please, Give Me Second Grace': A Study of Five Songs in Wes Anderson's *The Royal Tenenbaums*," in *CineMusic? Constructing the Film Score*, ed. David Cooper, Christopher Fox, and Ian Sapiro (Newcastle upon Tyne: Cambridge Scholars Publishing, 2008), 97–110.

21 Michael Long, *Beautiful Monsters: Imagining the Classic in Musical Media* (Berkeley: University of California Press, 2008).

22 Ben Winters, "The Non-diegetic Fallacy: Film, Music, and Narrative Space," *Music & Letters* 91, no. 2 (May 2010): 224–44.

23 *The Royal Tenenbaums* press kit, 19.

24 If *Rushmore* presents itself using the visual images of theater, *The Royal Tenenbaums* is rooted in literary imagery, while *The Life Aquatic* completes this narrative trilogy by invoking other models of cinema—of which, more below.

25 Many of the characters are connected with literary creations, and inserted shots provide us with their book covers and some associated sounds (gun shots and horses' hooves for Cash's novel, bookkeeping machines for Henry Sherman's book *Accounting for Everything*, etc.).

26 Zissou is clearly modeled on the legendary French explorer and aquanaut, Jacques-Yves Cousteau.

27 Carolyn Abbate, "Music—Drastic or Gnostic?" *Critical Inquiry* 30, no. 3 (Spring 2004): 524.

28 Mottram, *The Sundance Kids*, 394. Anderson also acknowledged the debt to Fellini in the *Life Aquatic* press kit, 50.

29 A similar, but less noticeable, use of this technique in *The Life Aquatic* occurs in the scene in Hennessey's underwater laboratory. In *The Darjeeling Limited*, principal film locations and their characters (including ones that have only been mentioned in dialogue) become 'impossible' separate train compartments, complete with rolling scenery behind. Anderson's camera travels along this imaginary train supported by The Rolling Stones singing "Play with Fire."

30 Mottram, *The Sundance Kids*, 392.

31 *The Life Aquatic* press kit, 40.

32 Anderson notes in the DVD commentary that the orchestral version is "what Zissou would do also … would want it to be more symphonic when the action kicked in."

33 *The Life Aquatic* press kit, 40.

34 Bowie's music is an integral part of the film, with Seu Jorge (as demolitions expert Pelé dos Santos) performing his songs in Portuguese on deck at various points.
35 De Nora, *Music in Everyday Life*, 47.
36 *The Life Aquatic* press kit, 41. 'Pelée' refers to the name of the character played by Seu Jorge.

Chapter 5

Kieślowski's *Musique concrète*

Joseph G. Kickasola

Film sound theorist Michel Chion writes: "[Krzysztof] Kieślowski endows noises and music—a solo flute or a slender soprano voice—with an energy that cuts through the general pall of the world."[1] Indeed, one of Kieślowski's more remarkable achievements is the way he utilized diegetic sounds—that is, the noises and music of the fictional world being presented—to revitalize and expand our sense of our own world, which he saw to be to be far more than just a Euclidean affair.

To achieve this, Kieślowski utilized a range of different techniques along the full range of the classic realist/formalist continuum. Categories like 'realist' and 'formalist' can be rather blunt instruments when approaching a nuanced director like Kieślowski, but to stick with those terms for a moment, it can be said that Kieślowski's feature film career moved from a more 'realist' chapter, as he came out of a documentary career in the late 1970s, into a more 'formalist' chapter, as he explored fictional narrative filmmaking. The lessons learned in the documentary period remained important to him, however, and his formalism did not become a simple 'art for art's sake' affair. Kieślowski found himself seeking expression of more universal and 'metaphysical' concerns, and in that endeavor he found the realist/formalist continuum to be constraining.[2]

Indeed, his sonic style in his late period (1991–4) took on something of a hybrid form through his embrace of both realist and formalist techniques, and one product of this hybridization was a more deliberate approach to sound effects and their relationship to the musical score. This hybridization increases the amount of semantic weight one grants to sound effects and music, and it expands their typical semantic roles. In other words, sometimes hearing itself, as a sensuous experience (and not just a semiotic/referential process), rises up, free from its typical subservience to the visual, and sounds and music begin to function as the central axis of meaning upon which a scene turns. As diegetic sound effects, they are 'realist,' but their stylized employment (often found in creative pairings with the visuals) marks them as 'formalist.' Likewise, as Kieślowski grew more adventurous with his sound work, he found the sounds of 'reality' (diegetic or not) to be useful as instruments in a type of aural symphony.

This marks a step beyond the typical Hollywood practice of writing an extra-diegetic score that simply amplifies the mood of a given scene. Indeed, Zbigniew Preisner's scores (for all Kieślowski's later films) are highly regarded, and Kieślowski even makes the music itself an essential 'player' in the diegetic worlds of *The Double Life of Véronique* (1991) and *Blue* (1993). Preisner has noted that Kieślowski often used music to express the inner life of his characters,[3] and musical moments (real and imagined) often became key factors in the direction, speed, and amplitude of the narrative.

Alternately, both Preisner and Kieślowski's sound recordist, William Flageollet, notes how Kieślowski sometimes refrained from music or any other obvious sound, demanding heavy silences between characters who were, appropriately, often debating heavy matters.[4] But even in such moments sound persists. The avant-garde composer John Cage has noted: "There is no such thing as an empty space or any empty time. There is always something to see, something to hear. In fact, try as we may to make a silence, we cannot."[5]

So the real dynamic that emerges here is not silence versus sound but, rather, which sounds capture our attention and why? Both Cage and Kieślowski understood this dynamic. Although we have no evidence that Cage and Kieślowski ever met or even knew of each other, there exist numerous parallels which will drive the analysis in this chapter: both were extraordinarily influential in their respective fields; both rejected the Scylla of sentimental conventions and the Charybdis of clinical, emotion-less formalisms; both understood the dramatic power of what R. Murray Schafer would call "the soundscape" of daily life;[6] and both understood (from different religious traditions) the human need to explore and understand larger, even spiritual dimensions of reality.[7]

And this takes us a step further, toward the culmination of a productive realist/formalist tension in Kieślowski's later aesthetic. What if the sounds of the film worlds themselves—the diegetic sounds—are artfully arranged such that they function *as* musical accompaniment through pronounced rhythm, timbre, etc.? This dynamic also describes an essential question driving the *musique concrète* movement, a movement with which Cage was heavily associated and with which Kieślowski's realist/formalist hybridization efforts might be productively aligned.

With Kieślowski, the *concrète* technique moves in a transcendent sort of direction, one that illuminates his entire aesthetic and supports his central, abiding concern: the existential question of whether or not reality is shot through with higher significance. Two scenes from two of Kieślowski's latter films—*The Double Life of Véronique* (1991) and *Three Colors: Blue* (1993)—demonstrate how sound effects can overcome their subservience to the image through *musique concrète* techniques, and how the music of "reality" can be expressively and formally employed to suggest the possibility of a higher, metaphysical reality.

In terms of Kieślowski's experimentation with audio, this is the top of the mountain, the culmination of Kieślowski's journey from objective, realist documentarian to spiritually probing and experimental formalist. To understand how he got there, we first need a better understanding of the *musique concrète*/cinema relationship and Kieślowski's use of sound as a de-familiarizing cue.

Musique concrète and Film Sound

Musique concrète is a loose designation for the work of certain twentieth-century musicians who sought to take sounds not usually associated with music and construct musical pieces from them. The 'father' of *musique concrète*, Pierre Schaeffer, titled one of his seminal compositions "Cinq études des bruits" ("Five Studies of Noises"). The most famous of these 1948 pieces was the first, made up of noises associated with the railway. Schaeffer soon moved away from what he called 'anecdotal' sounds (i.e., recognizable sounds) and pursued electronic manipulations of recorded sounds as well as electronically generated sounds, but his original legacy remained influential. Cage followed the same trajectory; he preserved a love for 'found' sources, and he pursued such sounds throughout his career.[8]

The following excerpt, from Cage's seminal essay "The Future of Music: Credo," is revealing, both in its direct reference to film and in its literary form, which is akin to cinema's mode of telling two (or more) stories at once by means of parallel editing:

I BELIEVE THAT THE USE OF NOISE

Wherever we are, what we hear is mostly noise. When we ignore it, it disturbs us. When we listen to it, we find it fascinating. The sound of a truck at 50 m.p.h. Static between the stations. Rain. We want to capture and control these sounds, to use them not as sound effects, but as musical instruments. Every film studio has a library of "sound effects" recorded on film. With a film phonograph it is now possible to control the amplitude and frequency of any one of these sounds and to give to it rhythms within or beyond the reach of anyone's imagination. Given four film phonographs, we can compose and perform a quartet for explosive motor, wind, heartbeat and landslide.

TO MAKE MUSIC

If this word, music, is sacred and reserved for 18th and 19th century instruments, we can substitute a more meaningful term: organization of sound.

WILL CONTINUE AND INCREASE UNTIL WE REACH A MUSIC PRODUCED THROUGH THE AID OF ELECTRICAL INSTRUMENTS[9]

It is instructive that Cage notes the importance of film technology in opening the door for *musique concrète*, and we might also note that early sound theorists and filmmakers tinkered with these ideas a decade or two before the most prominent *concrète* composers hit the scene. In addition to Walter Ruttman's image-less film *Weekend* (1930), a true progenitor of the *concrète* movement in its character as an urban sound collage, many avant-garde film artists (e.g., René Clair) and theorists were interested in what they called 'asynchronous' sound (that is, sounds mismatched with images that do not 'belong' to them in the real world). Sergei Eisenstein considered this to be a sort of 'counterpoint,' and he elevated it to the level of moral duty in order to preserve the artistic integrity of the visual image and not dilute its power. Eisenstein resisted sound but saw the contrapuntal or asynchronous soundtrack as its only legitimate use, and he only saw profit in sound's dialectical *tension* with the image.[10]

As John Belton and Elisabeth Weis have noted, classical film theorists (i.e., before World War II) were united in their discomfort with 'natural' synchronized speech on film.[11] Some theorists echoed Eisenstein in that they saw the rise of the sound film as a threat to the aesthetic gains made in the visual elements of film art. Rudolf Arnheim seemed to reject any film sound whatsoever.[12]

Others, however, struck a more optimistic posture, and Bela Balázs's understanding of the phenomenological significance of film sound holds the key to understanding the function of Kieślowski's *musique concrète*. Balázs stated:

> The sounds of our day-to-day life we hitherto perceived merely as a confused noise, as a formless mass of din, rather as an unmusical person may listen to a symphony; at best he may be able to distinguish the leading melody, the rest will fuse into a chaotic clamor. The sound film will teach us to analyze even chaotic noise with our ear and read the score of life's symphony. … The vocation of the sound film is to redeem us from the chaos of shapeless noise by accepting it as expression, as significance, as meaning.[13]

The parallel with the statement by Cage is obvious. Like Cage, Balázs advocated sound techniques that need not be slavishly representational and synchronous. He supported experiments with asynchronous sound, and he argued that the sound film gives us an opportunity to examine the world—real *or* imagined—in a more neutral context and thus become more aware of that which may have been previously submerged in our sensory experience.[14] We can hear sound *as* sound, and begin to understand what it might mean to us; art excels precisely where it opens up to us this neglected world.

Cage himself suggested something along those lines: "One may give up the desire to control sound, clear his mind of music, and set about discovering means to let sounds be themselves rather than vehicles for man-made theories or expressions of human sentiments."[15] He quickly moved to qualify this, noting that this does not mean emotion is absent from the experience but only that our cognitive categories for emotion have been disrupted and we are then free to perceive the sounds themselves anew and forge new associations. Cage's attempt to hear the sounds themselves without superimposing linguistic categories upon them is reminiscent of the philosopher Edmund Husserl's phenomenological 'bracket' which aims to reveal something like pure perception.[16] Likewise, this approach re-aligns sonic experience with the whole purpose of art, which is 'de-familiarization,' according to the formalist theorist Viktor Shklovsky:

> Habitualization devours work, clothes, furniture, one's wife, and the fear of war .... And art exists that one may recover the sensation of life; it exists to make one feel things, to make the stone stony. The purpose of art is to impart the sensation of things as they are perceived and not as they are known.[17]

This is precisely the value of Kieślowski's highly original and artistic use of *musique concrète* technique. Although Kieślowski is not as 'hands off' and aleatoric in his approach as Cage, and while he may not have asserted that 'perception' and 'knowledge' should be radically separated as Shklovsky seems to suggest, he nevertheless recognized and highlighted the value of the soundscape as encounter with the under-perceived and ever-expansive real.

Kieślowskian Sounds: As De-familiarization, Temporal Structure, and Counterpoint

It is important to note that Kieślowski's late 'formalist' aesthetic was not, in his view, an abandonment of his former 'realist' documentary principles. He saw the two modes as different yet consistent in their goal of the pursuit of truth about the world. For Kieślowski, a sign of artistic quality was the realization that an artist had formulated 'exactly the same thing' that he had experienced or thought "but with the help of a better sentence or better visual arrangement or better composition of sounds than I could ever have imagined."[18] Embedded within this phrase is the notion that 'reality' is not made up simply of 'objective' facts that can be captured in a documentary form; it also involves thoughts and feelings that real people, including the artist, have about those 'facts.'

To that end, the de-familiarization principle—essentially an 'unlearning' process as a means of achieving a new perspective on reality—becomes key in nearly all his aesthetic decisions, sound included. To better understand how he arrives at something like *musique concrète*, we should also understand some of the principles and techniques driving his other, less dramatic sonic choices. Then we can consider two films that use *concrète* technique more explicitly, as a means of temporal structure and counterpoint.

Aural De-familiarization

According to Michal Zarnecki, the sound recordist for his early documentary films, Kieślowski always had the reputation of being a 'co-author' with those artists with whom he worked. Likewise, according Zarnecki, Kieślowski never hesitated to 'correct' a mistake, and he "always" asked "if the sound was good after a take."[19] Characteristics of this sort are not unusual in good film directors, but they are important to note as we forge an understanding of Kieślowski and his relationship to sound. If, in fact, Kieślowski did not place the soundtrack in automatic subservience to the image, it may be that this aesthetic flows from his egalitarian, co-operative approach to his crew. From his early days in documentary Kieślowski was, in other words, open to what sounds—and those who work with them—could do.

His early feature films (made ca. 1976–85) show a growing interest in formal experimentation, and most of them fall along the lines of the de-familiarizing principle that Shklovsky describes: they surprise the viewer, causing something of a cognitive disconnect that forces the viewer to rethink his or her perception. Philosopher Kenneth Dorter elaborates on this idea, and on the notion that such artistic practices reveal hidden, less obvious truths about experience. Dorter mentions four levels of experience at which art seems to express a certain kind of truth: (1) our emotions, (2) cultural values, (3) sensory experience, and (4) the "elusive significance of our experience." All four levels are operative in Kieślowski's sound design, but Dorter's elaboration on point (3) best articulates the whole of the matter: "Art reveals something not only about the subjectivity of experience but about the experienced world itself, something that is not accessible to conceptual understanding."[20] He continues:

> Since in our normal experience qualities like color, shape, and sound are "absorbed" into the images of perceived things, they are experienced only derivatively—not in themselves but as submerged in the object. ... Art, however, can make the qualities of color, shape, sound, duration, weight, etc., stand alone as images themselves rather than as mere features of

normal physical things. Thus it can give us a framework within which to see these qualities in their own terms. … In this way art can *reveal truth about the world* by making conspicuous the primitive qualities of which our experience is composed but which are normally submerged in that experience.[21]

Kieślowski found that in addition to these qualities on their own terms, as once submerged but now revealed properties of the world, they could give sensuous intensity and shape to the narrative ideas put forward in a film and at the same time provide provocative and revealing occasions for audience mis-direction.

Indeed, even early in his feature-film career Kieślowski used sound effects to fool the audience and thus expand the audience's vision (and occasionally its conscience). Near the beginning of *Camera Buff* (1979), for example, there is a woman's scream which we presume—and fear—to come from the protagonist's wife; it turns out that the scream belongs to another woman in the hospital, and this forces the audience to consider suffering on a more universal scale rather than as a simple point on the trajectory of one character. Another example, from *No End* (1985), is more directly 'spiritual'; Ula hears a distinct ringing sound that she perceives to be the ghost of her dead husband rubbing the edge of a glass with his finger; later in the film the therapist that Ula observes is shown to be doing the very same thing, throwing into doubt the veracity of sound and vision.

This sort of doubt would prove productive in the later features, as Kieślowski strained to give the audience a sense that the universe is larger, more expansive, and more meaningful than was first supposed. For example, when Dorota goes to see her terminally ill husband in *Decalogue II* (1988), we see the husband (comatose or asleep) and then Dorota's anguished expression. This quiet moment lasts for some time, and what we don't see but only—and suddenly—hear is a disembodied voice telling Dorota to leave the jar of fruit that she had brought. The voice seems authoritative, and, because it comes from nowhere, initially it seems as though it might be the voice of God; it something akin to what Michel Chion calls the *acousmêtre*, a haunting, off-screen presence with the power to 'see all' and 'know all,' and possessing "omnipotence to act on the situation."[22] It would be too much to say that this belatedly revealed hospital patient (who never reappears, and about whom we know nothing) is some sort of direct symbol. But it could be argued that the consistent technique of surprise and de-familiarization, which results in a constant expansion of time and space in the mind of the audience, has the aggregate effect of generating a 'cosmic' or 'transcendent' sort of feeling throughout the film. One has the intuition that there is a larger, wider reality being considered here, even if this reality is not fully presented on screen. Disembodied voices also play crucial roles in *The Double Life of Véronique* (1991) and *Red* (1994), as Kieślowski considers the universal themes of human connection, God, doubt, fate, free will, and moral choice.

According to William Flageollet, the sound mixer on all the later films, Kieślowski often added noises for which the picture offers no referent.[23] For instance, in the first narrative scene of *Red*, Valentine's original conversation with her boyfriend is interrupted by the loud noise of an unseen helicopter, forcing her to close the windows; we hear this helicopter a few times throughout the film, but we never see it until the very end of the story, when we look back and realize that it functioned as a harbinger of disaster (and, for some characters, redemption). In *Blue* (1993), a typical 'establishing' night-time shot is held as we eventually hear the mysterious sound of a telephone ringing. Whose phone is this? And why are they calling so late? These questions are not answered until much later in the film, and the camera's relentless gaze at the city forces us to think in the broadest possible terms about all human beings and their need for connection.

Later in *Blue*, when Julie surveys an unfinished page of her late husband's music manuscript, the musical notation (in extreme close-up) gives way to the five lines of an empty staff, just as the music on the soundtrack yields to the sound of whistling wind. Since the scene takes place indoors, the emotionally hollow sound is diegetically impossible, yet it is appropriate for the moment. This sort of sonic contribution to the emotional meaning of the scene is what Chion calls "free counterpoint," like the example he gives from Andrey Tarkovsky's *Solaris*, in which the movement of a character's frozen body is complemented by the sound of breaking glass.[24]

At other times Kieślowski provides precisely the sorts of sounds that match the picture, without sentiment and without mercy. The killing of the taxi driver in *Decalogue V* (and its extended version, *A Short Film about Killing*, both 1988) stands among the most viscerally engaging and horrifying images in the Kieślowskian oeuvre. Where other directors might have sentimentalized the killing, exploiting or mollifying it through musical cues, Kieślowski is unsparing in the relentless, dispassionate, detailed sounds of slow, agonizing, undignified death. No sound of tension, scraping, hitting, flesh spattering, gasping, etc. remains unheard, as Kieślowski recognized this scene to be de-familiarizing all on its own. For most of us, the only horrifying deaths we have encountered have been on screen; what needed de-familiarization was the convention of *cinematic* death. In this instance, sound was key.

These sound effects, and their creative employment, all function to de-familiarize a scene, object, or event to which an audience member otherwise might not have paid careful attention. In this manner Kieślowski not only maintains the required attention but challenges the viewer to search for meaning in the moment, to extend his or her conception beyond a local, referential plot point, and to consider larger, metaphysical issues. In terms of audio, these principles reach their zenith in two examples that may genuinely be described as *musique concrète*.

Musique concrète as Temporal Structure

The first example speaks to the musical use of diegetic sonic material, which is to say that the sound achieves prominence in the scene through an emphasis on its rhythmic/temporal pattern and its timbral qualities. We might say the diegetic sounds provide a temporal frame for the images, even as they yield a sort of experiential theme or metaphor—the inexorability of fate.

At the opening of *Blue*, a traveling sequence beginning with a close-up of a car tire, no music per se is playing and very little dialogue is spoken. With the exception of the silent girl, the characters barely appear. The opening of *Blue* is sonically spare, yet we are reminded, as we recall Cage's words, that "there is no such thing as an empty space or any empty time."[25] Once we bracket away the expectation of extra-diegetic music that typically begins a film, we note the music of the soundscape. The natural sounds of the various shots beat a consistent, steady time. The pulsating whir of the car's tires, the whoosh of lamp posts as they are passed, the ominous drip of fluid from a faulty brake line: these elements form a continuous aural procession through the sequence, culminating in the curious but steady click of a ball hitting a stick as a boy plays a game on the side of the road. At the very moment he wins the game, the car passes and the other characters lose everything. The rhythm stops; after a pause there is a terrifying rupture, the nightmarish cacophony of squealing rubber, a barking dog, and crunching, twisted metal. As the result of a very deliberate editing choice, we hear these sounds play under the visual of the boy's face, and we absorb his transformation from delight to bewilderment to horror. Only after the boy's initial reaction do we see the mangled car as it collapses into its final resting position.

Although this occurrence seems to be a tragic 'coincidence,' the inexorable rhythm has suggested the opposite. To say the crash functions as a mere symbol of 'fate,' then, is to oversimplify. Yes, one can see an abstract idea like 'fate' being the point of the sequence, but what matters is that fate is *felt*, and that one intuits this inexorability through sensation and perception. Through the structuring and focusing of diverse everyday sounds, Kieślowski suggests that larger forces and issues are at work.

This subtle *musique concrète* is a remarkable inversion of how Eisenstein envisioned cinematic rhythm. Eisenstein, who began in filmmaking's silent era, regarded visual montage as the primary timekeeper, the driver of cinema's pace and life.[26] Montage of course occurs in the Kieślowski scene, but it takes a subservient role to the internal sonic rhythms of each shot, which, remarkably, all beat at approximately the same rhythm. Kieślowski takes what in other films have been subservient sonic *effects* and forms them into an intra-diegetic *sonic and metric dynamic*—a fate rhythm—that regulates the pace and, ultimately, provides the meaning of the scene. In *Audio-Vision: Sound on Screen*, Chion states that sounds temporalize images along several dimensions (i.e., it gives the image a sense of time).[27] It is fair to say that in *Blue* the sounds not only temporalize but also foundationalize the visuals, their assemblage, and what we expect from them.

Musique concrète as Counterpoint

In the world of narrative film, there are relatively few examples of *musique concrète* as asynchronous counterpoint. Experiments as suggested by the early film theorists are usually the domain of truly 'experimental' film. In Kieślowski's *Double Life of Véronique*, however, we see a fascinating exception to the rule.

This film is mysterious on many levels that cannot be fully explored here. In short, however, it is essentially a *Doppelgänger* story, and much of the film's action is about one character intuitively sensing the existence of the other. 'Intuition' and 'mystery,' therefore, are fully on display. In one scene, Véronique receives an anonymous package that contains an audiocassette. As she listens to the tape with a set of wireless headphones, Véronique wanders around her apartment and attends to mundane things (she drinks water, brushes her teeth, etc.); the audience, however, hears only the equally mundane yet foreign contents of the mysterious audiotape (pedestrian noises and echoes, what sounds like doors, a car, things being dropped, open, and shut, etc.). This piece of *musique concrète* climaxes, and ends, with the unexpected sound of an explosion.

This sequence creates a bicameral world that is at once marvelous and disconcerting. The effect is difficult to describe, but it serves as an amplification of the film's central theme of duality: the idea that two worlds (in this case represented by nonsynchronous aural and visual elements) could coexist. Indeed, the tape is like a transmission from another coexistent world, one into which Véronique is beckoned, and everything about the production of this scene reinforces that feeling.

Again, Chion's theories on sound give a little more articulation to this experience. He writes that sounds tend naturally toward 'synchresis' with images. In other words, sound and image weld a cause–effect relation, regardless of any logical connection between them; this effect is stronger in some cases than others, but the tendency toward synchresis is always present. Chion also writes about a process he calls "spatial magnetization."[28] In this situation, the recorded 'distance' and timbre of the film sounds make them appear to emanate from a source within the frame or at least from the immediate diegetic region off-screen, even though this is clearly not the case.

In the scene from *The Double Life of Véronique*, our logical understanding that the sound is clearly *not* emanating from the objects in the frame is synthesized with these psychological tendencies. The fact that most of the actual noises in Véronique's apartment are absent from the frame only bolsters the synthesis. The result is a "vast extension" of space in the experience (the creation of the "superfield," according to Chion); in the hands of a genuine artist, this sonic technique can actually *double* the size of the world rather than merely frustrate the audience's expectations. When this marvel occurs, the film has ascended to the level of what Chion calls the "phantom audio-vision," a term he reserves for the extraordinary sound design of the Russian filmmaker Andrey Tarkovsky. Chion's description of Tarkovsky's film *The Sacrifice* (1986) might very well apply here to Kieślowski:

> [O]ne can hear sounds that already seem to come from the other side, as if they're heard by an immaterial ear, liberated from the hurly-burly of our human world. … [I]t calls to another dimension, it has gone elsewhere, disengaged from the present. It can also murmur like the drone of the world, at once close and disquieting.[29]

The connection with Tarkovsky is significant, as both filmmakers had similar aims, and Kieślowski often expressed great admiration for the Russian master. Although Kieślowski's sound design is not always as adventurous as that of Tarkovsky,[30] it does share something of the same goal: to suggest a hidden dimension of reality.

To play devil's advocate for a moment, one might argue against a transcendent reading of the technique and suggest that the *musique concrète* in *The Double Life of Véronique* functions only as a sonic fissure or rupture. Just as Gilles Deleuze remarked that the *image crystal* is an instance in which time itself sometimes "rises up to the surface of the screen" through a tear in the illusionistic fabric of the visual cinema,[31] perhaps we see here a *bruit crystal* in which the illusionistic, synchronous world ruptures and sound comes to the surface. One might say this is an example of the constructed nature of cinematic sound enunciating its own construction, as John Belton argues it always—to some degree—does.[32] If this is the case, Kieślowski is joining Jean-Luc Godard and many of the other politically oriented, Brechtian-esque filmmakers of the 1960s and 1970s who were most interested in demonstrating how constructed the cinema is. We might also say this is 'contrapuntal,' in the sense with which Eisenstein used the term. Sound and image do not correlate with our immediate, temporal experience; rather, they stand in stark dissimilarity, as deliberate opposites in a dialectical tension.

But neither reflexive rupture nor Marxist dialectical aesthetics serves as the most helpful conception of the sound in this scene. Yes, we do feel the tug and pull of illusion and construction that emerges, particularly in the moments where Véronique rewinds the tape (and the spell of the illusion is temporarily broken, then re-instantiated). There is also, certainly, a sense of the dialectical tension that a contrapuntal arrangement can create. But here the essence of counterpoint, and of cinematic construction, seems not to highlight the distance between sound and picture but to create something larger, and richer, in their combination, as Balázs, Chion, and the screenwriters (Kieślowski and Krzysztof Piesiewicz) have suggested. Véronique's world has opened up, not closed down.

Nor do those materialist paradigms cohere with Kieślowski's pronounced existential concerns. Kieślowski is not as interested in revealing the material conditions of cinematic construction as he is in pointing to a larger truth about how we encounter the world through the mysteries of our own experience, a truth about how our pedestrian world intersects with, or opens up to, a larger reality that we cannot fully describe but can intuitively perceive. To put it another way, we can perceive the world in a narrow, goal-oriented way, and much of our experience is indeed like that. But we can also bracket away our narrowing, daily attitude and open up to perceiving *more* of reality than we typically permit ourselves. And with this we might begin to understand that many things in our experience can be known and learned intuitively, before and beyond the operations of language, science, and political control. Kieślowski was far from religious in any conventional 'church-going' sense, but anyone familiar with him or his work knows that he considered the materialist conception of the world to be dangerously reductive. At the very least, he believed in other ways of knowing, ways that are beyond words, dogma, propaganda, and news reports.[33]

Our experience of going through the *Double Life of Véronique* scene is not one of disconcertion or frustrating bafflement; it is an experience of wonder, appeal, and revelation. This opening up, of the world and of ourselves, was also something Pierre Schaeffer himself aimed for in his *musique concrète* and his writings on it. The notion of sounds divorced from subjugating visual forces lies behind his notion of 'acousmatics,' a term that can be traced back to Pythagoras's disciples, who reportedly heard their teacher's voice but never saw him, since he spoke from behind a curtain. Schaefferian acousmatics free us from the tyranny of the visual. Acousmatics are not, Schaeffer states, a study in 'subjectivity' or 'objectivity,' a study of sonorous objects that are completely graspable. "We can gain knowledge of them. We can, we hope, transmit this knowledge," he says.[34] In the end, Schaeffer's *musique concrète*, and Véronique's cassette, force us to "hear with another ear."[35]

The contrapuntal *musique concrète* of this scene thus suggests a wider world of experience, but it also suggests a wider epistemology. Again we see consonance with the Cageian aesthetic:

> Here we are concerned with the coexistence of dissimilars, and the central points where fusion occurs are many: the ears of the listeners wherever they are. This disharmony, to paraphrase Bergson's statement about disorder, is simply a harmony to which many are unaccustomed.[36]

Conclusion

Kieślowski's sonic aesthetic, particularly in his later films, uses sound effects to guide, amplify, and deepen the meaning of given scenes. His deliberate, stylized use of ordinary sounds empowers the soundtrack to rise from a position of subservience to the image and gain greater semantic weight. Likewise, his sonic aesthetic reaches its zenith in unusual examples of *musique concrète* that they flow from his overall aesthetic and philosophy and from his general approach to cinematic sound.

Musique concrète is significant because it is not mere ephemera. It is a framing and presentation of all that is sonically foundational in our experience. These artistic examples—both musical and cinematic—demonstrate how much epistemological weight sound 'effects' can carry. In the cinema of Kieślowski and other great film artists, the sonic foundations of experience sometimes step forward, announce themselves, and point to a greater reality. The sonic world—even the film score—can truly speak for itself in these instances, and the extraordinary experience of living *through* that 'speech' gives us evidence of sonic, sensory knowledge that cannot be dismissed as mere affect. The sonic world's phenomenological power is a fundamental display of the intentional self and world(s) in dynamic interrelationship. It is the ground of meaningful experience, as musicians and other artists have intuitively known for some time.

To return to the quote that began this chapter, Chion states: "Kieślowski endows noises and music—a solo flute or a slender soprano voice—with an energy that cuts through the general pall of the world." The context here is Chion's observations of several scenes in *Blue*: Julie's jarring encounter with baby mice in her apartment, her noticeable breathing as she bites into a lollipop, her sudden interruption by noisy children as she attempts to forget her husband while she is submerged in a swimming pool. Chion sees Kieślowski as using "sounds to break in with the force of life" (and he points out that Kieślowski was helped in this by the technological fidelity and presence of Dolby audio).

And this is Kieślowski's typical sonic aesthetic: familiar yet arresting sounds draw power from the friction points of brute reality and characters' intense internal aspirations. Although Kieślowski was not typically engaged in long stretches of *concrète* experimentation, we see in these particulars how his audio aesthetic flows from the more adventurous ideas that *musique concrète* engenders: that reality is there all the time, that we often fail to notice its significance, and that it is far more grand and rich than our dull, habitualized ears have permitted us to hear. And what if the formalism of art de-habitualizes us and re-introduces us to life? What if, with this re-introduction, we discover a wider, deeply significant, more expansive reality than we previously imagined? Kieślowski raises those questions, and he asks us to truly listen.

Notes

1   Michel Chion, *Film, A Sound Art*, trans. Claudia Gorbman (New York: Columbia University Press, 2009).

2   Kieślowski's interest in metaphysics is well documented. In summary, his posture is something of an anxious, searching agnostic. He once said: "The world is not only

bright lights, this hectic pace, the Coca-Cola with a straw, the new car .... Another truth exists ... a hereafter? Yes, surely. Good or bad, I don't know, but ... something else" (quoted in Annette Insdorf, *Double Lives, Second Chances: The Cinema of Kieślowski* [New York: Hyperion, 1999], xv. Originally from an interview with *Télérama* [Paris: September 1993]).

3   "Zbigniew Preisner," in *Film Music*, ed. Mark Russell and James Young (Boston: Focal Press, 2000), 161–3.

4   William Flageollet, "Insights into *Trois Couleurs: Rouge*," *Red* (DVD, Miramax, 2003).

5   John Cage, *Silence: Lectures and Writings by John Cage* (Middletown: Wesleyan University Press, 1961), 8. Cage goes on to tell the story of visiting a soundproof laboratory and still hearing overwhelming pulsing sounds. His guide at the lab explained he was hearing his own pulmonary and circulatory systems.

6   R. Murray Schafer, *The Soundscape: Our Sonic Environment and the Tuning of the World* (Rochester: Destiny Books, 1994).

7   Cage was a Zen Buddhist and Kieślowski was raised a Roman Catholic, although as an adult he definitively left the church and embraced a more personal, existential sort of agnosticism wherein he often vacillated between faith and doubt.

8   Elliott Schwartz and Daniel Godfrey, *Music Since 1945: Issues, Materials, and Literature* (Belmont: Wadsworth, 1993), 120, 249. Other *concrète* composers mixed recorded sounds and standard instrumentation (e.g., Edgard Varèse's *Deserts*, 1954, composed for taped factory noises, winds, and percussion). We could also survey the variety of *musique concrète* examples and their progeny through electronic music and present-day popular musicians who use *concrète* techniques (e.g., D.J. Spooky and Sonic Youth), but that would extend far beyond our purview. It is enough to say that *musique concrète* has proven one of the most influential musical ideas of the last sixty years.

9   Cage, *Silence*, 3.

10 Sergei Eisenstein, Vsevolod Pudovkin, and Grigori Alexandrov, "A Statement," in *Film Sound: Theory and Practice*, ed. Elisabeth Weis and John Belton (New York: Columbia University Press, 1985), 83–5.

11 Elisabeth Weis and John Belton, eds., *Film Sound: Theory and Practice* (New York: Columbia University Press, 1985), 82.

12 See Arnheim's *Film as Art* (Berkeley: University of California Press, 1957), 199–230.

13 Bela Balázs, *Theory of the Film: Character and Growth of a New Art* (New York: Dover, 1970), 198.

14 Ibid., 120.

15 Cage, *Silence*, 10.

16 Edmund Husserl, *Ideas* (New York: Collier Books, 1962), 99.

17 Viktor Shklovsky, "Art as Technique," in *Russian Formalist Criticism: Four Essays*, trans. and ed. Lee T. Lemon and Marion J. Reis (Lincoln: University of Nebraska Press, 1965), 11–12.

18 Krzysztof Kieślowski, *Kieślowski on Kieślowski*, ed. Danusia Stok (London: Faber and Faber, 1995), 193.

19 Interview with Michal Zarnecki, *The Scar* (DVD), Kino Video, 2004.

20 Kenneth Dorter, "Conceptual Truth and Aesthetic Truth," *Journal of Aesthetics and Art Criticism* 48, no. 1 (Winter 1990): 37–51.

21 Ibid., 39 (emphasis added).

22 Michel Chion, *Audio-Vision: Sound on Screen* (New York: Columbia University Press, 1994), 129–30.

23 Flageollet, "Insights into *Trois Couleurs: Rouge*."

24 Chion, *Audio-Vision*, p. 39.
25 Cage, *Silence*, 8.
26 Sergei Eisenstein, *Film Form: Essays in Film Theory* (San Diego: Harcourt Brace and Co., 1949), 72–5.
27 Chion, *Audio-Vision*, 13.
28 Ibid. 129–30. The other ideas in the paragraph are taken from pp. 63–70, 87, and 150.
29 Ibid., 123–4.
30 For an exceptional analysis of Tarkovsky's approach to sound as a means of expressing the spiritual realm, see Andrea Truppin, "And Then There Was Sound: The Films of Andrei Tarkovsky," in *Sound Theory, Sound Practice*, ed. Rick Altman (New York: Routledge, 1992).
31 Gilles Deleuze, *Cinema 2: The Time-Image* (Minneapolis: University of Minnesota Press, 1989), xi.
32 John Belton, "Technology and Aesthetics of Film Sound," in *Film Sound: Theory and Practice*, ed. Elisabeth Weis and John Belton (New York: Columbia University Press, 1985), 63.
33 For a full account of Kieślowski's approach to these matters, see Joseph G. Kickasola, *The Films of Krzysztof Kieślowski: The Liminal Image* (New York: Continuum, 2004), chapters 1 and 2.
34 Pierre Schaeffer, "Acousmatics," in *Audio Culture: Readings in Modern Music*, ed. Christoph Cox and Daniel Warner (New York: Continuum, 2004), 81.
35 Ibid., 81.
36 Cage, *Silence*, 12.

Chapter 6

Gus Van Sant's Soundwalks and Audio-visual *Musique concrète*

Danijela Kulezic-Wilson

One of the fathers of New Queer Cinema, uncontested master of sensitive portrayals of youth angst and alienation, musician, photographer, and novelist, Gus Van Sant is undoubtedly one of the most exciting and unpredictable American filmmakers working today. His black-and-white debut *Mala Noche* (1985) was part of the initial wave of small, low-budget features that challenged the vacant spectacles of 1980s Hollywood and launched the first golden decade of American Independent Cinema by abandoning the rules of classical narration and introducing provocative themes that addressed new audiences of ethnic and sexual minorities. Van Sant's subsequent features— *Drugstore Cowboy* (1989), *My Own Private Idaho* (1991), and *To Die For* (1995)—further established him not only as a prominent voice in New Queer Cinema but also as a poet of alienation and an astute observer of subcultures existing on the margins of society and of a celebrity and media-obsessed culture. At the end of the 1990s, as his collaboration with Ben Affleck and Matt Damon on *Good Will Hunting* (1997) turned out to be a crossover hit that won Oscars for Best Screenplay and, for Robin Williams, Best Supporting Actor, Van Sant found himself in the middle of Hollywood's race to catch up with the growing critical and financial success of the Indies. But instead of taking part in one of the numerous tame products resulting from studio attempts to marry Indie hipness with big budgets, Van Sant somehow ended up helming the most notorious project of the decade, a shot-by-shot remake of *Psycho* (1998), and then following it with another variation on the reclusive mentor/young prodigy theme in *Finding Forrester* (2000).

Two years later, however, when *Gerry* premiered at the 2002 Sundance Film Festival, provoking wildly contrasting comments and mass walk-outs, it was clear that Van Sant's flirtation with the mainstream was over and that the director had returned to his independent roots with an increased appetite for unconventional subjects and challenging stylistic methods. *Gerry*, a story about two friends who get lost in a desert, was the first in a series of films which would become known as the Death Trilogy as they were all inspired by real-life murders and deaths; the second film in the trilogy, *Elephant* (2003), was based on the tragic events of the Columbine High School shootings, and *Last Days*

(2005) was inspired by the final days of grunge rock star Kurt Cobain. In the ensuing *Paranoid Park* (2007), an accidental killing becomes the main incentive for a cinematic meditation on responsibility and guilt, and *Milk* (2008) tells the story of Harvey Milk, the openly gay political activist who was elected to a public office and later assassinated by a disturbed fellow politician.

The diversity of Van Sant's interests and the inconsistencies in the style and quality of his films are mirrored in his similarly diverse and variably successful approaches to employing music. The original scores for his films are quite conventional, but even within these there are notable differences; the satirical *To Die For* makes great use of composer Danny Elfman's playful style, for example, while *Milk*—also with music by Elfman—features one of the most sentimental scores in any Van Sant film to date. His films with compiled scores, though—notably the Death Trilogy and *Paranoid Park*, which are the focus of this study—involve deeply personal musical choices and experiments with *musique concrète*.

Along with a common thematic thread and a fascination with cinematic time, space, and the *photogénie*[1] of cinematic movement, the Death Trilogy films have in common striking soundscapes that combine diegetic sounds with *musique concrète* and pre-existent pieces of electroacoustic music. Conceived in collaboration with sound designer Leslie Shatz, who has worked with Van Sant since *Good Will Hunting*,[2] these soundscapes create distinctive sonic and musical environments for characters who are in some personal crisis or who are pushed to the edges of existential endurance. More than that, the use of natural sounds as primary compositional resources combined with a focus on the interaction of characters with their surroundings not only embodies the fundamentals of *musique concrète* philosophy; it also seems to connect in a number of ways with the films' underlying themes and aesthetic credos.

It would be correct to say that the relationship between narratives and soundscapes in Van Sant's films is reciprocal, but this would simply reassert the perennial division between film as a self-contained entity and soundtrack as its added attribute. It seems more interesting to note that in the Death Trilogy the correspondence between the style of the soundtracks on one hand and of the narrative themes and *mise-en-scène* on the other hand establish the principles of *musique concrète* as the dominant mode of expression, and not only in sonic terms.

In the same way that *musique concrète* is concerned with the expansion of the sonic palette and increasing listeners' awareness of what can be accepted and perceived as music, so Van Sant's exploration of cinematic 'present tense' through *photogénie*, camera gaze, and movement invites audience members to experience a film's entire audio-visual diegetic content as music. At the same time, his use of traditional musical genres often challenges mainstream scoring conventions by making diegetic performances the focal point of a *mise-en-scène* and by imbuing pre-existing extra-diegetic music with inter-textual and sometimes intensely personal meanings. Whether diegetic or extra-diegetic or borrowed from other films, whether pop, rock, or classical, whether stretching in long, uninterrupted sheets or reduced to little sonic islands surrounded by silence, the music in Van Sant's films, particularly in the Death Trilogy and *Paranoid Park*, embodies each film's most subtle secrets, concerns, and meanings.

Existential, Transcendental, Musical

Samuel Beckett once said that he never wanted to see *Waiting for Godot* adapted for the screen because he wrote the play for two "small men locked in a big space,"[3] and he felt that this symbolic image would be lost if the play were subjected to the close-ups and editing techniques of film. Rightly or wrongly, Van Sant's *Gerry* has often been compared to Beckett's breakthrough play, partly because of its absurdist approach to narrative (or "anti-narrative," as Jonathan Romney calls it[4]) but also because its two characters, both named Gerry, get lost in a desert while searching for a mysterious 'Thing.' Van Sant has never responded to such comments. Nevertheless, an image lingers with the filmgoer after watching the two Gerry characters stumble to exhaustion, dehydration, alienation from each other, and the eventual death of one of them: an image of two very small figures imprisoned by the vastness of the space in which they are lost.

Neither in *Godot* nor in *Gerry* does anything much happen in terms of plot. The characters wait and talk, or in *Gerry* they walk and occasionally talk, but whatever they are waiting for or looking for seems to be unattainable, as if reflecting the conviction of the works' creators that any truth worth conveying lies beyond the reach of language or cinematography. In both the play and the film what matters is the search, and the beauty and horror of the process, which *Gerry* communicates in masterly fashion by juxtaposing the slow disintegration of its protagonists and their relationship with mesmerizing images of moving clouds, the cycles of day and night, and stunning landscapes.

The focus on the process is of course intrinsically connected with a sense of passing time, and in *Gerry* as well as in the other Death Trilogy films Van Sant makes duration itself a significant constitutive device. According to Van Sant himself, the initial inspiration for adopting this approach in *Gerry* came after watching Béla Tarr's seven-hour *Sátántangó* (1994) and being fascinated not just by Tarr's "timing of the story" but also by the idea that the more one watches certain simple actions, like walking, "the more they grow in their illumination."[5]

On one hand, this unwavering enthusiasm for long, contemplative shots brings to mind André Bazin's theories of deep focus and his belief in the ability of a film image to reveal "the presence of the divine in the real world."[6] On the other hand, it also invokes what Paul Schrader calls the 'transcendental' style epitomized in the work of such European and Asian directors as Carl Theodor Dreyer, Yasujirô Ozu, Robert Bresson, and Andrey Tarkovsky.[7] In either case, the focus on the temporal aspect of film is crucial, because by allowing the "pressure of time" to fill a shot one can discover "something significant, truthful going on beyond the events on the screen."[8] In this sense, time is considered to be both an aesthetic category and a spiritual category, a "raw material" of the film that allows the viewing experience to be "transformed into a repeatable ritual which can be repeatedly transcended."[9]

A number of elements typical of 'transcendental' style as described by Schrader can be recognized in Van Sant's approach to the medium; most notable among these are the importance of filmic form, an inclination for long takes, and the so-called 'surface-aesthetics' of quotidian details. With the exception of Bresson and Tarkovsky, most of the filmic transcendentalists examined by Schrader did not pay much attention to sound design. It is precisely in the area of sound, however, that Van Sant's appropriation of the elements of the 'transcendental' style have produced the most fascinating results.

Musique concrète and various pre-existing electroacoustic compositions indeed provide the main material for the extra-diegetic scores in the Death Trilogy and *Paranoid Park*. Diegetically performed pieces of classical music and pop-songs are present in these films in an obvious, deliberate way, as any other cinematic element—an actor, a movement, or recurring images of passing clouds. Actual pieces of *musique concrète* and electronically produced tracks have a function similar to that of conventional extra-diegetic music in the sense that they work subliminally on the audience, blending with the *mise-en-scène* and the surroundings to create a mood without drawing attention to themselves. Even when they are in juxtaposition with images, which is often the case, their presence is rarely felt as an intrusion; they do not suggest obvious attempts at defamiliarization, and they do not come across as interpretative devices that signal that something out of the ordinary is taking place. In *Elephant*, for instance, tracks by German-Canadian composer Hildegard Westerkamp, the Japanese band Acid Mothers Temple, and even a recording of William Burroughs reading are interwoven with the *mise-en-scène* in such a way that it is sometimes hard to tell whether the perceived sound is the result of a slightly amplified diegetic soundscape or extra-diegetic *musique concrète*. Toward the end of *Gerry*, when the two protagonists are staggering through the desert feeling increasingly hopeless and dehydrated, the electronic soundscape devised by Van Sant and Leslie Shatz seems to emanate from the *mise-en-scène* as an embodiment of the characters' hallucinatory state, a sonic mirage of electronically produced noises mixed with the unearthly sounds of a cello and the wind.[10]

Van Sant's interest in elaborate sonic design based on *musique concrète* does not originate in the Death Trilogy films, however. His first film, *Mala Noche*, clearly demonstrates his interest in the metaphoric use of sound and the expressive properties of *musique concrète*, most notably in the sex scene between Walt (played by Tim Streeter) and his Mexican lover, which is dominated by the sounds of bells and trains. According to sound designer Leslie Shatz, even while working on the veering-toward-mainstream *Good Will Hunting*, Van Sant sometimes played with as many as fifty different tracks of *musique concrète* in order to create the meta-diegetic sound effects.[11] An example is the scene that depicts the fight on the basketball court, a scene that—with its use of Gerry Rafferty's hit ballad from the late 1970s, "Baker Street"—is also symptomatic of Van Sant's approach to pre-existing music.

The music starts at the exact moment that Will (played by Matt Damon) throws the first punch at a guy who used to beat him up in kindergarten. But the Rafferty song is quickly submerged into a distant echo by the sounds of swearing, amplified grunts and punches, and a mixture of unidentified noises that include sirens and bells.[12] The gentle, compassionate ballad stands in juxtaposition with the images of violence, but its choice must also have been inspired by the content of its lyrics, which describe people stuck in hard, hopeless lives. It is typical of Van Sant to choose musical pieces that in some way relate to his protagonists' situations, either through their lyrics[13] or through a connection known only to the director. Knowing the music's hidden or underlying 'meaning' is not essential for appreciation of the scene, however. In the case of the fight scene in *Good Will Hunting*, it is not a knowledge of the ballad's lyrics that throws us into the main character's state of mind; rather, we 'sense' the character's deep-seated anger—the cause of which is revealed only much later in the film—through the oddness of the sound design with its combination of the ballad's echo-like presence, the *musique concrète*, and the slow-motion action.

Musical material is often present in Van Sant's mind in the early stages of his conceiving a film, and sometimes the music's content determines visual imagery in advance of shooting. An example is the most memorable scene from *Paranoid Park*, which shows its teenage protagonist showering in his friend's house after accidentally causing the death of a security guard at a train-yard. In an archetypal attempt at purification, the boy stands under the stream of water and then, as if too weak to endure the pressure, slides down to the floor while the sound of water becomes increasingly loud and mixes with an electronic buzz and various noises of nature; one almost gets the impression that the birds painted on the shower stall's tiles have somehow come alive.

As in *Elephant*, Van Sant here chose to give the role of the tortured teenager to a non-professional actor (Gabe Nevins), thus encouraging an impassive performance in the tradition of classical transcendental style. Indeed, Nevins's face is so expressionless and difficult to read that the character's struggle with an unspeakable burden can easily be interpreted as vacuity or emotional numbness. The shower scene is *Paranoid Park*'s only moment in which audio-visual interaction releases some of the protagonist's emotional turmoil, a turmoil that through most of the film is hidden behind the character's blank face and scattered in a fragmented narrative. But knowing that the track used here is an excerpt from Frances White's *Walk through Resonant Landscape #2*,[14] which was earlier used in *Elephant* and later in *Milk*, suggests that elements of the music itself inspired the organization of this particular *mise-en-scène*, right down to the detail of pictures of birds on the tiles in the shower cabin.

Soundwalking

Musique concrète in Van Sant's films does not simply fulfill the role of an extra-diegetic score. Its philosophical underpinnings also permeate the Death Trilogy on the levels of narrative organization and the conception of film as an inherently musical form. Indeed, the idea of interaction with one's surroundings, which figures in many examples of *musique concrète*, is an important narrative theme in both *Gerry* and *Last Days*. It is expressed in the protagonists' attempts to relate with nature, which in *Gerry* symbolizes a means of survival and in *Last Days* represents an antidote to the complete social alienation of its principal character. It is also one of the implicit themes in *Elephant*, which does not search for conclusions or explanations for the school massacre but invites us to take part in careful, detached observation of the protagonists and the ways in which they relate to one other.

The significant aspect of this approach is that the process of observation itself becomes engrossing, drawing the viewer into the rhythms of walking, the sounds of water, wind, or branches and stones crackling underfoot, turning the viewer's prolonged gaze into a music-like experience. The secret of this method lies in liberating the viewer from the expectations associated with filmic continuity and its concern with 'what's coming next?' by developing a sense of contentment with the present tense.[15] But unlike cinema's traditional transcendentalists, who explore the present tense through a state of stasis, Van Sant is fascinated by the medium's kinetic properties. Through the desert and through school playgrounds and corridors, captured by smooth tracking shots in *Gerry* or by more intimate Steadicam shots in *Elephant*, Van Sant's protagonists walk incessantly, as if treading some new songlines for the lost, ill-fated, and lonely.[16] Their walks become the most potent source of actual *musique concrète*, in the process creating cinematic equivalents of what soundscape composers call 'soundwalking.'[17] In these cases, however, it is not the films' protagonists but audience members who get to be immersed in a process that encourages them to discover, through sound, the inner spirit of cinematic environments.[18]

On the other hand, Van Sant's fascination with the actual *photogénie* of cinematic movement can be traced to the influence of Hungarian director Béla Tarr; indeed, the first installment of the Death Trilogy pays an open homage to what some critics call the 'Tarr trudge,'[19] the charting of a lengthy walk that is devoid of dialogue but rich with diegetic sounds. But whereas in Tarr's films the trudge is typically incorporated into a sequence of even lengthier static shots, in Van Sant's *Gerry* and *Elephant*, and a bit so in *Last*

Days, physical movement remains the primary focus of cinematic attention. The continuous tracking shots or Steadicam shots in the Death Trilogy are not treated as generators of goal-oriented narratives; rather, they are offered as meandering lines of repetitive visual and sonic themes (as in *Gerry* and *Last Days*) or overlapping temporalities (as in *Elephant*). These shots result in something similar to what Jonathan Kramer calls music's "vertical temporality," a temporality in which dialectical, narrative linearity is suspended for the sake of the audience experiencing a sustained moment of time.[20] Patient and unbroken attention to those moments in time that are filled only with a character's mundane actions also reveals another dimension of the cinematically extended 'now'; this dimension involves an increased awareness of those special moments' *sounds* and their musicality—the music of an 'expanded present tense.' And this brings us back to fundamental principles of *musique concrète* and 'soundwalking.'[21]

The most often-cited example of this approach is a four-minute-long scene in *Gerry* that shows the two friends in close-up walking alongside one other, their heads bouncing in the frame first in sync, then out of sync, then in sync again.[22] Van Sant's focused kineticism—combining the visual rhythm of the characters' physical movement with the crackling sound of their boots on the ground—makes this scene the film's most musical and hypnotic moment. The scene's musicality is reminiscent of an earlier, similarly memorable example of audio-visual *musique concrète*: the ride in an open railway handcar toward 'the Zone' in Tarkovsky's 1979 *Stalker*, which is rhythmic, continuous, and deeply mesmerizing in its attention to the musicality of repetitive audio-visual movement. But while the scene from *Stalker* is stylized by mixing Eduard Artemyev's electroacoustic score with diegetic sounds and by moving the camera to explore the face of each passenger during their lengthy ride, in *Gerry* the full attention of the camera is just on the movement, the moment of time it occupies, and the diegetic sounds it produces. It represents the most concentrated example of how the expansion of the cinematic *now* creates the *music of here*.

From *Für Elise* to *Für Alina*

Unlike works of *musique concrète* that are blended with the *mise-en-scène*, musical pieces of a more traditional kind in the Death Trilogy are presented in such a way as to obtain the audience member's unflinching attention. When such pieces are employed extra-diegetically, as pieces by Arvo Pärt and Ethan Rose are in *Gerry* and *Paranoid Park*, respectively, they are foregrounded through the deletion of diegetic sounds. When they are presented diegetically, in on-screen performances in *Elephant* and *Last Days*, for example, there is an insistence on the pieces' full or at least seemingly full duration. Particularly in *Last Days*, the engagement of different characters with music is given center stage within the narrative, as when a mostly static camera observes one of the characters singing along with a recording of The Velvet Underground's "Venus in Furs," or when Michael Pitt, who plays the main character, performs his own music while a camera positioned outside the window retreats slowly in a four-and-a-half-minute-long tracking shot that gradually expands its frame to reveal an image of the whole house with its surroundings. In any other context these musical moments would be perceived as interruptions of the narrative, but in a film based on extremely long shots of the aimless wanderings or drug-induced stupor of the main character they become focal points of attention and also offer isolated glimpses into concealed affective undercurrents of the story.

Bearing in mind that significant portions of the music in *Elephant* and *Last Days* are employed diegetically and that in at least one scene in *Paranoid Park* the music was the inspiration for the organization of the full *mise-en-scène*, it is not that surprising that none of these films features originally composed music; it seems obvious that in most cases the presence of music was 'premeditated' and thus indispensable in the processes of pre-production and production. On the other hand, even though carefully selected soundtracks are essential for establishing these films' emotional and stylistic tone, the choice of musical pieces—ranging from Beethoven to Hildegard Westerkamp— is not only eclectic but sometimes truly eccentric; one gets the impression that some of the scenes were deliberately and even subversively left with a temp track, because it is hard to find any plausible explanation or narrative justification for having Nino Rota's famous themes from *Juliet of the Spirits* and *Amarcord* often positioned as meta-diegetic music in *Paranoid Park*.[23] However, knowing Van Sant's meticulous attention to detail and the fact that most of his musical choices are infused with some personal significance or employed as an homage, one suspects that Rota's music has a hidden meaning, in the same way that Beethoven's music as played by murderer-to-be Alex in *Elephant* is perhaps a nod to Stanley Kubrick and the murderer—also named Alex—in Kubrick's *A Clockwork Orange*.[24]

This does not change the fact, though, that for *Elephant* Van Sant chose the most popular of Beethoven's piano pieces, *Für Elise* and the *Moonlight Sonata*, which brings to the scenes featuring this music an enormous cultural and semiotic baggage of the sort that most directors would care to avoid. But Van Sant presents Alex's performances of these pieces in the same way that he presents quotidian moments in the lives of all the other teenagers involved in the tragedy—patiently and dispassionately, with long shots from an observant camera—and this somehow removes every trace of sentimentality from the music. At the same time, the diegetic performance of the *Moonlight Sonata* by a teenage murderer-to-be creates a structural rhyme with the same music's extra-diegetic appearance at the beginning of the film; here the *Moonlight Sonata* sounds not only melancholy but surreal, lingering as it does over the school grounds and corridors, combined as it is with Westerkamp's *Doors of Perception* and a dense pile-up of diegetic and extra-diegetic sounds.

Obviously, the popularity of certain musical pieces has never been enough of a reason for Van Sant not to use them in his own films, especially if for him the pieces carry some personal meaning. Arvo Pärt's compositions *Spiegel im Spiegel* and *Für Alina*, both employed in *Gerry*, were another potentially risky choice, since they have been used time and again in theater, television, and films.[25] In an interview for *Slant Magazine*, Van Sant laconically explained that he wanted to use Pärt's music because he had it with him while he was shooting the film.[26] Yet certain connections between the narrative themes of *Gerry* and Pärt's musical style suggest that behind this choice there might be a deeper meaning.

Für Alina (1976), for solo piano, and *Spiegel im Spiegel* (1978), for piano and violin, were the first of the Estonian composer's works to feature 'tintinnabuli,' a stylistic device in which one voice arpeggiates the pitches of the tonic triad while another moves in stepwise motion. As Pärt explained in an interview for BBC3, "tintinnabuli is the rule where the melody and the accompaniment [are] one. One plus one, it is one—it is not two. This is the secret of this technique."[27] This calls to mind the fact that the two friends in Van Sant's film are both named Gerry, and the word 'Gerry' has an almost ubiquitous meaning, being used as a noun and as an adjective throughout their conversations. Additionally, the title of *Spiegel im Spiegel* can be translated either as "Mirror in the Mirror" or "Mirrors in the Mirror," alluding both to the potentially infinite sequence of phrases that can be generated by the violin descending along the tones of the F major scale and to the fact that each phrase is a reflection of a previous one. Thus it seems that Van Sant's choice of music for *Gerry* was influenced not just by the distinctive mood of Pärt's pieces transferring a strange sense of timelessness to the images of two figures caught in a temporal and spatial limbo; the choice was likely influenced as well by an aspect of Pärt's style that aspires to transcend historical, aesthetic, and cultural limitations and to become, for the composer, the manifestation of worship.

While *Gerry*'s narrative ambiguities tap into spiritual undercurrents in Pärt's music on a more profound level than most previous examples of the music's appropriation, the positioning of Pärt's pieces gives them additional meaning in the context of film. It is notable that the opening shots of two friends who share the same name is accompanied by the piece for violin and piano, two distinctive instrumental voices which, according to Pärt, despite their idiosyncratic timbres, represent and make One. And like the voices in Pärt's *Spiegel im Spiegel*, the two friends, as their names suggest, at first seem inseparable and even indistinguishable. They drive, then walk together, then occasionally talk and joke even after they realize they are lost. They make plans for finding a way out of the desert and listen to one another's suggestions. As they become increasingly desperate, the process of disintegration creeps in, culminating in the shots of the two Gerrys sitting apart, the camera circling at an incredibly slow pace around each solitary figure to emphasize their isolation. This is only the second time that we hear Pärt's music, but in this case the music is *Für Alina*; following the camera's circular trail around the Gerrys, then spreading through the desert, the single timbre of the solo piano seems the epitome of melancholic recognition of human fragility and ultimate loneliness.

Conclusion

I started this investigation of Van Sant's sonic style by looking for elements of a Beckettian spirit in the directionless wanderings and air of existential angst that surrounds the characters in the Death Trilogy, but there is possibly more to this analogy than first appears. Although famously an atheist in private life, Beckett through his art searched for the ineffable and unknowable; this made him an artistic transcendentalist who was condemned to the life of a writer who believed that "all the words in the world will not suffice to adequately name the simplest of subjective experiences."[28] But Beckett believed in music, and he always looked to it as a model for playing with words when trying to address the ineffable. His experiments with language led to its musicalization, which subverted its primarily semiotic function and allowed for alternative modes of perception in which grunts, gestures, and silences were as important or as meaningful as words.

In his Death Trilogy, Van Sant takes a similarly subversive approach to narrative form in the sense that he does not offer logical or meaningful stories, does not provide any background or development of his characters, and does not offer any motivation for the characters' actions. Van Sant enraged some critics by tackling a subject as sensitive as the Columbine killings without even trying to propose any conclusive explanation for how a crime like that is possible or what might have caused it. What is perhaps even more infuriating to Van Sant critics is the fact that all those sudden, violent, unexplained, and meaningless deaths in the Trilogy come after lengthy sound-walks in a temporal limbo.

With regard to their attempts to abandon causality and reclaim the visceral sensuality of form and to musicalize it, sometimes at the expense of its narrative coherence, the main difference between Beckett and Van Sant is that Beckett was inspired by the music of Schubert and Beethoven while Van Sant is influenced by the governing principles of *musique concrète*. The interaction with one's surroundings and the exploration of natural sounds as primary compositional resources are notions as central to *musique concrète* aesthetics as to Van Sant's approach to form in the Death Trilogy. Van Sant examines the ordinary, and by looking and listening carefully he discovers beauty and musicality in a simple movement, in the sounds that boots make on the ground, or in the way the light dances on a car's windshield. He is drawn to characters who are on the verge of death without even knowing it; in those moments when the characters' connection with the world is about to snap, an intuitive glimpse of a void without light, sound, or movement is what makes the senses more alert and the presence of nature all the more imposing. Whether it is the sound of water from a shower or a waterfall, the crackling of branches in a wood, or someone playing Beethoven or singing a song by Lou Reed, Van Sant's films tell us that it is *all* music.

Notes

1   *Photogénie* is a term used by French filmmaker Louis Delluc to describe the ability of the camera to make images and people appear intrinsically attractive and present reality from a new perspective.

2   Although Van Sant's Indie works bear the unmistakable marks of an 'auteur' both in terms of choices of narrative themes and their audio-visual presentation, it is not possible to ignore the fact that over the years Van Sant has worked with quite a stable team of collaborators. In addition to Leslie Shatz, his other long-term associates include Danny Elfman, the composer who, starting with *To Die For*, has written the music for all of Van Sant's films that feature traditional original scores (*Good Will Hunting, Milk*); Elliot Smith, the singer-songwriter who Van Sant commissioned to write songs for *Good Will Hunting* and whose music was also used in *Paranoid Park*; Harris Savides, director of photography in most of Van Sant's films since *Finding Forrester*; and Christopher Doyle, director of photography on *Psycho* and *Paranoid Park*.

3   Beckett, quoted in James Knowlson, *Damned To Fame: The Life of Samuel Beckett* (New York: Simon & Schuster, 1997), 436.

4   Jonathan Romney, "Gerry," *The Independent*, August 24, 2003.

5   Van Sant, quoted in Ed Gonzales, "Gerrymandering: An Interview with Gus Van Sant," *Slant Magazine* (2003), available at: www.slantmagazine.com/film/features/gusvansant.asp.

6   Sylvia Harvey, "What is Cinema? The Sensuous, the Abstract and the Political," in *Cinema: The Beginnings and the Future*, ed. Christopher Williams (London: University of Westminster Press, 1996), 230.

7   Paul Schrader, *Transcendental Style in Film: Ozu, Bresson, Dreyer* (Cambridge and New York: Da Capo Press, 1972).

8   Andrey Tarkovsky, *Sculpting in Time*, trans. Kitty Hunter-Blair (Austin: University of Texas Press, 1986), 117.

9   Schrader, *Transcendental Style in Film*, 11.

10   The soundscape here seems quite elaborate, but according to Van Sant it does not include any pre-existing electroacoustic music and was created by him and Leslie Shatz during production and postproduction.

11   Gabe Klinger, "Interview with Leslie Shatz: Sound Auteur," *Fipresci* ('Undercurrent 1') (2006), available at: www.fipresci.org/undercurrent/issue_0106/shatz_klinger.htm.

12   The combination of sirens and bells is a sonic motif that has recurred in Van Sant's films ever since *Mala Noche*.

13   A typical example is the scene from *Paranoid Park* accompanied by Billy Swan's song "I Can Help," in which the boy burdened with a guilty secret is called to the principal's office. Significant narrative and affective weight is also given to the scene in *Milk* that shows the eponymous character attending a performance of his favorite opera, *Tosca*, its death scene foreshadowing his own tragic ending.

14   Frances White's series of 'walk-through' pieces are based on actual 'walks through' her 1990 installation piece *Resonant Landscape*. First set up at Princeton University and then at the Kelvingrove Art Galleries in Glasgow, *Resonant Landscape* is an interactive installation whose sonic elements include electronically generated

sounds and recorded 'natural' sounds. The complete version of White's 1992 *Walk through Resonant Landscape #2* is available on the CD *Centre Bridge: Electroacoustic Works* (Mode Records, B000SO01J8).

15 The question of temporality in contemporary non-mainstream cinema is an important one and, from my point of view, provides the main argument against David Bordwell's definition of new narrative approaches as *intensified continuity*. See Bordwell, *The Way Hollywood Tells It* (Berkeley, Los Angeles, and London: University of California Press, 2006).

16 The term 'songlines' derives from the culture of certain of Australia's indigenous peoples. Simply put, a 'songline' is a sort of map—most often represented not graphically but aurally, in both the words and music of a song—that depicts the travels across the landscape of a tribe's mythical ancestors. For a lyrical account of how these 'maps' are thought to be transmitted to modern humans via dreams, see Bruce Chatwin's *The Songlines* (London: Jonathan Cape Ltd., 1987).

17 'Soundwalking' is a term introduced by Canadian composer R. Murray Schafer in the late 1960s and early 1970s to describe the practice of focused listening during which one moves through an environment while paying complete attention to the environment's sound.

18 In an interview with Randolph Jordan, Hildegard Westerkamp explains that 'soundwalking' is a type of walk that "opens the environment up to us and connects us to our inner selves," while the walks of Van Sant's characters come from a place of "inner desolation/isolation and disconnect." Randolph Jordan, "The Work of Hildegard Westerkamp in the Films of Gus Van Sant: An Interview with the Soundscape Composer," *Offscreen* 11, nos. 8–9 (2007), available at: www.offscreen.com/index.php/pages/essays/jordan_westerkamp/. Thus it is important to note that, in the context of this chapter, 'soundwalking' stands as a metaphor for an approach to filmmaking—which includes all manipulative processes of post-production—in which the viewer's rather than the protagonist's attention is directed toward exploring the cinematic environment through its sound.

19 Michael Brooke, "The Weight of the World." *Sight and Sound* 19, no. 1 (2009): 54–5.

20 Jonathan D. Kramer, *The Time of Music: New Meanings, New Temporalities, New Listening Strategies* (New York: Schirmer Books; London: Collier Macmillan Publisher, 1988).

21 I first tackled this relationship between film's temporality and the musicality of diegetic sound in Van Sant's films in a short position paper titled "Sound Design Is the New Score," in *Music, Sound and the Moving Image* 2, no. 2 (Autumn 2009): 127–31.

22 This scene is an obvious homage to a similar 'trudge' involving two main characters, János and György, in Béla Tarr's *Werckmeister Harmonies* (2000). Another example, the scene that shows the two Gerrys from behind walking through a canyon while a strong wind blows tumbleweed around them, is a reference to the scene from Tarr's *Sátántangó* (1994) that introduces two antagonists walking down a windy street.

23 Vincent LoBrutto offers several guesses regarding the presence of Rota's music in *Paranoid Park*, including the possibility that the circus music suggests that the main character's life is a 'circus' or that the frisson between the musical content and the story represents Alex's confusion, but none of them is very convincing. *Gus Van Sant: His Own Private Cinema* (Santa Barbara, Denver, and Oxford: Praeger, 2010).

24 In her exploration of the connections between the characters from Van Sant's *Elephant* and Kubrick's *A Clockwork Orange*, Jessica Shine insists on associating Beethoven's music with *Elephant*'s Alex to the point that in the scene at the

beginning of the film, when the *Moonlight Sonata* is heard without Alex being present, she interprets the camera's gaze as Alex's point of view ("Beethoven, Noise, and Isolation in Gus Van Sant's *Elephant*," paper presented at the Annual Conference of the Society for Musicology in Ireland, University of Ulster, Magee, May 7–9, 2010).

25 *Spiegel im Spiegel*, for example, was used in Tom Tykwer's *Heaven* and Guy Ritchie's *Swept Away*, films that, like Van Sant's *Gerry*, date from 2002.

26 Gonzales, "Gerrymandering."

27 Arvo Pärt, interview with Anthony Pitts broadcast on BBC3, March 29, 2000.

28 Eric Prieto, *Listening In: Music, Mind, and the Modernist Narrative* (Lincoln and London: University of Nebraska Press, 2002), 267.

Chapter 7

Blowin' in the Wind

Music and Meaning in the Coen Brothers' Films

Matthew McDonald

> There ain't too much I can say about this song except that the answer is blowing in the wind. It ain't in no book or movie or TV show or discussion group. Man, it's in the wind—and it's blowing in the wind. Too many of these hip people are telling me where the answer is but oh I won't believe that. I still say it's in the wind and just like a restless piece of paper it's got to come down some time …
>
> Bob Dylan, *Sing Out!* (October–November 1962)

Before becoming the voice of his generation, Bob Dylan (born Robert Zimmerman) grew up in Hibbing, Minnesota, and the frustration expressed in the above passage reflects a distinctly Minnesotan conflict. A Minnesotan myself, I can say with authority that although not all of the stereotypes about our state are true—Garrison Keillor tends to exaggerate—many of them are. Minnesotans believe that the simplest explanation is the best and that a cigar is *always* just a cigar. We exalt stoicism as perhaps the greatest of all virtues, and we have a natural distrust of those who call excessive attention to their own opinions and feelings. Yet those feelings still roil beneath the protective padding of our ubiquitous parkas. With his irreverent response to questions about the meaning of his famous ballad, Bob Dylan represents the quandary of his native state. Everyone knows the song is profound, and intended to be so, but Dylan doesn't want to be caught trying too hard or feeling too deeply. So he is stuck stubbornly defending an untenable position. There's no metaphor, he insists; the meaning of the song is exactly what the song says it is. The answer is blowing in the wind.

About a half a generation later and 200 miles to the south, two other Minnesotan artists came to adopt similarly belligerent attitudes toward questions of meaning in their work. Joel and Ethan Coen's comments in a 1991 interview about *Miller's Crossing*, whose opening title sequence features the image of a wind-blown hat, are emblematic of their rejection of symbolism and metaphor:

ETHAN: Apparently, nobody wants to be satisfied with the movie, as if they absolutely need explanations beyond the images, the story itself. That always surprises me. [...]

JOEL: Everybody asks us questions about that hat, and there isn't any answer really. It's not a symbol, it doesn't have any particular meaning ....

ETHAN: The hat doesn't "represent" anything, it's just a hat blown by the wind.[1]

Wind is a favored sound effect in the Coen brothers' films. It is often the very first sound, typically heard against a black screen, emphasizing its lack of grounding in the world of images. For the Coens, as for Dylan, this unattached sound (one with inescapable sensory connotations for Minnesotans, for whom checking the wind chill is a daily winter ritual) suggests a void where interpretation might occur. Don't look too hard, it warns the viewer, because there's nothing to see.

Perhaps the most persistent critique leveled against the Coen brothers is that they are overly concerned with technical virtuosity and formal rigor, generating characters and scenarios that refer mainly to the cinema itself as opposed to the real world of human beings. As the interview cited above suggests, the Coens themselves have not shied away from the 'formalist' label: as a rule, they are more interested in talking about technique than meaning. Composer Carter Burwell and sound editor Skip Lievsay, both of whom have worked on all of the Coen brothers' films, have attested to the Coens' stance against interpretation. In a 2004 interview, Burwell claimed: "I've never heard Joel and Ethan get into hermeneutical discussions of any of their films, ever." And Lievsay remarked in 2003: "I wouldn't say that [my sound effects have any extra-filmic meaning]. In the service of the movie—we don't aspire to anything more than that."[2] But whereas Lievsay has expressed sympathy with the Coens' attitude toward symbolic meaning, Burwell's commentary on his music for the Coens' films has frequently suggested resistance to, even defiance of, the Coens' commitment to "what you see is what you get" filmmaking. Consider, for example, what Burwell had to say about his score for A Serious Man: "When music pointedly ignores the apparent proceedings of a film it implies that there's something else going on. Something that may be more important than what you see."[3] Similarly, in reference to his frequently ironic use of music, Burwell has explained that

> the music is telling you something different to what you are seeing on the screen. It tells you that something is happening which does not meet the eye. Yet because music is such an abstract art, it does not tell you what that "more" is.[4]

These statements fly in the face of the Coens' disregard for "explanations beyond the images," but they are not evidence of a creative rift. Seemingly everyone agrees that the Coens' films are richly symbolic, and it would be a mistake to let the Coens' formalist rhetoric convince us that they themselves do not share this view. The real difference between Burwell and the Coens is not creative but rhetorical: Burwell is completely comfortable acknowledging and discussing the films on a symbolic level, whereas the Coens, true to the Minnesotan stereotype, are not. This sort of reticence is reflected by the Coens' quintessential protagonists, characters such as Tom Reagan (Gabriel Byrne) in *Miller's Crossing* and Ed Crane (Billy Bob Thornton) in *The Man Who Wasn't There*, strong silent types whose cool demeanors point toward their intense inner lives while revealing nothing about them (indeed, for the Coens' characters, verbosity tends to be inversely related to depth of character). These characters provide a precise analogue for the Coens' films, which demonstrate formal control, visual economy and clarity, and superior cinematic breeding, capturing our imaginations while aspiring toward complete inscrutability. And just as these characters are defined by the intense conflict between their inner turbulence and outer calm, so are the films of the Coen brothers.

Music, as the inscrutable art form par excellence, provides the Coens with an ideal vehicle through which to smuggle the suggestion of symbolic meaning into their films. Music can imbue filmic elements with the aura of *meaningfulness* without providing concrete meaning. It provides 'something else,' the perfectly ambiguous phrase that Burwell uses above and elsewhere to describe the function of his music. Sound effects can function in a similar way, particularly musical sounds or sounds that work in conjunction with the musical score, as they often do in the Coens' films, where the entire creative team works in much closer collaboration than is typical.[5]

The absence of concrete meanings is not only a feature of the Coens' films, of course, but one of their primary themes. The Coens' art is meant to imitate life, where, in their worldview, things don't happen for a reason; they just happen. Music plays a crucial role here as well: it not only shrouds potential symbolic meanings with ambiguity but also draws attention to this ambiguity in various ways, actively calling into question the existence of stable or identifiable meanings. In the hands of Burwell and the Coens, music is like the wind: its sound is evocative, yet it points to a void.

A Hat is Just a Hat

If the Coens actually wished to discourage their viewers from interpreting Tom's hat in *Miller's Crossing* (1990) as a symbol, they failed miserably. An entire essay could easily be devoted to the hat's meaning and significance (and has, in fact, in Erica Rowell's "Miller's Crossing: A Hat," an enlightening study of how Tom's identity is tied to and expressed through his fedora[6]). The hat is something of a surrogate protagonist in the film, featured in numerous close-ups, often disassociated from its owner. A narrative thread can be spun around the question of whether or not the hat is resting upon Tom's head. For example, the hat sets the plot into motion, as Tom realizes early in the film that he lost it the night before in a drunken bet with his lover, Verna (Marcia Gay Harden). He promptly retrieves it, and we see him in a post-coital moment, not with Verna but with his hat, smoking a cigarette while he gazes at it (Figure 7.1a. Tom's image is in the bureau mirror.). Later, Verna throws Tom's hat on a chair as a prelude to romance. The camera focuses on the hat (Figure 7.1b) and then moves to a concurrent scene: Leo (Albert Finney), an Irish mob boss who regards Tom as a close friend and esteemed confidant, is fending off an attack from a rival Italian gang, forced to run outside in his pajamas, firing away with his Tommy gun, while Tom is otherwise engaged. When Leo, who is involved with Verna himself and plans to propose to her, learns of Tom and Verna's affair, he beats Tom thoroughly, knocking off Tom's hat in the process and throwing it back at him as a final punctuation (Figure 7.1c). Tom decides to infiltrate the rival gang, where he arouses suspicion and ultimately finds himself on the brink of execution; in the secluded woods of Miller's Crossing, his hat is tossed away as a prelude to a bullet in the head (Figure 7.1d), which he avoids in the narrowest of escapes.

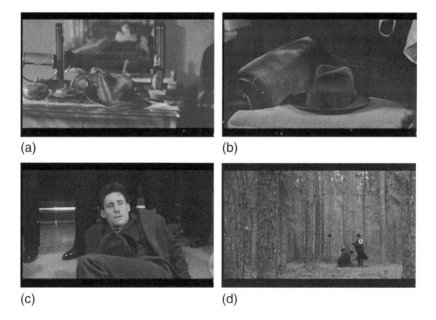

(a)

(b)

(c)

(d)

Figure 7.1 Four shots of Tom's hat in *Miller's Crossing*

Over and over again, Tom's hat is taken or taken off by Verna and thrown or knocked off by a rival. Tom's struggle to hold onto his hat is an attempt to remain a free agent in the world: to forfeit it would be to give himself over to a woman or to be bested by a man. In the simplest terms, losing the hat is a symbol of sex and death. This interpretation is suggested in a scene soon after Tom's beating at the hands of Leo, where Tom, in another post-coital moment, tells Verna of a dream:

TOM: I was walking in the woods, I don't know why. Wind come up and blew me hat off.

VERNA: And you chased it, right? You ran and ran and finally you caught up to it, and you picked it up but it wasn't a hat anymore. It had changed into something else—something wonderful.

TOM (GROWING ANGRY): Nah. It stayed a hat. And no I didn't chase it. Nothing more foolish than a man chasing his hat.

Tom is a surrogate for the Coens here, dismissing the hat's symbolic value much in the same manner that his creators have dismissed it: in addition to the comments cited above, Ethan Coen has referred to Verna's interpretation of Tom's dream as "gratuitous."[7] But Tom's irritation suggests that, for him, the interpretation is not gratuitous at all. Verna's words have touched a nerve; just as the Coens' irritation points toward their own ambivalence, Tom's uncharacteristically emotional response undermines his denial.

Further encouraging our skepticism, Tom and Verna's exchange references the wind-blown hat of the opening title sequence, providing an explicit invitation to read this image symbolically. The title sequence begins with a tracking shot of treetops in a forest, filmed from the ground (this shot is replicated later in the film where it is identified as Tom's point of view, as Tom is being led to his apparent execution at Miller's Crossing). Burwell's cue is a pseudo-Irish melody in 12/8 set to simple G-major harmony and scored primarily for strings, winds, and harp. A reduction of the second strain of the melody is shown in Figure 7.2.

At bar 8 of the figure, the music halts on a sustained dominant, at which point in the film the tracking shot of treetops dissolves to a static shot at ground level. Generically, a sustained dominant accompanying a cut to a new location would signal a shift from the title sequence to the story. Instead, a black fedora lands in front of the camera, and when it settles, the film's title appears above it (see Figure 7.3). At this point, the soundtrack undergoes profound changes. Diegetic sound is now heard, as the hat lands and wind blows in the trees. The Irish melody pauses on a high D, leaving the accompanimental triplets exposed and sounding alone over the bass (see bars 10–12 of the example). The harmonic simplicity of the Irish tune is temporarily abandoned as well, supplanted by pop-oriented progressions featuring parallel

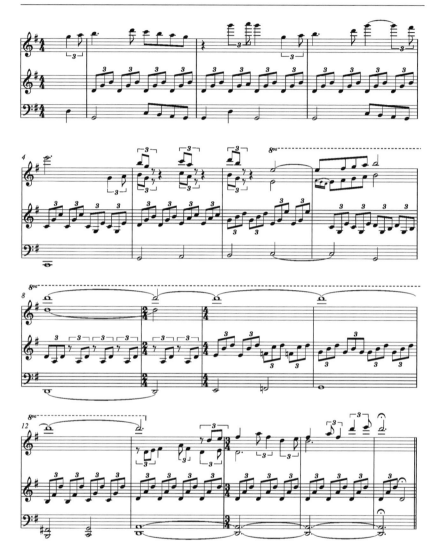

Figure 7.2 Music from *Miller's Crossing*, opening titles (transcribed by the author)

motion—vi-♭VII-I (bars 10–11) and iii-IV-V (bars 12–13)—and the only instance of non-diatonic harmony in the opening title music, the prominent ♭VII (F-major) chord.

At bar 12, the hat is blown away by a gust of wind; as we watch it drift slowly into the distance, the Irish melody and sustained dominant return (the latter with the same voicing), the music fades, and the next scene begins.

Figure 7.3 Miller's Crossing, main title

The resumption in bar 13 of the abandoned dominant of bar 8 marks the melodic and harmonic aberrations of bars 10–12 as constituting an ellipsis: this music is mysterious and foreboding, and to omit it would be to restore order and predictability to the credit sequence. The parenthetical nature of bars 10–12 underscores the image of the hat blowing in the wind as similarly parenthetical, an odd and unsettling detour in the transition from an otherwise unexceptional credit sequence back to the main story. Indeed, when the hat blows away, it leaves the frame as it found it, a static shot of a clearing in the woods. We are left to wonder whether the hat actually appeared or was an apparition, a dream.

These responses are shaped by the accompanying soundtrack, which is characterized by the fundamental tension between its apparent meaningfulness and its lack of identifiable meaning. The sudden contrast at bar 10 draws attention to the music that follows, but this music is characterized by the relative absence of signifying features: the Irish melody disappears, leaving an accompaniment with nothing to accompany, mingling with the empty sound of wind. The sense of absence is intensified by the orchestral swell in bar 8 (not shown in the figure) that features added brass and cymbals; this swell completely dissipates by the end of the bar, yielding to bars 10–12 as a hushed anticlimax. When the hat is dropped in front of our eyes with no associated head, its source unclear and its meaning elusive, the soundtrack pulls our response to the image in two directions. Like Verna, it urges us to interpret the hat; like Tom, it suggests that interpretation is futile. And like the Coens, it wants to have it both ways.

Was That a Sign?

Blood Simple (1984), the Coens' first feature film, begins with the sound of wind heard over a black screen, and the prologue and title sequence that follow (spanning about three minutes) are remarkable for the extent to which they continue to establish themes and stylistic traits that can now be regarded as fundamental to the Coens' films.[8] The prologue consists of several static long shots of inhospitable Texan landscapes—vast expanses of barren fields, a sprawling power plant set against gray skies, a burnt-out tire on an empty highway—accompanied by a drawling voice-over and the sound of wind (as well as screeching birds and thunderous oil drills), an audiovisual formula the Coens would return to at the beginning of *No Country for Old Men* (2007). The voice-over is spoken by Loren Visser (M. Emmet Walsh), an unscrupulous private detective who features prominently in the film. At the end of his short monologue, he explains: "Now, in Russia, they got it mapped out so that everyone pulls for everyone else—that's the theory, anyway. But what I know about is Texas. And down here, you're on your own."

With these words, both the credits and the story begin. We are taken to a highway at night, where Ray (John Getz) and Abby (Frances McDormand) are traveling in the rain. Ray drives the car while Abby drives the conversation, with Ray a reluctant participant. We learn that Abby is leaving her husband Marty (Dan Hedaya), who owns a bar and employs Ray. The couple is filmed from the back seat and, between them, on the windshield, we see the credits in blue; each name lingers on the screen for a few seconds and then, through an animated effect, appears to be cleared away by the windshield wipers (see Figure 7.4). The sound of the wipers is welded to the score, providing a mechanical beat to accompany the synthesized vocal melody and low bassline; the latter methodically repeats four-bar cadential figures in A minor. Eventually the music stops, but the sound of the wipers continues, decelerating slightly. When Abby notices that their car is being followed, Ray slams on the brakes, instigating a rapid series of cuts between the interior and exterior of the car. The sound of the wipers is displaced by screeching tires and running motors during the two exterior shots, and it is silenced entirely when Ray turns off the ignition.

Visually and sonically, these opening minutes portray Texas as land of desolation: the bleak landscapes; the haunting sounds of wind, birds of prey, and machinery; the impassive and monotonous musical score; and the isolation described by the voice-over ("down here, you're on your own"). This sort of environment haunts many of the Coens' films, most obviously the setting for *No Country for Old Men*, but also the hotel in *Barton Fink* (1991) and the endless fields of snow in *Fargo* (1996), and they are closely associated with the depraved characters they breed.

Environment in the Coens' films provides a setting for depravity and functions as its symbol: physical decay engenders and points toward moral decay.

Figure 7.4 Opening credit of *Blood Simple*, cleared away by windshield wipers

More broadly, the setting of each film signifies the meaningless void that surrounds any interpretation of the human actions taking place within it. In the voice-over that begins *No Country*, Sheriff Ed Tom Bell (Tommy Lee Jones) recognizes this void, which is implicitly linked to the empty vistas on display:

> There was this boy I sent to the electric chair at Huntsville here a while back. … Told me that he'd been planning to kill somebody for about as long as he could remember. Said if they turned him out he'd do it again. … I don't know what to make of that. I surely don't. The crime you see now, it's hard to even take its measure. It's not that I'm afraid of it. … But I don't want to push my chips forward and go out and meet something I don't understand.

Once again the Coens push their familiar disclaimer, here using the sheriff as the messenger: don't try to make sense of what you are about to see. This warning is embedded in the opening scene of *Blood Simple* as well, voiced by Ray, in his response to Abby's concerns about Marty:

ABBY: It's just … I don't know. Sometimes I think maybe there's something wrong with him. Like maybe he's sick? Mentally? Or is it maybe me, do you think?

RAY: Listen, I … I ain't a marriage counselor. I don't know what goes on, I don't wanna know.

Figure 7.5 Blood Simple, penultimate shot of prologue

Visually, the disclaimer is suggested by the paired images of a blank white billboard (in the penultimate shot of the prologue (Figure 7.5) and the windshield: the former is marked by the uncharacteristic absence of text, the latter by the uncharacteristic presence of text. The billboard, like Tom and his hat, draws attention to itself, asking to be read but revealing nothing. Abby and Ray's conversation near the end of the scene, as they move closer to consummating their affair, slyly reinforces the theme of empty signification:

ABBY: What was it back there?
RAY: Back where?
ABBY: That sign.
RAY: I don't know.

If the billboard suggests a tabula rasa, the act of cleaning the slate is drama-tized by the windshield wipers as they wipe each name from the screen. I failed to notice this effect the first time I watched the film; instead, my attention was drawn to the wipers by the soundtrack. When the music cuts out, the sound of the wipers remains, and the subliminal suddenly becomes obvious: in the opening cue the sound of the wipers had doubled as the percussion track. Because we have been conditioned to hear the wipers musically, when they are heard alone they maintain their musicality. It is thus unsettling when, after the car screeches to a halt, the sound of the wipers cuts in and out in synchronization with the editing of the images: musical sound is now treated as mundane sound. The absence of the score draws our attention to the sound of the wipers as potentially meaningful (just as the sudden absence of melody draws attention to the hat in the title sequence of *Miller's Crossing*), but the subsequent disruption in the soundtrack robs the sound of the wipers of both its musicality and its connection to the brooding score, undermining any meaning it might have acquired via association with that music.

Windshield wipers are not seen or heard again in the film, but their circular motion and metronomic whooshes establish a motif that is taken up by ceiling fans.[9] After hiring Visser to trail Abby, whom he suspects of infidelity, Marty learns of Abby and Ray's affair; he sits silently brooding in his office, where a ceiling fan can be seen and heard spinning above him, emitting muffled beats reminiscent of the wipers. "Marty—thought you were dead," says one of his employees, in a bit of ironic foreshadowing: Marty will later be shot by Visser while sitting in the same chair. As Marty continues to sit in his office, the image and sound of his fan are juxtaposed with those of the ceiling fan in Ray's bedroom, where Abby lies awake; this suggests that, despite their separation, the husband and wife are still intimately connected. In his score for this scene, Burwell arranged for piano his cue for the opening title sequence, and his commentary on this music reinforces his desire for music to add 'something else':

> the music has nothing to do with what anyone on screen is doing. It does imply there must be something going on that isn't being seen on the screen, there's something else happening, and the characters aren't privy to it. But the music has nothing to do with them, it's like a watch that's unwinding somewhere, and we don't know what will happen if it should ever stop ticking.[10]

An even better metaphor, perhaps, is a beating heart: Abby's and Marty's hearts, it seems, still beat as one—until one of them stops ticking.

Aware of Abby's affair, Marty hires Visser to murder Abby and Ray, but Visser decides it is more convenient to fake the murders and kill Marty after receiving payment. He shoots Marty in his office, and the sound of the fan that haunts the scene, as though a surrogate for Marty's heartbeat, is silenced by the gunshot. After several seconds, however, the sound returns, slowed considerably—sure enough, Marty is critically wounded but not yet dead. We learn this when Ray, happening upon Marty's body and thinking that Abby is the murderer, cleans up the crime scene and drives away to dispose of the body, only to discover that Marty is still breathing. Later, in a Hitchcockian turn, Visser realizes that he has left his engraved lighter in Marty's office and fears that Abby may have discovered it; he now must devote himself to the pursuit of Abby and Ray. Finding Ray's apartment empty, he telephones Abby; she answers, and (like the audience) hears nothing but Ray's ceiling fan. Abby associates this sound with Marty and assumes he is calling from his office;

by this time Marty is dead, but the telltale heart beats on. This is the first of several instances in which Abby believes she is in Marty's presence. She encounters Marty face to face in what is subsequently revealed to be a dream, and in the film's final scene she mistakes Visser for Marty as Visser comes to her apartment, shoots Ray, and attempts to kill her as well. Abby ultimately shoots Visser in the abdomen, without seeing him, and declares: "I'm not afraid of you, Marty"; Visser laughs and responds: "Well ma'am, if I see him, I'll sure give him the message."

And thus Marty lives on in Abby's mind. Abby, like all the main characters in *Blood Simple*, fails to interpret correctly what she hears and sees. Windshield wipers and ceiling fans provide enduring symbols of this confusion: the blurred image of rotating blades, the blurred pulses of their rotations (as realized by Lievsay), the sound of the fan that provides Abby a false signal of Marty's presence on the telephone.

This last-mentioned sound may suggest Abby's visceral connection to Marty, but Abby can trust the sound of the fan no more than she can trust her own heart, and no more than we can trust the opening scene's windshield wipers, which trick us both visually (wiping away the credits) and aurally (disguising themselves as percussion). The most basic meaning of these symbols, it seems, is the uncertainty of meaning and the unreliability of filmic signification—a characteristic theme for filmmakers who live and breathe in the realm of self-reference.

From Hades to The Haight

Among the many memorable characters of *A Serious Man* (2009) is the prologue's rabbi, who is taken for a dybbuk (the spirit of a dead person that inhabits the body of a living one). Whether or not the rabbi is actually a dybbuk is left unresolved, just as the relationship of the prologue (set in nineteenth-century Poland) to the rest of the film (set in 1960s Minnesota) at film's end remains obscure. On a snowy evening, Velvel (Allen Lewis Rickman) returns home to his wife, Dora (Yelena Shmulenson), with the happy news that he has just stumbled upon an old family friend, Treitle Groshkover (Fyvush Finkel), and has invited him to their home for soup. Dora is not pleased: she believes that Groshkover died three years ago of typhus, and thus she is convinced that her husband has encountered a dybbuk; "God has cursed us," she declares. When Groshkover arrives at the door, Dora sizes him up and then attempts to prove her suspicion by stabbing him in the chest with an ice pick. After he stumbles out the door, bleeding through his shirt, the husband and wife exchange opposite accounts of the ramifications of what has just transpired:

VELVEL: We are ruined. Tomorrow they will discover the body. All is lost.
DORA: Nonsense, Velvel. Blessed is the Lord. Good riddance to evil.

The opening title sequence follows over a black screen, and we are then transported to the main story, the unraveling life of Larry Gopnik (Michael Stuhlbarg), a middle-aged Jewish man and modern-day Job living with his family in suburban Minnesota. Do Larry's troubles somehow relate to the curse of the dybbuk? If so, was it Velvel's hospitality or Dora's lack thereof that is to blame?

These questions, too, are left unanswered. Predictably, Joel Coen has downplayed the relevance of the prologue to the rest of the film: "[The prologue] doesn't have any relationship to what follows, but it helped us get started thinking about the movie."[11] Elsewhere, he was a bit more forthcoming:

> You can look at the prologue retrospectively and say that it plunges you into the story full on as being a story about Jewish people. That's as opposed to a story about the Midwest, as opposed to a piece of Americana, as opposed to a specific community in 1967. ... But this tells you upfront. This is a story about a Jewish community and Jews.[12]

Clearly, the prologue seeks to lend mythological weight to the more modern events that follow and to suggest that Larry's tribulations are part of a long history of Jewish suffering. Burwell's music for the prologue fulfills a similar purpose. The opening cue (see Figure 7.6), scored for violin and harp, recurs in varied forms throughout the film. The violin melody evokes Jewish folk music via its use of the locrian mode, which features flattened second and fifth scale degrees. Burwell has linked this melody and its accompaniment directly to the film's protagonist: "Something about the relentlessness of this theme seemed right for the helplessness of Larry Gopnik against the unwinding of his life."[13] Burwell's characterization of this music as 'relentless' points to its function as an expression of the weight of history, the sense that the script of Larry's life has already been written. The harp ostinato is crucial here; it cycles in apparent indifference to the violin melody, and this effect is even more pronounced elsewhere in the film.

To my ears, however, the mythological quality of Burwell's music stems primarily from its similarity to the opening music of Stravinsky's *Orpheus*. Figure 7.7 compares Burwell's harp ostinato (in its first iteration) to that of the first tableau of Stravinsky's ballet score (bar 1 is shown, but this ostinato recurs in the final tableau as well); Burwell's tempo is 1–2 beats per minute

Figure 7.6 A Serious Man, opening cue (transcribed by author)

Figure 7.7 Comparison of harp ostinati from (a) *A Serious Man* and (b) Stravinsky's *Orpheus*

Figure 7.8 Comparison of (a) Burwell's score for *A Serious Man* (excerpt; transcribed by author) and (b) Stravinsky's score for *Orpheus*, bars 5–7 (reduced to three staves)

faster than Stravinsky's indicated tempo of ♩=69. Figure 7.8 compares a later variant of Burwell's cue (heard when Larry watches the next-door father and son playing catch) with an excerpt from the first tableau of *Orpheus*. (Note that in my transcription of Burwell's cue, for the sake of legibility, I have normalized the piano's rhythm to fit the metrical scheme of the other instruments; the actual rhythm of the piano melody is more fluid.) Burwell's string and harp accompaniment strongly evokes the texture of Stravinsky's score; in particular, Burwell's harp ostinato and overlaid melody (now scored for piano) are anchored by open harmonies that, like Stravinsky's, move in parallel motion in the lower strings.

For those who hear *Orpheus* in Burwell's score, the mythological aspects of the film narrative are enhanced, with the mode and original instrumentation of Burwell's upper melody helping to identify the mythology as specifically Jewish. Furthermore, the story of Orpheus has particular resonance with the film's prologue and main story. Both the Orpheus myth and the prologue explore the blurry boundary between the tangible world and the afterlife. Orpheus's heroic journey to the underworld to recover Eurydice fails abruptly when, against the orders of Hades and Persephone, he turns to look for her, and this failure can be understood as a lack of faith: he does not adequately trust the gods. A lack of faith is also explicitly the failure of Larry Gopnik, who continually questions God and is unable to "receive with simplicity everything that happens" to him, as the film's epigraph (quoting the medieval rabbi Rashi) advises.

Orpheus is ultimately torn to pieces and carried off by the sea and wind; at the end of *A Serious Man*, after Larry has apparently been diagnosed with a fatal illness, the final image features an approaching tornado. The entire film is a crescendo of trouble, and the sound of this tornado can be heard as the inevitable continuation of the prologue's first sound, that of the wintry wind that accompanies Velvel as he makes his way home. Much earlier in the film, however, a more direct and palpable connection between the prologue and main story is forged sonically.

The opening cue (Figure 7.6) returns at the end of the prologue and grows more intense until being cut off by the sound of the door, slammed by Dora after Groshkover stumbles back into the cold; the screen goes black and the title sequence ensues, with orange text over the black background. The slamming door produces an unnaturally reverberant sound suggestive of an epic event, and this sound functions as a pivot between the prologue music and the music of the opening titles; it initiates an extremely slow beat articulated by sparse echoes of the slamming door and rattling cowbells. This unusual soundscape gradually thickens and quickens, subtly morphing into a simple four-bar groove played by a traditional amplified rock ensemble. The groove builds momentum and ultimately leads into the beginning of "Somebody to Love" by Jefferson Airplane, one of the premier psychedelic bands in San Francisco during the Summer of Love. Specifically, we hear the cut from their 1967 album *Surrealistic Pillow*, soaked in reverb. As the song begins, a pinpoint of light emerges in the center of the black screen and slowly expands into a translucent orange circle. We soon find ourselves traveling through some sort of tube that fills the screen: it is the ear canal of Larry's thirteen-year-old son, Danny (Aaron Wolff), who is sitting in Hebrew school, listening to "Somebody to Love" via the earpiece connected to his portable radio. The film cuts to a close-up of Danny's ear and follows the cord, slowly making its way from the earpiece to the radio sitting on his desk; we now hear the song only faintly, from the perspective of Danny's classmates. When the instructor discovers the radio, he rips the earpiece from Danny's ear, in the process disconnecting the cord from the radio; the song now blares from the radio itself, inciting chaos in the classroom.

Music and sound lead us through time and space from *A Serious Man's* prologue to its main story, via the transitional space of the title sequence. The reverberant sound of the slamming door is transformed into the sound of Danny's radio; the music does not enter Danny's ear but seems to emerge from it. The dominant metaphor is that of birth: ear canal as birth canal, earphone cord as umbilical cord, radio as infant; when the teacher cuts the cord, the radio lets out a primal scream. We are witnessing the birth of 1960s counterculture via one of its most emblematic songs; when the students hear the sounds of Jefferson Airplane, they immediately revolt.

During the classroom sequence, close-up shots of Danny's ears and eyes, tuned in to the music and turned on by pot, are juxtaposed with shots of his fathers' ears and eyes, scrutinized by a doctor as the father sits through a mundane physical. Larry is a victim of the 1960s, apparently on the wrong end of the generation gap: the world is going to hell, and he is powerless to stop it. A subtle but powerful indication of the societal degradation that surrounds and terrifies Larry is encoded in the soundtrack: the tune of "Somebody to Love" emerges as though a riff on the Jewish melody of the prologue. The shared profile of these melodies is outlined in Figure 7.9, which compares three four-note motives from each melody; each motive features descending minor thirds, either from scale-degree 3 to 1 or from 5 to 3. One might note, in

Figure 7.9 Comparison of Jefferson Airplane, "Somebody to Love" (excerpt on upper staff; transcribed by author), and recurring melody from *A Serious Man* (lower staff)

particular, the prominence at the apex of each melody the flattened fifth scale degree that emphasizes the melodies' modal flavor. The Jewish connotation of this feature in Burwell's melody morphs into the blues-based inflection of Grace Slick's vocal, and thus the film's main culture clash—Jewish culture vs. counterculture—is embedded in the soundtrack.

Toward the end of A Serious Man, the Coens are intent on ironizing the score and undermining any deeper level of meaning we might try to find in it. Danny, after his Bar Mitzvah, is granted a rare visit to the mysterious Rabbi Marshak, who throughout the film has been touted as the ultimate font of wisdom and whose council Larry was denied at his time of greatest need. As it turns out, Larry wasn't missing much: the elderly Marshak delivers the most absurd of all the pronouncements made by rabbis throughout the film. He recites to Danny, deliberately and with great seriousness, the lyrics of "Somebody to Love" (which, presumably, he has heard on Danny's radio): "When the truth is found to be lies ... and all the joy within you dies ... then what?" He returns the confiscated radio and offers no answer to this apparently empty question. His only parting advice is perfunctory: "Here—be a good boy."

Although this scene is built up as the climax of the film, its point is not to deliver answers to the existential questions that have been tormenting Larry. The words of wisdom that Marshak offers Danny are not as important as the radio he returns to him. With radio in hand, in the film's final scene Danny returns to the classroom and once again listens to his music; his story has come full circle. And it is the same for Larry.

In Larry's final scene, just when his life finally seems to be taking turns for the better, he receives a phone call from the doctor who examined him at the beginning of the film; once again, his conversation with the doctor is intercut with shots from Danny's classroom. The doctor wants Larry to visit him immediately to "discuss some X-ray results," and Larry instantly recognizes the dire implication. As with Danny, nothing much has changed for Larry over the course of the film: his life is still in shambles, and despite his persistent attempts he still hasn't gained any insight as to why this is so. The parallels between the beginning and ending of the film drive home this point, and the ending provides satisfying formal closure. But the ending is not at all satisfying in terms of the narrative, and surely it is not meant to be. How do you end a film about a quest for meaning that goes absolutely nowhere, about characters who fail to undergo change? To put the question another way: when all the hope within your protagonist dies—then what?

The soundtrack provides two answers that, at the end of the film, are heard together. As Danny witnesses the impending catastrophe, once again we hear the voice of Grace Slick escaping from his earpiece: "You better find somebody to love," she wails over the final shot. But A Serious Man is having none of this sense of redemptive possibility: the music and its message are overwhelmed by the sight and sound of the approaching tornado. The tornado's whirling tunnel echoes the opening image of Danny's ear canal and is accompanied by the same lo-fi rendition of "Somebody to Love": birth has cycled to death, and Fate has asserted itself with great force but without logic and proportion.

As the lyrics to the "Dem Milner's Trern," the Yiddish song that weaves throughout the score, instruct: "The wheels turn, the years pass, without end or purpose." Like the deity of the Hebrew Bible, the Coens proclaim their ability to defy our insistence on legible meaning, sweeping away the very notion of narrative just as surely as the tornado will sweep away the already devolving structures of Larry's life and community. Here, as in all of the Coens' films, there is to be no answer found "blowin' in the wind." But urged on by the films themselves, and especially by the films' soundtracks, we will continue to look—and listen—for it.

Notes

1 Jean-Pierre Coursodon, "A Hat Blown by the Wind," in *The Coen Brothers: Interviews*, ed. William Rodney Allen (Jackson: University Press of Mississippi, 2006), 43, 44.
2 Randall Barnes, "Collaboration and Integration: A Method of Advancing Film Sound Based on the Coen Brothers' Use of Sound and Their Mode of Production," Ph.D. diss. (Bournemouth University, 2005), 508, 481.
3 Carter Burwell, "Carter's Notes," available at: www.carterburwell.com/projects/A_Serious_Man.html. The notion that film music should actively generate meaning would seem to be a general principle for Burwell. Elsewhere, he has stated simply: "I would say that I like writing music which contributes something to the film that isn't otherwise there" (Barnes, "Collaboration and Integration," 525).
4 Philip Brophy, "Carter Burwell in Conversation: Music for the Films of Joel and Ethan Coen," in *The Coen Brothers' Fargo*, ed. William G. Luhr (Cambridge: Cambridge University Press, 2004), 132.
5 The specifics of how the Coens collaborate with Burwell and Lievsay is a primary focus of Barnes, "Collaboration and Integration."
6 Erica Rowell, *The Brothers Grim: The Films of Ethan and Joel Coen* (Lanham: Scarecrow Press, 2007); see in particular 72–8 and 81–4.
7 Coursodon, "A Hat Blown by the Wind," 44.
8 My discussion of the film is based on the re-edited version, as released on the director's-cut edition DVD (Metro-Goldwyn-Mayer, distributed by Twentieth Century-Fox Home Entertainment, 2008).
9 Rowell, who unabashedly mines the Coens' films for symbolism, discusses these ceiling fans in *The Brothers Grim*, 16 and 27–8.
10 Burwell, "Composing for the Coen Brothers," in *Soundscape: The School of Sound Lectures 1998–2001*, ed. Larry Sider, Diane Freeman, and Jerry Sider (London and New York: Wallflower Press, 2003), 196.
11 "A Serious Man Production Notes," available at: www.filminfocus.com/article/a_serious_man_production_notes?film=a_serious_man.
12 Dave Calhoun, "The Coen Brothers Discuss 'A Serious Man'," available at: www.timeout.com/film/features/show-feature/9032/The_Coen_brothers_discuss-A_Serious_Man-.html.
13 Burwell, "Carter's Notes."

Chapter 8

Sound and Uncertainty in the Horror Films of the Lewton Unit

Michael Lee

In the aftermath of RKO taking heavy financial losses on expensive productions, the studio hired Val Lewton to form a production unit tasked with
producing low-budget horror films to emulate the lucrative business in horror
done by its rival, Universal. Between March 1, 1942, and August 17, 1945
the Lewton Unit at RKO produced eleven low-budget features, nine of them
marketed as horror films. The first, *Cat People*, did remarkably good business,
and the series as a whole fared well financially.

In recent decades, the Lewton Unit has won admiration within the critical
community. Val Lewton has been the subject of numerous monographs
(the first published in 1973 before the explosion in critical scholarship on
low-budget films and the most recent by an influential art historian[1]), a large
body of articles, two feature-length documentaries, several film festivals and
retrospectives, and a few college courses. As Lewton produced a modest body
of work, one might reasonably ask what all the fuss is about. The answer may
lie in his unit's ambitious effort to reform a genre's conventions in ways that
touch all facets of filmic style.

Lewton took the soundtracks of his films very seriously. On *Cat People*, for
example, he took heat from RKO's chief of production for having hired John
Cass, the film's sound recordist, for three extra days of work to experiment
with reverberation effects and to record both real lions and the cat impressions
of vocal effects actress Dorothy Lloyd.[2] Such meticulous construction of sound
effects typified all of Lewton's productions, and it underscores the heavy
burden placed on sound within Lewton's filmic style.

Similarly, Lewton took the unprecedented step of employing senior composers on RKO's staff to write original scores for all of his films. Most films
budgeted at $150,000, the limit that RKO placed on Lewton, drew almost
entirely on the studio's library of cues. On learning of Lewton's desire for new
scores, RKO executives urged him to use cues from earlier films.[3] But of
Lewton's films, only *The Seventh Victim* (1943) contains any recycled music. In
a move that may be unprecedented in 'B' budget horror productions, Lewton
invited composer Roy Webb to "attend story sessions to contribute ideas for
linking visuals with music."[4]

Lewton's promotion of exacting efforts resulted in soundtracks that drew the attention of Joel Siegel, author of the 1973 *Val Lewton: The Reality of Terror.* Siegel claims that "Lewton's films were easily identifiable by their attention to detail, their unusually literate screenplays, [and] their skillful, suggestive use of shadow and sound."[5] While much has been made in the critical literature of Lewton's 'dark patches,' those heavily shadowed regions of the screen wherein his cinematographers and lighting designers led their audience to project its fears, examination of the unit's use of sound has been limited mostly to discussions of the so-called 'bus,' a sound editing trick where a sudden loud sound and abrupt edit cause the characters and audiences to jump with fright. Yet the 'bus' constitutes only one of the myriad ways in which the Lewton Unit imaginatively employed sound to distance their films stylistically from the generic conventions it inherited.

Lewton began producing in 1942, when the horror genre had entered into a period of stylistic stability fostered by the renewed interest of Universal Studios. After a two-year hiatus from the genre, Universal returned to horror in 1939 with the lavish production *Son of Frankenstein.* In this and subsequent horror offerings, Universal provided audiences with abundant exposure to familiar monsters and to new ones such as the Wolf Man, who quickly became popular through his appearances in almost semi-annual sequels. Universal's monsters intrude into an imaginary European landscape in which two distinct audiences saw their wishes fulfilled. The first audience came to see normalcy threatened by a monstrous force and drew pleasurable reassurance from the monstrous force's inevitable containment. The second audience, made up mostly of marginalized young males, enjoyed the pageantry of a disorderly, monstrous force unleashed on the normal world. For members of this latter group, the inevitable containment of the monster perhaps led to feelings of regret, but they were recompensed by the extensive production of sequels that reminded them that the monsters were never completely defeated. With both of these audiences, the genre's central signifier of course was the monster itself.

Suggestion over Depiction

The Lewton Unit shunned that central signifier in a style predicated on suggestion over depiction. Lewton told the *Los Angeles Times*: "We tossed away the horror formula right from the beginning. No grisly stuff for us. No masklike faces hardly human, with gnashing teeth and hair standing on end. No creaking physical manifestations."[6]

Since the horror genre requires a threatening force, abandoning the genre's main semantic element meant that something had to take its place. Lewton's threats vary from film to film. *Cat People* (1942) offers the story of a troubled Serbian woman named Irena who fears that, because of an ancient curse, she may transform into a panther should she find herself aroused sexually or by jealousy. Whether she is or is not a Cat Person is debatable. William Paul has persuasively argued that by carefully destabilizing the trustworthiness of the image track for the audience, the film in fact depicts no Cat Person.[7] And if no monster appears in *Cat People*, then none appears anywhere in Lewton's series, for of all the cycle's threats surely Irena comes closest to monster status.

Cat People revolves around the collision of Irena's self-doubt with the certainty manifested in Irena's bland husband, his female workplace confidante and later love interest Alice, and the womanizing psychiatrist who is hired to treat Irena. They are all absolutely sure that no Serbian curses can plague modern New York. But their certainty proves brittle, unappealing, and disastrously unable—over the course of the film—to provide Irena with needed aid.

This clash of the certain with the uncertain informs most of the Lewton Unit's output. Their second film, *I Walked with a Zombie* (1943), is a hushed meditation on uncertainty that ends with no satisfactory explanation for the mindless state of Jessica, the film's lovely zombie. The film contains many attempts at explanation, but none satisfactorily accounts for her condition. The Lewton Unit's third film, *The Leopard Man* (1943), stresses the communal nature of violence as its mild-mannered, seemingly harmless killer is driven to his actions by forces unknown and likely unknowable. The film's recurring image of a ball dancing at the apex of a fountain serves as a metaphor for the film's thesis that its characters know little of the forces that move them. *The Seventh Victim* (1943) provides a series of epigrams subtly configured to interrogate the logical framework for conventional certitudes about human happiness. And so it goes throughout the series, each film not just undermining the certitudes of its characters but also challenging those of its audience.

One of the unit's last and most troubled productions, *Isle of the Dead* (1945), foregrounds the theme of uncertainty and links it to positive human emotions. A small group of travelers find themselves trapped by plague on a tiny Greek island. The plague appears simultaneously explicable as a disease transmitted by fleas and as evidence of divine judgment on a group that harbors evil. Each character who fears the plague dies of the plague. Each character who fears evil dies—he or she believes—at the hands of an evil entity. The film's three uncertain characters, those who take no stand on what the group should fear most, survive to the film's melancholy close, their preference to take life as it comes apparently having paved the way to their salvation. One of the survivors cites life's uncertainty as the rationale for embracing love. Linking uncertainty with love constitutes a powerful departure from uncertainty's usual function in Hollywood films. Indeed, most Hollywood films of this period actively avoid uncertainty by uniting all aspects of production in the service of its eradication.

The Lewton Unit explored the ways in which sound can serve a cinema of uncertainty built on suggestion rather than depiction. What follows will survey how the unit's innovative use of sound—comparable to its vaunted use of shadow—reinforced its larger thematic goals.

The 'Bus'

On one occasion Lewton described the formula for his horror films this way: "Our formula is simple. A love story, three scenes of suggested horror and one of actual violence. Fadeout. It's all over in less than 70 minutes."[8] Especially in his scenes of suggested horror, Lewton relied heavily on sound.

The Lewton Unit's first scene of suggested horror—in *Cat People*—resulted in the much-discussed 'bus.' As Alice walks at night across the Central Park transverse, Irena follows her at a distance. Film editor Mark Robson cuts between shots of each woman walking through pools of street-lamp-generated light separated by deep shadows. As edited, the sequence provides no clear indication of the proximity of the two women. But the soundtrack consists entirely of the clacking of high-heeled shoes echoing crisply off the transverse's stone walls, and this allows the audience to experience, with Alice, the pursuer's proximity. When Alice notices the sound of her pursuer's shoes fall silent, she hears rustling in the hedge adjoining the stone wall. She becomes frightened and hurries. She stops at a street lamp and hears nothing; just as her tension builds to a peak, the soundtrack is saturated by the loud noise of a bus's pneumatic brakes. During the film's first showings, observers note, at this point audience members jumped out of their seats.[9]

More than a cheap thrill, the 'bus' entwines the sound effect into the Lewton Unit's larger thematic goals. J.P. Telotte describes the technique as one that undermines audience complacency.[10] An everyday object suddenly becomes frightening, and as a result the audience is uncertain as to what to trust.

All of Lewton's horror films contain 'bus' effects. In *The Seventh Victim*, a previously unseen dog disturbs a trashcan. In *I Walked with a Zombie*, a bird noisily and unexpectedly trills and flutters its wings. In *The Body Snatcher* (1945), a cabman's horse snuffles noisily and shakes its head. In *The Leopard Man*, a 'bus' effect is triggered by the sound of a train passing overhead; in *Curse of the Cat People* (1944), the effect is triggered by the sudden and noisy adjustment of a window shade.

Sound effects had served the horror-film genre long before Lewton's 'bus.' But in earlier films the sources of frightening sound effects seemed more stable. As semiotic elements of the horror genre, the sound of thunder and wind, of creaking doors and floorboards, of noisy scientific machinery, of a woman's shrill scream, and so forth, had served Universal and other studios quite well, and all of these have roots in Gothic literature. What differentiates the 'bus' effects deployed at RKO from earlier sonic signifiers of fear is not just their diversity but also the familiarity of their apparent sources. In earlier horror productions, audiences anticipated and even hoped for thunderclaps and creaking doors. In contrast, Lewton's 'bus' effects came as complete surprises. Rather than echo clichéd Gothic formulations, they took elements of everyday life and 'defamiliarized' them. The Lewton Unit sought to relocate horror from the chronologically vague and largely European settings popular at Universal to a familiar and modern America. The 'bus' reinforced the thematic logic of that change.

Sound Collage: Nightmare, Memory, and Impossible Space

Other menacing sound effects proliferate in the Lewton films and complement the 'bus' device, but they tend to feature everyday sounds transformed in meaning by the fears of overwrought characters. One example is the rhythmic clacking of a loose chain on a truck fender in the scene from *Curse of the Cat People* in which Amy, the film's child protagonist, runs away from home during a snowstorm. She and the audience hear the noise in the distance. As the noise presses closer, it changes into the sound of the rhythmic hoof beats used earlier to reinforce Amy's nightmare after she heard an aging stage actress tell a particularly vivid version of the tale of the Headless Horseman. In the snowstorm scene, Amy cowers on a snowy bridge listening to the oncoming sound, certain that the storybook terror of her nightmare approaches. When the sound's source is revealed as the wholly explicable tire chain, Amy's childish terror is replaced by the audience's very real fears associated with a child lost in the snow on an icy road.

The nightmare that precedes this scene on the bridge and fosters the confusion of metallic clanking for the hoof beats of the approaching Horseman typifies scenes throughout the Lewton horror productions in which sound effects heard in nightmares echo in the waking world and vice versa. Daytime elides into nightmare, nightmares elide into daytime. For example, Irena has a nightmare in *Cat People*. In it we hear repetitions of the psychiatrist's earlier line: "The, uh, key." The image track shows the key to the panther's cage as it turns into a sword, and the psychiatrist as he turns into King John, the slayer of those marked with Irena's curse. Actor Tom Conway's reading of the line, with its insertion of an "uh," provides a rhythm that merges beautifully with the ostinato in Roy Webb's extra-diegetic music, an ostinato based on a snippet of a lullaby hummed earlier by Irena that is now reduced to a pattern of just a few notes stacked shrilly on one another. The resulting sonic collage of the repeated line superimposed on music suggestive of the tread of cats affords entrée into Irena's psyche and punctures the boundary of waking life and nightmare.

A similar sonic collage supports the image track showing the exterior of a cataleptic woman's coffin in *Isle of the Dead* as a few droplets of water fall from the ceiling of the dank crypt. The sound of the wind, the dripping and its echoes, and a descending ostinato pattern in Leigh Harline's score are eventually joined by the murmuring of the woman buried alive inside the coffin. Earlier in the film she had complained to the now dead doctor that she suffered from cataleptic trances and that she had recurring nightmares of being buried alive. Now her nightmare is realized as an arresting mix of sounds unfolds. The boundary between life and nightmare blurs as she lives her darkest fears.

The most detailed sound collage found in the Lewton Unit's output does not reference a nightmare. *The Seventh Victim* opens with Mary, the film's young protagonist, heading up the stairway at her boarding school, Highcliff Academy, to see the headmistress. Mary is about to learn that her sister is missing. Mary's journey to find her sister will feature many missteps, perhaps the most serious being her falling in love with her sister's husband. Worse, the audience will be taken on a journey in which over the course of Mary's fruitless search the bases for human happiness will be challenged. This information is all foreshadowed in John C. Grubb's elaborate sound collage as Mary first ascends the stairway.[11]

Only one element of the collage—the sound of girls' voices conjugating the Latin verb for "to love"—appears in the shooting script for *The Seventh Victim*, and perhaps this sound is presented as though it is being heard through a classroom door. Beyond that, however, the collage defies the spatial logic of the image track as many classroom lessons are heard simultaneously while none at all appears on the image track. In one classroom French rather than Latin is taught, and the verb being conjugated is "*recherche*": "to search." In another classroom there is a stern correction to an inaccurate recitation of the American presidents in chronological order. In still another classroom there transpires a music lesson, with up-and-down scales being sung at successively higher pitch levels. This musical exercise will never find a point of rest and can only halt arbitrarily; the scale relates to the staircase, but the chromatic harmonic progression foreshadows the futility of Mary's search for a satisfactory resting point. Perhaps the most telling overheard lesson involves a girl's voice reciting the final verse of Oliver Wendall Holmes's poem "The Chambered Nautilus," with its exhortation to "leave thy low-vaulted past." Mary is on the point of departing Highcliff forever and embarking on a journey comparable to the one proposed in the poem.

The soundtrack in this sequence from early in *The Seventh Victim* cannot possibly be providing the audience with Mary's actual aural experience, although she does react with an amused smile to the scolding from the American history teacher. The collage thus establishes itself as the stuff of memory rather than experience; actress Kim Hunter, who played Mary, provided the voice reciting Holmes's poem, and Mary cannot be both in class and on the stairs. The collage anticipates the events of the film: a girl searching for her sister instead falls in love and makes many mistakes in a ceaseless journey comparable to that of the chambered nautilus. Holmes's penultimate line, "Till thou at length art free," points toward death; Mary's journey will resemble her sister's, whose journey ends in suicide. Along with providing the audience with a forecast of the film's plot, the collage—which defies the unities of time and space—fuels audience uncertainty by destabilizing the soundtrack as a reliable source of information.

Sound Effects and Their Structural Absence

Sound effects complement the Lewton Unit's stylistic preference for sugges- tion over depiction. In stark contrast to what typically happens in Universal Studio's horror cycle, many horrific elements in Lewton's horror films are heard and not seen. Examples abound. In *The Seventh Victim*, the sound of a chair tipping over behind a closed door serves as the one scene of "actual violence" that signifies the missing sister's long-anticipated suicide. In *The Body Snatcher*, the street singer's off-screen performance of the aptly chosen air "Will Ye No Come Back Again" is interrupted as the murderer cups his hand over her mouth; the image track shows only the empty street down which the murderer followed the singer, and the murder plays out only on the sound- track. In *The Leopard Man*, there is a memorable variation of this approach, when a young girl is slain outside the front door of her house while her mother and brother listen helplessly.

Shadows frequently dominate the image track of Lewton's films. These shadows, as Telotte has argued, provide the Lewton productions with struc- tural absences.[12] The dark is not merely the absence of something to see; rather, it is a structural absence that signifies the inability to see what lies in the dark. The logical equivalent to a darkened image track is a silent sound- track. Menacing silences proliferate in the Lewton Unit's horror sequences. The best of these silences gesture sharply toward a presence that the listener somehow misses. The scene in *Cat People* when the young woman suddenly no longer hears the footsteps of her pursuer is a prime example; rather than being reassured that her troubles are gone, she must instead wonder what new form her troubles have taken, and the silence she hears constitutes a menacing structural absence.

In the climactic sequence of *The Seventh Victim*, the missing sister, Jacqueline, has a similarly frightening moment. Intending to do her harm, a man follows her at night. Jacqueline turns into a maze of alleys and can no longer see her pursuer, but she can hear the soft tread of his gumshoes. Then, when she suddenly no longer hears his tread, she finds herself in a worse position; she still senses his presence but no longer knows where he is. Sight and sound having abandoned her, she backs herself to a wall and begins feeling her way toward a blind corner. The extended shot of her fingertips probing the wall—before reaching her pursuer's jacket—underscores her sense of abandonment.

In *The Ghost Ship* (1943), a terrifying moment finds a crewman on a mer- chant ship in the chamber where the ship's anchor chain is stored. The ship's murderous captain shuts and locks the door to the chamber, trapping the crew-man inside. As the ship's huge anchor chain begins to fill the chamber, the crewman realizes that he will be crushed to death and screams to his shipmates for help. But the sound of the gigantic chain fills the entirety of the sound-track, and the audience watches helplessly as the dying man's screams are never heard. The image tracks of many horror films show many screaming people whose cries are supported by the soundtrack. In this scene from *The Ghost Ship* the Lewton Unit gives the screamer no support at all; the disturbing absence of sonic support is created not by silence but, rather, by a smothering presence of diegetic noise.

Deliberate absences of 'supportive' sound—for purposes related to a narra-tive's structure—find their way into several of Lewton's other films. One of the most notable examples occurs in the climactic sequence of *The Leopard Man*, when the roles of the main characters are reversed and the audience joins with the terrified killer as he listens to the menacing silence of the museum. 'Silent' moments like these offer the audio parallel of the Lewton Unit's vaunted shadows; they indicate not nothing but, rather, something quite terrifying that we cannot perceive.

Diegetic Music

All of Lewton's productions prominently feature diegetic music. Much of it obeys conventions long established for low-budget films. Scottish airs sung by the street singer at the beginning of *The Body Snatcher*, for example, help establish the setting as Edinburgh as effectively as the title superimposed on the stock shot of Castle Rock. Similar justifications motivate the Spanish music heard in the El Pueblo nightclub in *The Leopard Man*, or the organ grinder in the zoo in *Cat People*. Diegetic music helps establish a sense of place and even of time, a crucial function in films with meager budgets.

What differentiates these snips of diegetic music from comparable music in other studios' films is the Lewton Unit's attention to detail in their selection. For example, the organ grinder at the zoo in *Cat People* is playing a sped-up version of Lyonel's opening lines of the Act Three quintet, "May Heaven Forgive Thee," from Friedrich von Flotow's 1847 opera *Martha*. At this exact point in the opera, Lady Harriet has just publicly accused Lyonel of insanity, and the chorus has obliged her by binding Lyonel with ropes. Now fettered like a madman, Lyonel sings to Lady Harriet, who came to him in disguise only to fall in and out of love with him. These are his words in translation as sung during the passage quoted on the monkey organ:

Ah, may Heav'n above forgive you,
That my life you could destroy!
'Twas your pleasure to deceive me,
With my breaking heart to toy.[13]

In his monograph on the film, Kim Newman reads the character Oliver—Irena's suitor and eventual husband—as having fundamentally deceived Irena.[14] That deception begins at their first meeting as the monkey-organ music grinds on the soundtrack. Newman observes that Oliver, being already emotionally attached to his co-worker Alice, came to Irena dishonestly. Later Oliver and Alice will falsely accuse Irena of insanity, and they will work with Irena's psychiatrist, Dr. Judd, to have her committed to an asylum. The quotation from *Martha* foreshadows and, more importantly, interprets the action in *Cat People* in a way that anticipates Newman's analytical observation of many years later.[15]

Similar moments when the diegetic music links thematically to the film as a whole can be found in many of the Lewton Unit's productions. For example, Natalie, the one-armed member of the urbane devil cult depicted in *The Seventh Victim*, kills time while waiting for Jacqueline to kill herself by playing the piano. She nonchalantly tickles a series of augmented triads. With its stacking of three pitches a major-third apart, the augmented triad looks on paper invitingly like a major or minor triad. But its structure lies entirely outside the boundaries of diatonic music. Its famous earlier appearances often coincide with supernatural contexts, such as the conjuration theme from Paul Dukas's *The Sorcerer's Apprentice* (1893).[16] The urbane cult looks like a group of typical Manhattanites, but their appearance, like Natalie's chord, is deceiving.

The diegetic music heard in *I Walked with a Zombie* serves the specific structure of the film while simultaneously reinforcing the Unit's preoccupation with uncertainty. Very little actually happens in *I Walked with a Zombie*. In place of action, the film bursts with narrations of what happened before the film began. In trying to determine how Jessica became a zombie prior to the film's start, it pits two explanatory systems against one another. One system is rational and takes on the trappings of Western civilization and a few of its myriad assumptions of how the world works; the other system looks for answers in Voodoo and the supernatural.

Resulting from this clash of systems, a series of doublings arises. There are two zombies, Jessica, the beautiful wife of an English sugar planter, and Carrefour, the descendant of slaves brought long ago to the island. Each resides in a fort; Jessica in Fort Holland, where her husband makes his home, and Carrefour at the Houmfort, where the rituals associated with Voodoo unfold. Each zombie walks to the other's fort. Each fort has a doctor, a physician who treats Jessica and the leader of the "better doctors" associated with Voodoo. Each fort houses musical instruments with Fort Holland's piano doubling the Houmfort's drums and conches. Interestingly, both forts also house Aeolian instruments: a primitive Aeolian flute made from a gourd is both heard and seen during Jessica's walk to the Houmfort, and as Carrefour's shadow haunts Fort Holland a breeze transforms Jessica's gilt harp into an Aeolian harp.[17] Aeolian instruments, sounded by the action of natural wind blowing across strings or holes, were traditionally used to capture the voices of the spirit world; their use here, in a film that features two voiceless zombies, is extraordinarily apt.

Likewise apt are the film's diegetic musical performances, which lend support to both rational and supernatural perspectives. The "Fort Holland Song" sung and composed by a calypso singer named Sir Lancelot offers a prime example of the local perspective. According to *The Hollywood Reporter*, Lewton hired Haitian musician LeRoy Antoine to serve as "technical advisor on *I Walked with a Zombie*," and "Antoine will also teach the negro actors Haitian rhythms for use in the voodoo ceremony."[18] Antoine had co-authored a book on music in Voodoo ritual that contained not only some of the drumming patterns heard during the film but also the text and melody to the song "O Legba" that is performed in the film.[19] Antoine supervised recording sessions on October 20 and 24, 1942, when his arrangements of the traditional Haitian songs "O Marie Congo," "O Legba," "Wallee Nan Guinan," and "Levee Dumbala" were recorded along with the drummers whose work haunts much of the film's last half.[20] Unlike Sir Lancelot, Antoine does not appear in the film, but his work informs its soundtrack.

The so-called rational perspective finds support when Paul Holland, Jessica's husband, plays Chopin's Prelude in E Major. The screenplay called for Liszt's "Liebestod," a peculiar suggestion since Liszt wrote a "Liebestraum" while Richard Wagner wrote a famous "Liebestod," albeit not for piano. In the context of the film, Chopin provides a richer hermeneutic field than does either Liszt or Wagner.[21] Musicologist Jim Samson has carefully documented the reception history of Chopin's music, linking it with "the poetic, suggestive of the sublime and mysterious, distilled to intimacy."[22] Chopin's historical situation allows the viewer to link Holland not only with the rationality of the Western perspective but also with the subjective and Romantic ideals that demonstrate how conflicted the Western perspective can be. This echoes the film's larger handling of the dichotomy of superstition and reason by demonstrating how fragile are the certitudes stemming from reason, no matter how certainly its advocates present themselves.

The Ghost Ship depicts a young officer named Tom who knows that the captain of his merchant ship is a murderer. Tom tries to convince his crewmates of what he knows, but they refuse to listen to him, not because what he says is so fantastic but because they like their jobs and do not want any trouble. Consistently the indifferent crew members use music to block out the terrifying reality unfolding all around them. We encounter this when Tom's best friend wears headphones and listens to dance music as he shuffles about the radio room with an imaginary partner. For the radio operator, music provides a pathway to escape from his duty to his friend. We encounter it again when crew members play harmonica to cover over Tom's overtures for support; the same harmonica is later used to accompany Sir Lancelot, who composed two calypso numbers for *The Ghost Ship*, as he sings while the captain is trying to murder Tom. In both cases, the stark juxtaposition of cheerful sounds with terrifying events crystallizes the use of diegetic music as a pleasant distraction that blocks out harsh reality.[23]

In these and other examples, diegetic music serves large thematic issues and overarching narrative structures. The finely wrought details of these moments constitute a hallmark of the Lewton Unit's sonic style.

Roy Webb

The soundtracks of all of Lewton's productions at RKO benefited from lavish orchestral scores. The simplest explanation for this lies in the fact that RKO's music library lacked cues germane to the horror genre. With their remote settings and ambitious subject matter, the studio's earlier horror productions—such as *The Most Dangerous Game* (1932), *King Kong* (1933), and *The Hunchback of Notre Dame* (1939)—differed drastically in tone from Lewton's films, and thus their scores by Max Steiner and Alfred Newman were simply unsuitable for recycling.

A full account of the remarkable features of Roy Webb's scores for the Lewton Unit falls outside the scope of this chapter. A few illustrations must represent the general rule that these scores highlight the central thematic issues of the films. More than providing apt accompaniment for the mood or action in specific scenes, Webb's scores are filled with carefully composed music designed to recapitulate and even clarify the narratives of their respective films. Lewton's inclusion of Webb in story meetings may explain why the composer took such care in crafting music uniquely suited to each film. Two examples chosen from dozens will demonstrate this point.

In *Cat People*, Webb provides a score peppered with leitmotifs. The most ubiquitous of these quotes the French lullaby "Do, do l'enfant do," heard first in the film's main title cue and later from the lips of Irena as she hums it to herself in the dark. Fragments of this melody haunt Webb's score in scene after scene; they appear in ten of the fourteen cues he composed for the film.

After the opening credits, Webb's first presentation of the tune coincides with Oliver asking Irena if she loves him. "Do, do l'enfant do" insinuates itself into the scene in a sweet orchestration for strings, harp, and flute, stably harmonized in the key of F Major. On later appearances, the tune is invariably associated with Irena. As her psychological state deteriorates over the course of the film, the tune receives increasingly strident harmonization, abandoning the stable tonality heard earlier first for polytonality and later for discordant versions that defy tonal description.

In Webb's cue "Too Late," we hear the lullaby doubled into a G-flat Major chord in first inversion moving to E-flat Major over a disturbingly unrelated descending harmonic progression beginning on a G-sharp diminished chord; this polytonal music appears on the soundtrack with Irena's whispered ranting as the image track shows her clawing the sofa's upholstery after Oliver has indelicately admitted his love for Alice. In the brief cue "Cat Theme" that underscores the later image of Irena peering into a restaurant to find Oliver and Alice in intimate, late-night discourse, Webb presents the lullaby rocking back and forth between two dissonant pitch-class sets; the harsh, atonal effect marries well with the disturbing image of Irena's deterioration into madness.

Just as Webb's tonal handling of the lullaby becomes more strident, his orchestrations become stranger and stranger. Two in particular merit notice. During Irena's interview with Dr. Judd in his office we hear Webb's cue "Needful Help," in which the lullaby motif is doubled at the fourth in timpani tuned extremely high and further doubled by the glassy timbre of violins in false harmonics. This material is accompanied by a dissonant hexachord played on the novachord, an early analogue synthesizer. In the scene where Irena murders Dr. Judd, we hear the tune starkly plunked on solo marimba, an instrument whose Latin flavor is apt to confuse the listener in this context. Unusual instruments and peculiar techniques continue to deform the lullaby, transforming it into something ever more frightening.

These later cues provide a stark contrast to the sweet orchestral version of the lullaby heard during Oliver's proposal. Later, however, we discover that the music heard during the proposal was not underscore but a diegetic recording. This becomes clear late in the film as Dr. Judd, Alice, and Oliver wait for Irena to come home so they can commit her to an asylum. Alice kills time listening to Irena's records. She plays the exact bit of "Do, do l'enfant do" that was heard during the proposal scene until Oliver says "let's not play that" and abruptly lifts the needle off the phonograph disc. Only at this point do we learn then that the sweet music that accompanied Oliver's proposal came from a record in Irena's collection. Her lullaby leitmotif thus becomes something 'frozen,' identical in its rigidity to the understanding of her by Oliver, Alice, and Dr. Judd. The film's belated revelation that music heard earlier was actually diegetic rather than extra-diegetic possibly has no precedent. Meticulous in its handling of music, the Lewton Unit was also highly original.

The Seventh Victim tells the story of a young woman, Mary, who discovers that her missing sister, Jacqueline, married without telling her, gave away her business to a relative stranger, and became enmeshed in a devil cult. The cult, which provides the film's putative horror element, has pledged itself to two mutually exclusive rules: they will punish with death anyone who "speaks of their being or their deeds," but they will not engage in violence. As Mary falls in love with Jacqueline's husband, the cult hounds Jacqueline until finally she hangs herself. Enmeshed within this story are numerous ideas that point toward the film's larger theme of fruitless striving for happiness.

Webb's score fixates on this larger theme by relentlessly providing melodic material misshapen by perpetually ascending harmonic motion. Whereas 'arch shapes' dominate most melodies, in his music for *The Seventh Victim* Webb assiduously eschews them. And his ascending antecedent phrases are almost never balanced with descending consequents.

Webb establishes his approach in his "Main Title" cue. After the 'V' for Victory theme—a chattering, dissonant gloss on the opening of Beethoven's Fifth Symphony composed by Webb for RKO's wartime productions—Webb cadences deceptively from an E-flat Minor seventh chord over an A-natural pedal to D-flat Minor, the key of the "Main Title" cue. From here the ascending melodic material commences. The first phrase begins with ascending intervals moving up the D-flat Minor scale; this melody, an ascending scale soon to be echoed in the singing lesson in the film's opening sound collage, offers a simple signifier for striving. Then the winds enter, ascending step-wise from F-flat to A-flat. The next two measures provide a slightly embellished restatement of the initial material until the winds ascend to the unexpected chromatic tone of A-natural; this is a significant move, a musical 'misstep' that overshoots the expected dominant and effectively links the underscore to the important theme of 'missteps' in the film's narrative. Over the next eight measures of his "Main Title" music (see Figure 8.1), Webb extends the idea of relentless ascent. Few of his scores fixate so insistently on such a fine connotative detail.

The film's opening scene finds Mary, after her ascent up the stairway, confronted by her school's headmistress. Upon learning that her older sister is missing, Mary resolves to go to New York to find her. Webb's cue, "Principal's Office," underscores the conversation between Mary and the headmistress. Webb deploys his musical signifier of fruitless striving here by having the violins ascend up a C Minor scale but stopping on the leading tone. By having his melody end inconclusively on the leading tone, Webb supports the film's narrative theme of incomplete and unsatisfactory searches.

In the next cue, "Room Number 7," Webb continues to develop the idea of ascending but inconclusive scalar figures. The cue underscores the scene in which Mary at last convinces the owners of a boarding house to open the room

Figure 8.1 Roy Webb: "Main Title" from *The Seventh Victim*, melody mm. 3–8

that her sister rented but never visited. After the door is opened, the camera's gaze shifts from a lone chair to a noose hanging above it, and with this Mary discovers the first sign of her sister's fixation on death. In Webb's cue, the ascending minor-mode melody is doubled at the second and the fourth, while below a series of dissonances sound in an iambic rhythm. Indeed, throughout the film Webb uses that same iambic rhythm to signify death, most notably after the suicide of Mary's sister.

Throughout his score for *The Seventh Victim*, Webb wisely develops his humble musical materials. His economical score meshes beautifully not just with the film's larger themes but also with its smaller details.

Sonic Style and the Lewton Unit

In a 1973 book fundamentally concerned with visual and narrative innovation, Joel Siegel identified sound as a crucial element of Lewton's style, yet (apart from a discussion of the 'bus' technique) he neglected to delve into the films' soundtracks. This flaw mars the literature on the Lewton Unit in general. Surely an innovative filmic style involves *all* aspects of filmmaking, including elements of the soundtrack.

A filmic 'style' requires recognizable elements that recur from film to film within a filmmaker's oeuvre. By this definition, RKO's Lewton Unit—with its repeated use of the 'bus,' of sound collage, of the soundtrack's structural 'absence,' of violence made audible but not visible, of diegetic music aptly chosen for its explanatory potential, of extra-diegetic scores consistently measured to highlight a film's thematic potential—surely employed a sonic style. It was a style of great sophistication, comprehensively enmeshed in and ably reinforcing Lewton's cinematic goals.

Notes

1   These are Joel E. Siegel, *Val Lewton: The Reality of Terror* (New York: The Viking Press, 1973), and Alexander Nemerov, *Icons of Grief: Val Lewton's Home Front Pictures* (Berkeley: University of California Press, 2005).
2   George Turner, "A Retrospective of the 'Original' Val Lewton's *Cat People*," *Cinefantastique* (May–June 1982): 26.
3   Edmund G. Bansak, *Fearing the Dark: The Val Lewton Career* (Jefferson: McFarland Publishers, 1995), 127.
4   Ibid.
5   Siegel, *Val Lewton: The Reality of Terror*, 23.
6   Ibid., 31.
7   See William Paul, "What Does Dr. Judd Want? Transformation, Transference, and Divided Selves in *Cat People*," in *Horror Films and Psychoanalysis*, ed. Steven Jay Schneider (Cambridge: Cambridge University Press, 2004), 159–75.
8   Siegel, *Val Lewton: The Reality of Terror*, 31.
9   DeWitt Bodeen, "Val Lewton Proved that Even Low-Budgeted Films Can Have Artistic Integrity," *Films in Review* (Fall, 1963): 216. Charles Higham and Joel

Greenberg, *The Celluloid Muse: Hollywood Directors Speak* (London: Angus and Robertson, 1969), 217–18.

10 J.P. Telotte, *Dreams of Darkness: Fantasy and the Films of Val Lewton* (Urbana: University of Illinois Press, 1985), 14.

11 I attribute this collage to Grubb for his having executed it. The idea may have belonged to Mark Robson or Val Lewton. It does not appear in the shooting script.

12 Telotte, *Dreams of Darkness*, 21–8.

13 Translation from librettist Wilhelm Friedrich's original libretto by Stephen Smith found in the Berlin Classics compact disc release of a 1944 production of *Martha*, 0021632BC.

14 Kim Newman, *Cat People* (London: British Film Institute, 1999), 18–21.

15 Lewton's final draft for the script for *Cat People* reads: "Over the scene is the wheezy music of the Triumphal March from 'Aida,' as played on a hand organ." Someone in the Music Department substituted the apt scene from *Martha* for the familiar but thematically unhelpful music called for in the script. Roy Webb seems a likely candidate as he had regularly attended the opera with his mother in New York City. At least three productions of *Martha* had taken place in that city during his period of youthful opera-going.

16 See Carlo Caballero, "Silence, Echo: A Response to 'What the Sorcerer Said,'" *19th-Century Music* 28, no. 2 (Fall, 2004): 171–6, for a captivating discussion of Dukas's conjuring motive and its link to the supernatural.

17 This small figure clearly mattered to Lewton, who describes it in his final draft of the screenplay. Lewton obviously had a love for the British poet Samuel Taylor Coleridge, who is quoted at length in Lewton's later film *The Seventh Victim*; one imagines that Coleridge's poem *The Aeolian Harp* (1795) might have been a Lewton favorite.

18 *Hollywood Reporter*, October 29, 1942.

19 Laura Bowman and LeRoy Antoine, *The Voice of Haiti* (New York City: Clarence Williams Music, 1938).

20 Logs indicated Antoine's presence on the set and in recording sessions, and his arrangements are located with the musical materials in the Fine Arts Special Collections Library of the University of California, Los Angeles.

21 Again, attributing responsibility for a substitution can be difficult. Norm Bennett played piano on the set the day the scene was shot. Perhaps he made the substitution thinking the screenplay gave an erroneous instruction.

22 Jim Samson, "Chopin Reception: Theory, History, Analysis," in *Chopin Studies 2*, ed. John Rink and Jim Samson (Cambridge: Cambridge University Press, 2006), 3.

23 The handling of music in *The Ghost Ship* anticipates the scene in *The Good, the Bad and the Ugly* (1966) when the prison commander uses his orchestra of prisoners to drown out the sounds of his torturing their fellow inmates.

Chapter 9

Conducting the Composer

David O. Selznick and the Hollywood Film Score

Nathan Platte

In a filmmaking career that stretched from the early 1920s through the 1950s, David O. Selznick produced some of Hollywood's most celebrated films, including *King Kong* (1933), *Gone with the Wind* (1939), *Rebecca* (1940), *Since You Went Away* (1944), and *Duel in the Sun* (1946). In early 1949, two newspaper articles confronted the renowned producer's influence in film music and offered startlingly different conclusions.

In the *Washington Post*'s "Movie Music Makes Progress," Selznick is depicted as a mover and shaker in the brief but volatile history of film music. Selznick not only receives credit for introducing orchestral underscore to sound films, but he is also touted as a leader in film music promotion and aesthetics:

> Selznick's latest innovation in motion-picture music is to be found in his production, "Portrait of Jennie." ... Because of the ethereal aspect of the story, Selznick decided to score "Portrait of Jennie" solely with the music of one of the French masters, Claude Debussy.[1]

Compared to "'Hearts & Flowers' played by a bored pianist," argued the writer, Selznick had taught audiences to "enjoy motion-picture music as an art form in its own right."[2]

Writing for *Rob Wagner's Script*, music critic Lawrence Morton painted a bleaker picture: "[Selznick] set upon [Debussy's] music with the fury of the Bacchantes, and with cries of 'Evoe! Evoe!' he tore it to shreds, dismembered it as the Thracian maidens dismembered Orpheus."[3] The use of Debussy in *Portrait of Jennie*, argued Morton, was regressive rather than innovative:

> Now comes Mr. Selznick, at this late date, with a revival of the musical techniques of the theatre organist of the 'twenties. The score for *Portrait of Jennie* is the kind we used to hear in a hundred Bijou Theatres on a hundred Main Streets across the nation. It is a potpourri, a pasticcio, a hodgepodge, a patchwork, a grab-bag, a paste-and-scissors job. All that differentiates it from its ancestors is its slick pretentiousness.[4]

The articles betray strong biases,[5] but they effectively encapsulate two points that any discussion of music in Selznick's films must confront:

1. Even without formal musical training, Selznick held so strong a sway over the music in his films that it could even overshadow the musicians involved. Morton's article tellingly bears the title "Selznick's Debussy," and the quotations above give the impression that Selznick scored *Portrait of Jennie* himself. (Indeed, one must look closely at both articles to find the name of Dimitri Tiomkin, who arranged the score.)
2. Selznick's influence over film music was contentious, drawing both praise and condemnation from composers and critics.

Given Selznick's strong presence in the scoring process and wide recognition in the press, it might seem a simple task to delineate the producer's musical style. In the case of director John Ford, Kathryn Kalinak has argued that

> the similarities among the scores of Ford's westerns, the striking recurrence of the same songs, across numerous genres, produced by different studios in different eras and scored by different composers, as well as the extent to which many of the songs are not typical or used conventionally, has convinced me that there is a kind of music that I am prepared to describe as Fordian.[6]

Might a similar argument be made for Selznick? Not as easily. Most of the common musical traits found in Selznick's films are either too general or too specific to be noticed even by careful listeners. He preferred long musical scores to short ones, for example. He also made sure that his composers stocked their music with associative themes, in large part because he could dictate themes' placement and narrative function without having to use musical jargon. On the other end of the spectrum, he also liked recycling a small body of individual cues across multiple films. Unless one watches specific films back-to-back, however, these reuses are apt to go unnoticed.[7]

Although Selznick's style is not immediately discernible from the soundtrack alone, it is nonetheless expressed loudly and clearly through the production process itself. Selznick's style, in other words, can be 'heard' in the production files that show his persistent involvement throughout the scoring process. Observing Selznick's influence in the process, as opposed to just the final product, is thus perhaps all the more appropriate.

Selznick's eligibility for auteur status—a title normally reserved for directors—has always been tenuous, and Matthew Bernstein argues persuasively that even creative producers like Selznick should not be viewed through the same critical lens reserved for auteur directors like Ford and Hitchcock.[8] This is not a mark against Selznick but an acknowledgment that his versatile talents in multiple genres make it harder to set his work, including his involvement with music, in a neatly prescribed category. In an article on Victor Fleming, a director who collaborated with Selznick on *Gone with the Wind*, David Denby notes:

> [Fleming's] absence from the list of the blessed suggests a flaw in auteur theory and not in Fleming—a prejudice against the generalists, the non-obsessed, the "chameleons," as Steven Spielberg called them, who re-created themselves for each project and made good movies in many different styles.[9]

Selznick, like Fleming, "made good movies in many different styles," and his contributions to film music help to illuminate how he achieved this feat. Selznick's powerful presence shaped the creative dynamic of film scoring while eliciting different responses—musical and otherwise—from composers; tapping into the energy and conflict of these collaborative relationships brings Selznick's sonic style into greater relief. This chapter offers a broad view of Selznick's methods and musical tastes as they changed over his career, and it concludes with a case study of the controversial *Portrait of Jennie*. Featuring Debussy's themes as arranged by Dimitri Tiomkin, *Portrait's* musical peculiarities accentuate both the producer's substantial contributions and the limits of his authorial voice.

Cuing Music at RKO and MGM

The son of mogul Lewis J. Selznick, David O. Selznick grew up in the film business; he was in his early twenties when his first short films were released in 1923. Consequently, Selznick's introduction to film music came during the silent era, and his appreciation for these films and their music continued throughout his career.[10] Notes on film scoring from Selznick, however, do not surface until 1935, when the producer left the studio system to become an independent producer. Nevertheless, initial mentions of Selznick's interest in film music arise as early as 1932, when he was a young executive producer at RKO. Upon arriving at the studio, Selznick quickly established a relationship with the studio's music director, Max Steiner, who had distinguished himself as a conductor, arranger, and composer of musicals in Europe, New York, and Hollywood. After Steiner provided credits music for Selznick's first RKO film, *The Lost Squadron*, the producer asked for more in his next film, *Symphony of Six Million*. As the *Los Angeles Times* reported:

> An "operatic underscoring" is the technical designation of the musical complement composed by Max Steiner for RKO Radio Pictures' "Symphony of Six Million." The underscoring ... is a combination of Steiner's compositions and his own orchestrations of Hebrew classics,

including Eli, Eli, Kol Nidre, Hatikvah, and Auf'n Pripitochok. [Steiner] credits the original idea for this treatment to David O. Selznick, executive vice-president in charge of RKO production.[11]

It was an unusual idea for 1932, when most films contained little extradiegetic orchestral music, but it was not completely without precedent. Earlier films from Paramount, such as *Fighting Caravans* (1931), had already incorporated wall-to-wall background scores.[12] But *Symphony* ultimately proved more influential. The nonstop musical accompaniment of *Fighting Caravans*, which plays at a low volume for much of the film, was hardly noticed in the press.[13] For *Symphony*, however, Steiner and Selznick had done more than simply drop a music track behind the film's story. They had successfully determined which scenes would benefit most from music's presence and—just as important— absence. Indeed, the mere inclusion of music in certain scenes of *Symphony* helps contrast and characterize narrative space. Scenes that take place in or around the protagonist's home receive music; when the protagonist violates his own promise to serve his local community as a doctor and moves uptown to a ritzy office, the music stops.[14] Unlike the virtually ignored *Fighting Caravans*, critics marveled at the music in *Symphony*:

> The Radio people who are responsible for underlaying it throughout with a splendid musical score have pointed the way which may be followed with profit by others. It was composed by Max Steiner, and as an example of thematic music is worthy of study. In the silent days we had music throughout the picture. ... With the coming of "talkies" and their early imperfections, dialogue and the rasping of mechanical contrivances all but eliminated music. Lately, it has been brought in occasionally, possibly during a silent scene, or a big moment. Here in "Symphony of Six Million" it is used in almost every foot, and for the very deliberate purpose of building and sustaining emotional values of both the dialogue the incidental background noises and the picture itself.[15]

Selznick's support of Steiner's work in *Symphony* was not an isolated incident but, rather, the beginning of a collaboration that would span twelve years. Shortly after *Symphony*, Selznick and Steiner began work on *Bird of Paradise*. When Steiner asked the producer how much music he wanted, the producer is said to have responded: "For my money, you can start on the first frame and finish on the last."[16] He nearly got his wish. Aside from one scene, music plays throughout the entire film. Even though *Bird's* score more closely resembled *Fighting Caravans* in length, improved dubbing technology allowed the music to be played at a higher volume without obscuring dialogue. Several scenes with reduced dialogue or sound effects gave Steiner's vivid music additional exposure, prompting critics to once again praise the composer for music that recalled silent-era accompaniments.[17]

With Selznick's continued support, Steiner provided elaborate scores for *The Most Dangerous Game* (1932) and, most famously, *King Kong* (1933). Due to a lack of surviving production files, it is harder to judge Selznick's personal involvement with the music in these films (he served as executive producer for both), but his push for music in *Symphony* and *Bird* abetted Steiner's efforts with the later films, which grew increasingly ambitious in their complexity. "There were a great many individual mistakes in the orchestra," wrote Murray Spivack in the recording log for *Most Dangerous Game*, "which were not due to lack of rehearsal. These should be considered unavoidable, inasmuch as the musicians were working from 10:00 A.M. to 6:00 A.M. [20 hrs], and the music was extremely difficult."[18] Selznick's support for these scores also registers through increased financial support. Recording logs, for example, reveal that the size of the orchestra for each production grew, from only thirty musicians for *Symphony* to forty-six in *Kong*.[19] Collectively, all four Selznick–Steiner films marked a triumph for extra-diegetic orchestral music and set a standard to which other studios and composers aspired.

A newspaper interview with Steiner from this period gives a valuable glimpse of the close working relationship composer and producer enjoyed. According to the article, Steiner explained that

> David O. Selznick came to the conclusion that any music, whether classical or popular, that is known—even if not by name—to the general public, is distracting. He said to me one day:
> "Steiner, when a tune has been heard before, the people in the audience search their memories. They say, 'where did we hear that before? Just what is that melody?'"
> Selznick, who is extremely sensitive musically, also said he thought music should fit the precise action, mood, and even words in a screen play, and obviously should be especially composed.[20]

Symphony, of course, had featured familiar Jewish melodies, but the other Steiner scores had followed Selznick's prescription to favor original material. But if this is how Selznick felt about music at the end of 1932, it is not how he would discuss film music in 1937, when in a letter to Katharine Brown he would enthusiastically encourage the use of pre-existent music.[21] At some point, then, Selznick changed his mind. Herbert Stothart, Selznick's next music director, is the one who helped change it.

In 1933, Selznick moved from RKO to MGM, where he produced eleven films in two years. Just as he helped jumpstart Steiner's compositional work at RKO, so Selznick now turned to MGM's chief composer, Herbert Stothart. Like Steiner, Stothart came from Broadway to Hollywood in the late 1920s. He had been working at MGM since 1929, but his career as a film composer only began gathering momentum after working with Selznick on *Nightflight* (1933) and *Viva Villa!* (1934). It is a telling coincidence. Selznick, for his part, valued Stothart's contributions and made efforts to have the composer assigned to his pictures. Of the scant archival material documenting their work together, two letters from Selznick express his enthusiasm for collaborating with Stothart:

> Dear Herb:
>
> I've just heard that in accordance with my request I have you again on "Vanessa." I can't tell you how pleased I am and am looking forward to working with you again.[22]

For *A Tale of Two Cities*, Selznick exclaimed that he was "delighted with the assignment of Mr. Stothart."[23] Indeed, Stothart appears to have effected one especially important change in the producer's view of film music: namely, that the skillful incorporation of pre-existent classical, popular, and folk music into a score had the potential to better connect with audiences than original music. This approach differs markedly from the methods evinced in Steiner's music for the island adventure films at RKO. For Stothart, however, the interweaving of strong music into film scores was not just a preference; it was an artistic responsibility. "The public today," wrote Stothart, "is benefiting by the greatest works of the greatest composers, woven into the drama of the screen and giving it new effectiveness, while the drama itself is creating a new sense of music appreciation."[24] Stothart put this philosophy into practice, incorporating the music of Wagner into Selznick's *Vanessa: Her Love Story* (1935) and Tchaikovsky into Selznick's *Anna Karenina*. After Selznick left MGM, Stothart continued working classical and popular works into *Romeo and Juliet* (1936), *The Wizard of Oz* (1939), *Mrs. Miniver* (1943), *Song of Russia* (1944), and *The Yearling* (1946), among others.

While Selznick's changing views concerning pre-existing music is surprising in light of Steiner's assertions from 1932, the benefits of arranging familiar melodies for film would not have been a hard sell: it had already worked in Steiner's *Symphony of Six Million* and had been a common practice during Selznick's training in the silent era. After Selznick left MGM in 1935 to become an independent producer, Stothart's ideas would continue to influence Selznick's scoring notes for years after.

The Prestigious Independent

Still in his early thirties, Selznick followed his father's example in 1935 by establishing his own production company: Selznick International Pictures. From RKO through MGM Selznick had focused increasingly on prestige pictures—expensive films that featured major stars, high production values, and pointedly artistic aspirations, usually expressed through stories based on literary adaptations. At Selznick International Pictures, the producer planned to make prestige pictures the mainstay of his operations. Background symphonic scores would enhance both the production values and artistic aura of Selznick's releases, and it is with these productions that Selznick's participation in film scoring becomes easier to observe.

One simple yet crucial facet of the scoring process that Selznick closely monitored was the selection of composers. At first, Selznick worked exclusively with Steiner, whom he borrowed from RKO to score his first independent feature, *Little Lord Fauntleroy* (1935), and then hired full-time as Selznick International's music director. Serving as Selznick's de facto composer further enhanced Steiner's reputation and press coverage on films like *Garden of Allah* (1936) and *A Star Is Born* (1937),[25] but Steiner began working at Warner Bros. in 1936 and accepted an ongoing contract with that studio the following year when tensions between him and Selznick prompted a temporary separation. (Selznick still borrowed Steiner from Warner Bros. to score later productions, including *Gone with the Wind* [1939] and *Since You Went Away* [1944].) Steiner's assignments at Warner Bros. meant that Selznick could not always secure his preferred composer, and MGM kept Herbert Stothart similarly busy. Consequently, Selznick expended considerable effort trying to find available composers who possessed sufficient experience and stamina to withstand the producer's demands.

Successful collaborations with Franz Waxman (*The Young in Heart* [1938], *Rebecca* [1940], *The Paradine Case* [1947]) and Tiomkin (*Duel in the Sun* [1946], *Portrait of Jennie* [1948]) resulted in multiple engagements, but other composers, like Alfred Newman and Miklós Rózsa, did not return. Selznick also terminated some composers' contracts mid-production if he felt their music violated his expectations. Selznick rejected Alexandre Tansman's score for *Since You Went Away* and hired Max Steiner in the eleventh hour to write an entirely new score; Leith Stevens had just begun recording his music for *The Paradine Case* (1947) when he was jettisoned and replaced by Waxman; Bernard Herrmann wrote a handful of cues for *Portrait of Jennie* before leaving the production to Dimitri Tiomkin. In all three cases, collaborations with new composers soured and Selznick hired someone who had worked for him previously. Contributing to Selznick's highly publicized prestige pictures consequently held the potential for either great success or humiliation. Selznick's composers knew they had to follow his directions closely.

Selznick communicated his ideas on music through scene-by-scene instructions that were dictated to secretaries and then given to the composer. Some scoring notes were drafted during conferences with the composer; others were drafted before a composer had even been selected.[26] Although the length and detail featured in these notes differs from production to production, a general trajectory is observable: as Selznick's experience as an independent producer grew, so too did the length of his scoring notes.

Selznick's musical observations for *Little Lord Fauntleroy*, which are his earliest surviving scoring notes, are therefore rather succinct. The producer drafted several sets of notes in January of 1936.[27] Each set is two pages long and dictates which scenes are to have music and when the music should begin and end. While simple in concept, Selznick's scoring notes convey his ideas on how music should work within the drama. For *Fauntleroy*, Selznick determined that music would enhance scenes of tear-jerking sentimentality and depictions of royal living, thereby setting these portions of the film apart. The producer made sure anything smacking of villainy did not receive music. When the grouchy Minna arrives, falsely asserting her son's right to Ceddie's lordship, Selznick ordered the music out. Consecutive scenes concerning the bogus claimant constitute the longest stretch of music-less film. Much like *Symphony of Six Million*, in which the absence of music emphasizes the protagonist's estrangement from his own ideals, the withholding of music in *Fauntleroy* reinforces the intruders' illegitimacy.[28] Selznick had initially requested music for a scuffle early in the film between Ceddie and a gang of jealous Brooklyn boys. Steiner wrote a 'hurry' cue for the scene, but even this jot of ill-willed aggression clashed with the film's musico-dramatic paradigm. The cue was removed, and it is the only substantial cut made in the entire *Fauntleroy* score.[29]

When the producer tackled *Gone with the Wind* several years later, the expanded length of his notes signaled a much greater level of investment. Scoring notes from previous pictures had never exceeded four pages, but for *Gone with the Wind* Selznick's numerous scoring notes had to be collated into a thirteen-page document dated November 6, 1939.[30] The very next day Selznick dictated another twelve pages of instructions.[31] To these were added shorter installments over the ensuing weeks. Although time would not afford Selznick the luxury of dictating such elaborate and detailed notes for all subsequent projects, the precedent and success of *Gone with the Wind* set a new standard of involvement to which the producer would aspire on *Since You Went Away* (1944), *Duel in the Sun* (1946), *Portrait of Jennie* (1948), and *A Farewell to Arms* (1957).

Selznick's scoring notes for *Gone with the Wind* once again reflect a sensitivity to music and its relationship to characters and narrative space. Explaining his rationale for switching between extra-diegetic music for Melanie and Ashley and diegetic music for Scarlett with her beaux at the Twelve Oaks barbecue, Selznick wrote:

> this few hundred feet is important in that it is the only glimpse we get of the rich and aristocratic side in the whole picture plus being the introduction of the Ashley–Melanie relationship and plus being our first opportunity to contrast Melanie and Scarlett musically and therefore, [make] the most lasting impression.[32]

Selznick also prompted other important changes, such as the addition of voices to the tune of "Dixie" heard during the film's foreword (a memorable touch) and Steiner's revisions of the final sequence between Scarlett and Rhett.[33] In such instances, Selznick did not merely prescribe a desired musical effect; he also reacted to what the composer had already realized. Upon listening to a selection of newly recorded cues for *Gone with the Wind*, Selznick remarked:

> I am very much afraid that we may be overdoing the Mammy theme, and I wish that you would have [music director] Lou [Forbes] or someone check carefully where we are using it in proximity to this use, both before it and after it. … The trouble is that we are forced to do the picture backwards and sideways and we have no accurate perspective on where and how often we are using the themes, and where and how often in relation to each other. And I think Lou ought to prepare a chart immediately showing the use of all the themes, reel by reel, so that we can take one look at this chart and see where there is any danger of repetition or too much use too close together.[34]

Whether Lou Forbes made a chart or not, Selznick's attention to thematic placement demonstrated unusual sensitivity to music's affect and structural balance within the film.

Of course, such close attention to the film's orchestral underscore could also prompt resistance from composers. Rózsa bristled when he received Selznick's notes for *Spellbound* (1945) and later claimed that he "completely disregarded all [of Selznick's] 'musical' ideas."[35] (Comparison between Selznick's notes and Rózsa's music quickly disproves this assertion; Rózsa in fact followed Selznick's instructions closely.) Scrawling on the back of a cue for *Since You Went Away*, Steiner vented his own frustration at the producer's requests for rewrites: "Alteration #64!!!! MUSIC BY DAVID O. SELZNICK."[36] For *Duel in the Sun*, Tiomkin had to rewrite many of the film's cues. The composer retold this unfortunate circumstance in a humorous anecdote in his memoirs, although one doubts that at the time Tiomkin found the situation funny.[37] On the positive side, these same composers all seemed to approach Selznick's notes as a hurdle worth mounting. Passages in Rózsa's, Steiner's, and Tiomkin's scores for Selznick evince similar efforts to follow and elaborate upon the producer's instructions (often by inserting additional themes or setting multiple themes in counterpoint). In this respect, Selznick's intense involvement paid off in unexpected ways. His instructions presented a challenge to composers; they responded by overachieving.

An important recurring theme that arises across the producer's scoring notes is a repeated call for pre-existing music. These suggestions range from the simplistic, such as Selznick's request that Steiner use "Auld Lang Syne" as an associative theme in *Fauntleroy*, to the elaborate, such as Selznick's request that *Gone with the Wind* be supported with a tapestry of period-appropriate music.[38] In between these extremes are many scoring notes in which Selznick encouraged—in the spirit of Stothart—the inclusion of familiar works that audiences might recognize and enjoy. When *Intermezzo* (1939), a film about two classical musicians, received positive notice in the press, Selznick expressed gratitude to music director Lou Forbes and Max Steiner:

> The score on *Intermezzo* is receiving a great deal of comment and extraordinary favorable attention, for which I thank and congratulate you both.
>
> The outstanding point that has been commented on by so many, and that certainly has served to make the score so beautiful, is its use of classical music to such a great extent instead of original music hastily written. This is a point on which I have been fighting for years with little success.[39]

With his final Hollywood film, *Portrait of Jennie*, Selznick would at last have the opportunity to realize this ambition to its fullest extent.

A Hollywood Finale

David O. Selznick's wistful *Portrait of Jennie* begins with billowing clouds that circle to the music of Debussy's *Nuages*. As an unseen narrator contemplates notions of time and timelessness, the clouds part to reveal a hazy view of Manhattan as seen from the sky. This nebulous introduction sets the tone for the rest of the film: characters move about dimly lit locales, musing vaguely on the ability of love and art to defy the progression of time. The music of the film contributes to the haze and disorientation, in part because the score features the gauzily textured works of Claude Debussy, whose meandering melodies and idiosyncratic harmonic progressions withhold the grounding of regular phrases and cadences. Yet even these familiar Debussy pieces possess an uncanny quality, distorted by composer Dimitri Tiomkin for the context of the film. Seeking to articulate this unusual ambience, one critic described *Portrait of Jennie* as "brave and tender, wrapped protectively in the wispy dress of fantasy."[40]

The score for *Portrait* is one of the most ambitious and complex musical projects of Selznick's career, and it yields valuable insights under careful scrutiny. Months before *Portrait's* scoring began, Selznick anticipated that the film would require the services of a musician willing to tackle "difficult music problems" as the film's "quality is straining for something extraordinary in music."[41] Perhaps because the film was so different from previous productions and its fantasy-based story was so vulnerable to disdain, Selznick turned to the score with unprecedented vigor, hoping to improve—and perhaps redeem—a production that had been plagued with difficulties.[42]

Portrait of Jennie follows the life of Eben Adams (Joseph Cotten), a struggling New York City artist who decides to paint a portrait of Jennie, a young girl he has met in the park. Every time Eben sees Jennie, however, she has aged noticeably; she claims that she is "hurrying" to catch up with him. As Jennie approaches Eben's age, the two fall in love. Then Eben learns that Jennie is a ghost from the past—she died in a hurricane at Land's End Light in the 1920s. Adams visits Land's End Light on the anniversary of her death and reunites with Jennie before she is swept away by a tidal wave. In the film's epilogue, Adams's portrait of Jennie is shown hanging at the Metropolitan Museum of Art, where it is visited by young women who admire Adams's artistry and his muse.

For *Portrait* Selznick considered no fewer than eleven different composers, including Stothart Steiner, Gian Carlo Menotti, Benjamin Britten, and Deems Taylor.[43] He initially settled on Herrmann. In February of 1947 Herrmann wrote a song that Jennie sings in the film, so in July of 1948 he was rehired to write the rest of the score. But when Herrmann abruptly left the production for unknown reasons (perhaps chagrined by Selznick's persistent involvement), Selznick hired Tiomkin to arrange a score based on themes of Debussy.[44] Although the idea of using Debussy had been suggested to Selznick by screenplay writer Francis Brennan, the approach connected both with contemporaneous scores like that of David Lean's *Brief Encounter* (1946, a film featuring a score based entirely on Rachmaninoff's Piano Concerto No. 2) and, more importantly, silent film practices. As Kurt London noted in his 1936 survey of silent-era accompaniment: "There were cinema conductors who avoided compilations and accompanied good films with fragments out of the works of one single composer. This happened at times with music by Debussy and Tschaikowsky."[45] Lawrence Morton's accusation that Selznick had plundered musical techniques of the silent era for *Portrait* was absolutely correct. It was also more appropriate than Morton acknowledged: *Portrait* relied upon other antiquated cinematic techniques (color tinting, old-fashioned camera lenses, and D.W. Griffith-inspired special effects) to tell a story in which past and present melt together; the musical score helped further the effect.

There are eight sets of music notes for *Portrait*, with dates ranging from July 21 to October 2, 1948. With the exception of the first set, which appears to have been supplied by Herrmann before it was annotated and expanded by Selznick, all the other notes come from Selznick. The documents reveal many interesting details, such as a "Key to themes" in the notes from July 31, 1948, which lists five pieces by Debussy and specifies their extra-musical associations. From this page one learns that excerpts from *Prelude to the Afternoon of a Faun* signal "Jennie's comings and goings" and her "prescience," whereas *The Girl with the Flaxen Hair* represents "Eben the artist re[garding] Jennie: sketches, portrait, etc."[46] This notion of a musical piece emphasizing a character's subjectivity recurs in numerous scenes in which the music fulfills a meta-diegetic function. For Eben and Jennie's "First Meeting in the Park," for example, Selznick instructed that "After [they] rise from [the park] bench, trail into small thin prelude to Jennie's song, as though tune in her head." Later, Selznick asked Tiomkin to "score as if tune in [Adams's] head" and "JENNIE'S SONG in Eben's thoughts to bring in Jennie musically."[47]

Like Steiner's early 1930s scores at RKO, which had contrasted narrative space through the presence and absence of music, so Selznick's notes for *Portrait* evince a keen appreciation for music's power to both delineate and blur multiple levels of fantasy. On the one hand, Selznick specifies that either musical silence or traditional Irish music (Eben's cab-driving buddy is Irish) signal 'real' world scenes in which Jennie is absent. Scenes in which Eben and Jennie are united—either in thought or actuality—feature Debussy-infused underscore. Music cues featuring "Jennie's Song" (originally composed by Herrmann and later inserted among Debussy-based passages) signal yet another level: the mysterious past from which Jennie is able to occasionally emerge and transcend.

Selznick used different types of music to characterize the fluid shifting between Adams's 'regular' life and Jennie's supernatural intrusions; he also manipulated the diegetic and extra-diegetic musical boundary to give the film's supernatural ambience an especially unstable character, heightened to a large extent by the privileging of Adams's subjectivity through the voice-over narrations and musical underscore. In one montage, for example, Adams explains in a voice-over that "my memory was beginning to play tricks on me. I was seized by memories so urgent that they were more real to me than what was before me." After this statement, Adams is shown listening in a concert hall to an adapted and densely re-orchestrated passage of *Prelude to the Afternoon of a Faun*. Adams's voice continues over the music: "Everything reminded me of Jennie." His remark causes the bombastic orchestral sounds to fade mysteriously away, allowing an eerie rendition of Jennie's song performed on novachord and violin harmonics to emerge. Oddly, this new music, which seems to reflect a melody heard in Adams's head, matches with the emphatic gestures of the orchestra conductor. In this scene and others, the division between diegetic, extra-diegetic, and meta-diegetic becomes increasingly vague.[48]

Although through his prolific notes Selznick clearly directed the placement and narrative function of music, Tiomkin played a key role in the selection of Debussy's works. Scoring notes from Selznick that predate July 30 are devoid of references to Debussy, although they do specify the placement of music within scenes and the inclusion of associative themes (i.e., "Dark water theme" "Jennie youth theme"). Writing at 6:00 in the morning on July 31, Selznick noted that he and Tiomkin had spent the entire night selecting Debussy pieces to satisfy the score's thematic outline. The session had proven exhilarating for the producer, who exclaimed: "The music of the picture in my opinion has every chance of being the most distinguished and revolutionary score ever written."[49] Thus, while Tiomkin played a critical role in helping select Debussy works and excerpts, these selections had to be fitted to a thematic scheme previously drafted by Selznick.

Considering this tight framework, Tiomkin responded with admirable creativity. Working with only six of Debussy's compositions,[50] Tiomkin utilized melodic relationships embedded in Debussy's original pieces to draw musical ties between themes that shared interrelated extra-musical associations. For example, Tiomkin takes two distinct but related passages from the First Arabesque (mm. 1–17; mm. 39–46) and employs them as Jennie's "youth" theme and Jennie's love theme, respectively. By emphasizing certain shared melodic traits across the themes, Tiomkin strengthened the score's thematic coherence while also thickening and redesigning Debussy's textures.[51] As Lawrence Morton indignantly but rightly observed, *Portrait of Jennie* does not feature the music of Debussy but, rather, the themes of Debussy. Yet, in spite of Morton's abhorrence, some critics, like Selznick himself, found the transformation of familiar music into the new medium appropriate if not exactly groundbreaking: "Debussy's music—'lifted' by Hollywood for years, now openly acknowledged—becomes another shimmering Hollywood score 'written and conducted' by Dimitri Tiomkin, celestial chorus and all. It will heighten the popular response to this strange and beautiful 'portrait.'"[52]

In the end, *Portrait* was a testament to both the producer and the composer/ arranger. The score represented Selznick's most detailed and invested musical efforts, and Tiomkin's arrangements had encapsulated—as much as any single score could—ideals of film music that Selznick had fashioned, championed, and honed since the 1930s. Considering that *Portrait of Jennie* would be Selznick's last American-made film, its score represents a fitting farewell to the Hollywood sound that Selznick had helped shape.

Notes

1 "Movie Music Makes Progress: 'Hearts & Flowers' to Debussy," *Washington Post*, January 9, 1949.
2 Ibid.
3 Lawrence Morton, "Selznick's Debussy," *Rob Wagner's Script*, March 1949, 36.
4 Ibid.
5 In tone and content, the first article reads like a studio press release; it may well have been one. Morton, meanwhile, had committed many of his recent writings to illuminating the artistry of contemporary film scores. In this respect, he and Selznick (hereafter abbreviated as "DOS") stood on common ground, but their aesthetics were diametrically opposed. Selznick's conservative tastes, which evinced themselves in *Portrait of Jennie* in a Debussy-based score, were anathema to Morton, who believed film music's future had to rely upon original efforts that engaged with modern musical trends. See Lawrence Morton, "The Music of *Objective Burma!*," *Hollywood Quarterly* 1, no. 4 (July 1946): 378–95.
6 Kathryn Kalinak, *How the West Was Sung: Music in the Westerns of John Ford* (Berkeley: University of California Press, 2007), 12.
7 Selznick, for example, liked a theme from Steiner's music for *A Star is Born* (1937) titled "Janet's Waltz." (The theme is associated with the character of Esther;

"Janet" refers to Janet Gaynor, the actress playing Esther.) "Janet's Waltz" is used in Selznick's *Rebecca*, thereby replacing Franz Waxman's original music in one scene. The waltz is also reworked in Steiner's score for Selznick's *Since You Went Away* (1944).

8   Matthew Bernstein, "The Producer as Auteur," in *Auteurs and Authorship: A Film Reader*, ed. Barry Grant (Malden: Blackwell Publishing, 2008), 180–9.

9   David Denby, "The Real Rhett Butler," *The New Yorker* 85, no. 15 (May 25, 2009): 78.

10 Selznick expressed his admiration for silent-era filmmaking to Kevin Brownlow, who published the producer's fond recollections in *The Parade's Gone By* (New York: Alfred A. Knopf, 1968), 431. In 1941 the producer also advocated for the preservation of both silent and sound film scores at the Museum of Modern Art, a remarkably prescient recommendation. See the letter from DOS to John Abbott, 19 February 1941, reprinted in *Memo from David O. Selznick: The Creation of "Gone with the Wind" and Other Motion Picture Classics, As Revealed in the Producer's Private Letters, Telegrams, Memorandums and Autobiographical Remarks*, ed. Rudy Behlmer and Roger Ebert (New York: Modern Library, 1972), 308.

11 "Picture to be Given Operatic Underscore," *Los Angeles Times*, April 3, 1932, B18.

12 Another reason the music for *Fighting Caravans* likely went unnoticed is that the music's authorship was both collective and hidden. Nine composers worked on the score, but none was listed in the film's credits: John Leipold, Max Bergunker, Emil Bierman, A. Cousminer, Karl Hajos, Herman Hand, Emil Hilb, Sigmund Krumgold, and Oscar Potoker.

13 One rare notice in the press has been identified by James Wierzbicki. See *Film Music: A History* (New York and London: Routledge, 2009), 123.

14 This musical divide is later broached to great dramatic effect at an important turning point in the story. When the protagonist's girlfriend takes the unprecedented step of visiting his uptown office to remind him of his responsibility to his home community, the extra-diagetic score accompanies her entry into his office, signaling the penetration of a professional sphere that had previously been kept separate.

15 Leo Meehan, "'Symphony' Rated As Classic," *The Hollywood Herald*, March 23, 1932.

16 Max Steiner, "Notes to You: An Unpublished Autobiography," 1963–1964, Max Steiner Collection, L. Tom Perry Special Collections Library, Harold B. Lee Library, Brigham Young University, Provo, Utah (hereafter abbreviated as "MSC"), Box 1, Folder 1, 113–14.

17 See Robbin Coons, "Vidor Uses Technic [sic] of Silent Days," undated clipping in Scrap Book 1, MSC, Oversize Box 8.

18 Murray Spivack, "Recording Breakdown," August 13, 1932, RKO Studio Records, Performing Arts Special Collections, University of California, Los Angeles (hereafter abbreviated as "RKOSR"), Box P-18, Folder A602.

19 RKO Daily Musicians' Reports for *Symphony of Six Million*, RKOSR, Box P-16, Folder A 585. See also Rudy Behlmer, "King Kong: The Eighth Wonder of the World," liner notes for Max Steiner, *Original Motion Picture Soundtrack: King Kong*, Rhino Movie Music, 1999, compact disc.

20 "Classical Composers Banished from Hollywood," *Los Angeles Times*, October 16, 1932, B10.

21 DOS to Katharine Brown, August 30, 1937, David O. Selznick Collection, Harry Ransom Humanities Research Center, The University of Texas at Austin, Box 1237, Folder 3. (Hereafter, citations of documentation from this collection will be shortened to the following format: "HRC 1237:3.")

22 DOS to Herbert Stothart, January 16, 1935. The author thanks William Rosar for sharing a digital scan of the memo.

23 DOS to Victor Barravale, April 24, 1935. A digital scan of the memo was shared by William Rosar.

24 Herbert Stothart, "Film Music," in *Behind the Screen: How Films Are Made*, ed. Stephen Watts (London: Arthur Baker Ltd., 1938), 139.

25 See, for example, a cover story provided by the composer himself about his work with Selznick: Max Steiner, "Music Hath Charms," *Box Office*, August 22, 1936, 1.

26 *Since You Went Away*, for example, has scoring notes of both types.

27 "LITTLE LORD FAUNTLEROY, Musical scoring to be made for," January 8, 1936; David O. Selznick, "LITTLE LORD FAUNTLEROY, Music Notes," January 23, 1936; David O. Selznick, "LITTLE LORD FAUNTLEROY, Music Notes," January 31, 1936, HRC 463:6.

28 This phenomenon exemplifies Mark Slobin's concept of *erasure*: "Who gets sound-space and who gets silence carries major cultural meaning" (Mark Slobin, "The Steiner Superculture," *Global Soundtracks: Worlds of Film Music* [Middletown: Wesleyan University Press, 2008], 22).

29 Max Steiner, "Reel 1, Part III," *Little Lord Fauntleroy*, MSC Volume 101.

30 "GWTW Music Notes, Compiled," November 6, 1939, HRC 413:5.

31 "Gone with the Wind Music Notes Corrected by DOS," November 7, 1939, HRC 413:5.

32 "Gone with the Wind, List of Scenes for Possible Scoring," November 30, 1939, HRC 413:5.

33 See DOS to Lou Forbes, November 10, 1939, HRC 1237:3 and "Notes on Music, For Maxie to Re-Write, in Order of Importance," December 4, 1939, HRC 413:5.

34 DOS to Lou Forbes and Max Steiner, November 17, 1939, HRC 1237:3.

35 Miklós Rózsa, *A Double Life* (New York: Wynwood Press, 1982, 1989), 147.

36 Max Steiner, "Reel 12, Part 4, Alteration," MSC Volume 141, back of single-sided page 1.

37 Dimitri Tiomkin and Prosper Buranelli, *Please Don't Hate Me* (Garden City: Doubleday & Company, Inc., 1959), 220–2.

38 DOS to Max Steiner and Lou Forbes, October 9, 1939, reprinted in *Memo*, 225–6.

39 Ibid.

40 Reviewing *Portrait of Jennie*, one critic wrote: "The late Percy Hammond, review-ing for the *N.Y. Herald Tribune*, used to employ the phrase 'brave and tender play' to describe a drama that showed sensitivity but failed to provide a valid dramatic experience in the theatre. *Portrait of Jennie* is brave and tender." *Fortnight* 6, no. 1 (January 7, 1949): 31, in *Selected Film Criticism, 1941–1950*, ed. Anthony Slide (Metuchen, NJ: Scarecrow Press, 1983), 192.

41 DOS to Milton Kramer, HRC 1151:9.

42 The filming of *Portrait* is not addressed here, but the film's various hitches and obstacles during production are summarized by Thomson (see 498–502) and are covered in detail in John Matthew Miller, "David O. Selznick and His *Portrait of Jennie*" (master's thesis, University of Texas, 1987). Shooting on location in New York was particularly difficult and the camera work of cinematographer Joseph August was not always deemed satisfactory by Selznick (see David Thomson, *Showman: The Life of David O. Selznick* [New York: Alfred A. Knopf], 498–9). Problems were further aggravated by trouble off the set, such as the alcoholism of managing producer David Hempstead and threats of suicide from Jennifer Jones, the leading lady.

43 The list of composers considered by Selznick for *Jennie* includes, but is not limited to, Bernard Herrmann, Herbert Stothart, Max Steiner, Hugo Friedhofer, Richard Hageman, Roy Webb, Franz Waxman, Aaron Copland, Gian Carlo Menotti, Benjamin Britten, and Deems Taylor. Selznick also considered engaging Toscanini to conduct the score as "clearly, the job would not require very much of Toscanini's time" (DOS to Milton Kramer, undated, HRC 1151:9).

44 For more on Herrmann's involvement, see Thomas DeMary, "The Mystery of Herrmann's Music for Selznick's *Portrait of Jennie*," *The Journal of Film Music* 1, no. 2/3 (2003): 153–82.

45 Kurt London, *Film Music: A Summary of the Characteristic Features of Its History, Aesthetics, Technique; and Possible Developments*, trans. Eric S. Bensinger (London: Faber & Faber Ltd., 1936), 60.

46 "'JENNIE'—MUSIC NOTES," July 27, 1948, Dimitri Tiomkin Collection, Cinema-Television Library, Edward L. Doheny Jr. Memorial Library, University of Southern California, Box 49, 2.

47 Ibid.

48 Robynn Stilwell insightfully suggests that such musical passages of diegetic/ non-diegetic ambiguity might be theorized as spanning a "fantastical gap," an idea that works particularly well in the case of *Portrait*: "Like any liminal space, [it] is a space of power and transformation, of inversion and the uncanny" (Robynn J. Stilwell, "The Fantastical Gap between Diegetic and Nondiegetic," in *Beyond the Soundtrack: Representing Music in Cinema*, ed Daniel Goldmark, Lawrence Kramer, and Richard Lepper [Berkeley: University of California Press, 2007], 186).

49 DOS to Paul MacNamara, July 30, 1948, HRC 944:4. Although the memo is dated July 30, Selznick admits in the text of the memo that it is early morning and that he has stayed up all night. The memo was likely written early on July 31.

50 Tiomkin had wanted to use more, but Selznick could only afford to pay permissions fees for six works: Arabesques Nos. 1 and 2, "The Girl with the Flaxen Hair," *Prelude to the Afternoon of a Faun*, and "Clouds" and "Sirens," both of which are from *Nocturnes*.

51 Tiomkin's adjustments in orchestration have received both praise and criticism from modern scholars. See William Rosar's comments in DeMary, "The Mystery of Herrmann's Music," 177; Sarah Reichardt, "Commodity vs. Artwork: Timelessness and Temporality in the Music for *Portrait of Jennie*," paper presented at The Hollywood Musical and Music in Hollywood conference, Boulder, Colorado, 2001.

52 Philip K. Scheurer, "Sentiment, Showmanship Unusual Blend in 'Jennie,'" *Los Angeles Times*, December 27, 1948, 15.

Chapter 10

The Stanley Kubrick Experience

Music, Nuclear Bombs, Disorientation, and You

Kate McQuiston

The evidence for Stanley Kubrick's importance and influence as a director of English-speaking cinema in the second half of the twentieth century lives in numerous pages in the scholarly and critical literature dedicated to the man and his craft, on fan web pages and in the blogosphere, and in perennial homages, parodies, references, and imitations in popular culture. Kubrick is famously preoccupied with man's individual and collective self-destructive tendency. His films witness the spectacular unraveling of the best-laid plans, failsafe devices, robberies, computers with no record of error, and men who become perfect killing machines. Characters' personalities are flattened out in favor of a focus on the social hierarchies and other systems that circumscribe them; workings of the military and issues of class difference recur across his oeuvre. Kubrick's world is harsh, but often beautiful and not without hope. His visual language includes languid tracking shots, expansive pacing, meticulously crafted lighting and effects, and an array of striking frame compositions—the product of a photographer's mind, and ready-made for iconic posters—that suggest his intensive care for the overall look of things. But counting and cataloging these attributes still does not add up to Kubrick. Most important in Kubrick is really what cannot be seen and what is not said—the deep substrata of human drama, moral fissure, and psychology. He seems to want us to be uncomfortable enough that we long remember and mull over his cinematic confrontations with difficult themes and problematic characters.

If the essence of Kubrick eludes what we can objectively describe and account for, as I suggest, what place might music have in spectators' experiences of his films? This chapter explores how music plays a major part in Kubrick's distinctive style and 'feel.' As an invisible and nonverbal art that nevertheless can readily communicate and connote, music asserts itself uniquely in Kubrick, often along the lines of both familiarity and surprise.

On the Audience and the Role of Music

Music in Kubrick is illuminated by the expectations the director had of his audience and his tendency to think in musical terms. On the matter of audience involvement, Kubrick remarked:

> Nobody wants to be told anything. And anything they discover for themselves has the difference between a nuclear bomb and a firecracker, in terms of its ability to energize their sensibilities. If you discover it for yourself, it's everything, and if somebody tells it to you you don't want to know it.[1]

For Kubrick, explication was the enemy of art, and he expected his audience to be attentive, involved, and curious, to be looking for something other than a pat story line, or a world in which things are indeed what they seem. His films are for searchers and ponderers, for people who like puzzles and games, and who enjoy playing "Name That Tune."

The main problem that Kubrick must solve in his filmmaking, therefore, is one of striking a balance between giving us just enough to put things together but not so much that we sit back and stop thinking. His goal is one of affect—of stirring something up—without crowding the spectator out of his own space in which he can play and create meaning. Music, an art known to prompt a similar, open-response opportunity for its audience, is uniquely qualified among the cinematic elements to engage the spectator with respect to the entire film. What's more, music is the only element, with the debatable exception of voice-over narration, that has the privilege of permeating the film's entire atmosphere both diegetically and on *our* side of the screen. K.J. Donnelly's description of music in film as having supernatural qualities is a fitting tribute to its uncanny and unbridled qualities.[2] Because of its multivalence, music is cinema's rogue element; depending on its context, it can act like a magical or multiply bondable molecule. In Kubrick, music often plays 'out in the open,' and just as often it grabs our attention for its style or mood in combination with the images and drama.

But even the answer to the question "What makes a Kubrick film sound like a Kubrick film?" cannot be simple. Consider the eclectic array of the films, and the fact that they run the gamut of five decades and the technological trappings that came with them. Each film has its own aural world, made up of music, sound, and voices, and across the films the musical selections seem to have little in common: Wendy Carlos's bending pitches and morphing electronic timbres; popular songs; original music by Gerald Fried, Nelson Riddle, and Jocelyn Pook; arrangements by Laurie Johnson and Leonard Rosenman; waltzes; dance band tunes; an array of classical music. The list as a whole hardly describes the 'sound' of Kubrick. Nor does the mention of any single work borrowed from the concert hall. For example, Bartók's *Music for*

Strings, Percussion and Celesta in Spike Jonze's *Being John Malkovich* (1990) animates the film's characters (literally) and the quirky surrealism of the narrative, but it is a far cry from the same music's turn in Kubrick's *The Shining* (1980); for Martin Scorsese's psychodrama *Shutter Island* (2010), music supervisor Robbie Robertson chose the very same Ligeti composition, *Lontano*, featured in Kubrick's *The Shining*, and yet *Shutter Island* does not look or sound at all like the work of Kubrick.

Kubrick's sonic style is best detected in how the films *feel*; Kubrick films feel "a little bit off," as *New York Times* critic A.O. Scott succinctly puts it, and "our disorientation is the strongest evidence of the filmmaker's mastery."[3] How Kubrick orchestrates this peculiar balance between control and subjectivity, a sense of disorientation that is nonetheless compelling and aesthetic, relies on an interplay of cinematic parts that depends on the selection and, more important, the implementation of music.

Disorientation, however, is a tool wielded not by Kubrick but by his spectators. Kubrick's is a cinema of inference, even when the narrative seems clear, and it is also a cinema of *aesthetics*. It is cinema to be *sensed* as understanding takes a back seat, or comes upon reflection. Kubrick said that "a good film, like a piece of music … should be able to be seen more than once,"[4] and he likened the act of watching and rewatching a film (if it had "substance") to the way "you re-read a book or hear a piece of music."[5] He occasionally spoke about music's special powers, and about the limitations of words. In an interview with William Kloman, for example, he said:

> There are certain areas of feeling and reality—or unreality or innermost yearning, whatever you want to call it—which are notably inaccessible to words. Music can get into these areas. Painting can get into them. Non-verbal forms of expression can. But words are a terrible straitjacket. It's interesting how many prisoners of that straitjacket resent its being loosened or taken off.[6]

In an interview with Joseph Gelmis, Kubrick touched on the topic again: "Movies present the opportunity to convey complex concepts and abstractions without the traditional reliance on words. I think that *2001*, like music … is able to cut directly through to areas of emotional comprehension."[7]

If we're watching and listening to the films again and again, as Kubrick hoped we would, we begin to notice things—moments of synchronization of music and image, for example—that, once detected, become indispensable to our experience, if not our understanding, of the scene and of the entire film. These moments—those described as ironic, surprising, uncanny, uneasy, hilarious, delightful, disruptive—so many of which involve music, are the little loose threads Kubrick hopes we will pull in attempts to find a way 'in.' The likelihood that many of the classical works probably don't initially register for most audiences as 'borrowed' does not stop this music from having a profound effect on the listener for other reasons, and it does not mean that the listener cannot later discern musical functions and significance.

The films have given rise to abundant and varied discussion, and *2001: A Space Odyssey* (1968) in particular has been analyzed, explicated, and unraveled by all manner of approaches. The point seems to be the inquiry itself, and the joys of speculation and discovery. David Patterson has called *2001* "the quintessence of the filmic Rorschach," and his analogy easily describes the wide responses just to the movie's use of Johann Strauss's *Blue Danube Waltzes*.[8] Patterson's own discoveries of musical interrelationships across *2001* of course depend upon the multiple viewings that Kubrick had in mind, as well as upon score study at a level of detail worthy of classics in any genre—the kind of attention that gives its object a life of its own.

Kubrick marvels at questions of *how* we perceive and respond to film, and high on his agenda is the hope that we notice and enjoy these things. Rather than question 'meaning' in *2001*, Kubrick prefers that audiences seek 'experience,' and this word perhaps best frames response to his entire oeuvre. What he says regarding *2001* applies here: "Our interest, in the film, is more in *man's response* to his first contact with an advanced world."[9] This is both a subject and an experience that he wants for his audience, just as the Ludovico treatment in *A Clockwork Orange* (1971) is both displayed and meted out.

All of this room for subjectivity and indeterminacy would seem to challenge the image of Kubrick's famous control over every aspect of his filmmaking, his pursuit of perfection, and his reputation as an *auteur*. But for Kubrick, a good film leaves blanks for the audience to fill in, and leaves them free to discover the films for themselves. These factors have greatly played into the cult status his films have attained—'cult' appropriately evoking the spiritual and the mysterious, and befitting the ritual of repeated viewing.

The Music Lover behind the Camera

Among directors of English-speaking cinema, Kubrick is well known for employing large swaths of concert-hall music whose turns in Kubrick's films live on in popular culture. More important than any aspiration to 'high art' is Kubrick's sheer love of music. He was ever listening to music, and buying new recordings, in every genre. He listened with his films in mind, and he was as sensitive to composers as he was to performers. In *2001* it is not simply Strauss's *Blue Danube Waltzes* that the audience hears; it is the *Blue Danube Waltzes* as interpreted by Herbert von Karajan and the Berlin Philharmonic. Likewise, the movement from an obscure Vivaldi cello sonata featured in *Barry Lyndon* (1975) comes across with singular beauty in Pierre Fournier's playing. For *Eyes Wide Shut* (1999), Kubrick narrowed his choice for a recording of Mozart's *Requiem* down to three, and then he had to pick one—a task that must have been both difficult and delightful for such a music lover.

Kubrick played music on the set to get actors into the right mood for a scene, and he attended recording sessions whenever he could. Musical selections for the finished films were a matter of taste, but they had to meet numerous other requirements. His audition process was rigorous and depended upon factors that varied from case to case; the music might have to fit the diegesis, match the source material, impart particular connotations, or provide a certain mood and tempo, or it might simply have to fit the length of a particular scene. And it might need to do *all* of these things. Extensive documents in the Kubrick Archive in London, and in particular a large notebook devoted to planning the music for *Barry Lyndon*, attest to the attention Kubrick and his production team devoted to the aesthetic, legal, and mechanical issues of incorporating music into a film.

Not surprisingly, Kubrick was concerned about how things sounded in the theater. He was so enthusiastic about Dolby Stereo Optical Sound when it became available that he sent letters to Mel Brooks, Mike Nichols, Irwin Allen, Roman Polanski, William Friedkin, George Lucas, and Woody Allen. "If you have heard Dolby Stereo Optical Sound, and like it," he wrote, "would you be willing to write a short blurb for Dolby to use in a trade ad, the purpose of which is to help convince theater owners they should equip themselves to run it?"[10] For *Barry Lyndon*, Kubrick went to unusual lengths to proscribe and ensure the conditions of exhibition. With prints of the film came letters addressed to the projectionist with a litany of precise requirements pertaining to sound, including instructions for the playing of an enclosed LP record or tape in the theater during the intermission.[11] As is evidenced in memos, he also sent men, in the manner of secret agents, out to theaters all over the United States and Europe to check that these conditions were met. In a memo dated September 7, 1977, and titled "Barry Lyndon – Investigation and checkout 'Look' Theater, Stockholm, complaint," Ray Lovejoy reports:

> The pre-performance music was identifiably Barry Lyndon—and also fed through to the foyer, where the audience mingled enjoying a last cigarette, etc., prior to taking their seats. This was repeated in concept during the intermission, there being a no smoking ban in the cinema.

Such measures bespeak not only Kubrick's high expectations of everyone who had a hand in bringing the film to fruition but also his passionate interest in the realization of a fully developed aesthetic world for his audience.

Existing Works

There is no doubt that an existing piece of music can help at the box office. It is a trick as old as cinema itself, and still alive and well, as evident in the seemingly relentless use of pop songs in contemporary film. Whether the borrowed material comes from the repertoire of popular song or classical music, films have long benefited from its recognizability and artistic cachet.

Kubrick's achievements with music have been somewhat overshadowed by the attention devoted to his infamous rejection of original music that Alex North wrote for *2001: A Space Odyssey* in favor of existing works; Kubrick's decision was a great disappointment to North, in spite of Kubrick's declared intention, at the start of the project, to attempt to get rights for the existing works that he wanted to use. Kubrick's process of musical selection and securing rights for *2001* has been the subject of several recent studies.[12] For some, his rejection of North in favor of classical works may have cast classical music as the arch enemy of the contemporary composer, although the persistence of Beethoven, Mozart, and countless other composers of the past and the relative scarcity of living composers on the programs of symphony orchestras worldwide has been in evidence for decades, and Kubrick's later films involve both original and existing music. Kubrick's greatest offense (to those offended) with *2001* may have been that he succeeded with the choices he made—Richard Strauss and Johann Strauss Jr., Ligeti, and Khachaturian—and one must wonder what the terms and tenor of the musical choice debate would be like had *2001* been a flop. Kubrick was surely pleased to be entwining his own work with that of his favorite composers, and he took great pains to choose and employ these composers in his films. Directors who borrow music stand to benefit from the great likelihood that the spectator will encounter this music again in another context, recognize it, and remember the film in which he or she first heard it; the music is a form of free and serendipitous—yet uncontrollable—advertising.

Among Kubrick's classical picks are many relatively little known works, and this raises questions, especially in cases in which audience familiarity seems unlikely, as to what factors motivated the choice of one work over another. At one point in the making of *Barry Lyndon*, for example, Kubrick wanted to use Vivaldi's *Four Seasons*, but he changed his mind, likely when he ran into legal difficulties, or found something more favorable. There is correspondence in the Kubrick Archive that concerns the need for the consent of the musicians' union in order for a recording of the *Four Seasons* to be used in the film, but this seems inconclusive.[13] Failure to reach an agreement, or a timeline too short to allow him to secure consent, may have steered Kubrick toward other solutions. In any case, it is easy to imagine a slow movement from the *Four Seasons* substituting for the arrangement of a movement from a Vivaldi cello sonata that accompanies the melancholy scenes following the wedding of Barry and Lady Lyndon. Paul Bazelaire's sensitive arrangement and the emotion of cellist Pierre Fournier's performance amplify the music's expressive powers to near-romantic levels. Elsewhere in the same film, Kubrick passes over the more familiar passages of Mozart in favor of the more pedestrian and less remarkable march from *Idomeneo*. Perhaps for the transitional moments when this excerpt is used, any other Mozart work would have been overqualified—too interesting, too lyrical—for the job.

Kubrick studied other filmmakers and was keenly aware of his contemporaries and their use of music. One of Francis Ford Coppola's most celebrated moments is his use of Wagner's *Ride of the Valkyries* in *Apocalypse Now* (1979), and this impressed Kubrick. The striking music in William Friedkin's *The Exorcist* (1973), particularly the music by George Crumb and Krzysztof Penderecki, clearly influenced the soundtrack for *The Shining*. Kubrick's attention to other directors, and his tendency to use musical ideas to describe them, suggests he saw the director's role as similar to the role of the composer in previous eras. In an interview before the release of his *Full Metal Jacket* (1987), Kubrick mused:

> Now, I would say that Coppola, if you are going to compare [directors] to composers, I would say that Coppola would be like Wagner and I would like to think of myself as Mozart. I like to have that precision and the correctness—classical rather than romantic.[14]

In the sense that Kubrick plays with the topics his borrowed music evokes, and considering his sensitivity to careful musical alignment with images, "classical" is indeed a fitting term. Yet considering the potential surprises and sometimes sly humor in his image-music pairs, Kubrick would seem to be less like Mozart and more like Haydn.

Richard Wagner, a giant of the classical world and monumentally important forerunner of twentieth-century concepts about film music, was evidently a preoccupation of Kubrick, although for whatever reasons Kubrick never featured Wagner's music in his films. For *Dr. Strangelove* (1964), correspondence in the Kubrick Archive shows that the director had planned at one point to use Wagner, but it is not clear which music Kubrick had in mind, or which scenes. Anthony Burgess's first screenplay draft for *A Clockwork Orange* specified: "Another day of treatment, shots of people burning in bombed city streets, interspersed Nazi smiles and laughs of triumph, set to 'Wagner's fire music from *Götterdämmerung*.'"[15] A notebook Kubrick kept in 1980 devotes eleven pages to Wagner's *Ring* cycle; it details plot points, character motivation, and mythological precedents, and it traces causes and effects over the course of the entire colossal opus. The purpose of this exercise is unclear, although one possibility is that Kubrick had it in mind for a future project, possibly his unfinished 1990s project—titled *Aryan Papers*—about the Holocaust. Kubrick may have been hesitant to release the film on the heels of Steven Spielberg's phenomenally successful *Schindler's List*, which came out in 1993; after all, Kubrick's hopes of making a movie about Napoleon had been similarly discouraged by the appearance in 1970 of Sergei Bondarchuk's *Waterloo*.

For the scenes in *Eyes Wide Shut* that include Györgi Ligeti's *Musica ricercata*, Kubrick had first intended to use just the piano accompaniment of Wagner's song "Im Treibhaus," from the song cycle *Wesendonck Lieder*;

he decided against it because he felt the music was "too beautiful."[16] Appropriate to the film's plot, however, the *Wesendonck Lieder* were born of Wagner's love for a woman other than his wife; appropriate to the many uncertainties in *Eyes Wide Shut*, it still is not known if Wagner's affections for Mathilde Wesendonck ever led to an affair.

We might be tempted to compare the very controlling Kubrick with Wagner, but his openness to improvisation and collaboration make him quite unlike Wagner. Kubrick's self-comparison with Mozart is in several ways more apt. Mozart was a freemason, and Kubrick resembles a freemason both in his intellectual vigor and curiosity and in his secretive, artistic collaboration with the many bright minds in his company. Whereas Wagner's mythical worlds and music exist unto themselves, Mozart's operas play with musical styles and details of contemporary culture that his audience knew and encountered everyday, and certain Mozartean elements—capitalization on the recognizable music, humor, self-reference—are also found in Kubrick. But where Kubrick departs from Mozart, of course, is in his confrontations with that central modernist trope, the ugliness and violence of man.

If we survey Kubrick with classical music in mind, we find works that cover a wide range of likely recognizability. At one end of that range, Strauss's *Blue Danube Waltzes* and Beethoven's Ninth Symphony are probably the most recognized, and thus the most discussed. The use of Beethoven in *A Clockwork Orange* proved especially provocative, mainly because of the music's association with the violent protagonist Alex. Champions of Beethoven were faced with the uncomfortable fact that, while Kubrick might be exposing new audiences to Beethoven, he was linking the music with a dangerously seductive criminal; it is not the context most people would have thought of, and probably not one many Beethoven fans would espouse, despite its historical resonance.[17] The negative reaction to Alex's love of, and association with, Beethoven, and the casting of Beethoven as the handmaiden of Alex's violent impulses, recalls the response in the musicological community to Miloš Forman's 1984 film *Amadeus*.

Robert L. Marshall describes the outcry over the "liberties" in *Amadeus* that distorted facts of the composer's biography and the complaints about the film making Mozart a victim of commercial interests.[18] Marshall defends the film, however, reminding us that Mozart himself depended upon commercial interests. Indeed, as is well documented in letters he wrote to his father, Mozart was always mindful of the public's taste—he might have been thrilled at the resurgence in the popularity of his music through Forman's film. Those who would decry *Amadeus* in the name of preserving historical truth (or for the sake of some other personal investment in a composer and his image) miss the advantages such a film can afford. Marshall gets at what's really at stake:

> [I]f, armed with the shield of their poetic licenses, [authors and film directors] are going to trash the facts of history and, along the way

perhaps, cast a baleful light on the reputations of great and famous men, then they had better be prepared to redeem the historiographical insult with a sufficient portion of poetic truth, justice, or some other compelling form of adequate compensation.[19]

In Marshall's view, the return on *Amadeus*, which he considers a thoughtful drama, was an enormous surge of popular interest in Mozart, and well worth the film's inaccuracies.

For those in the audience who know and love the music they suddenly hear in a Kubrick film, the experience could be, as Marshall has it, an "insult," for being new and seemingly against the grain. Alex in *A Clockwork Orange* experiences an extreme version of such a situation when Beethoven's music appears in a Nazi propaganda film he is forced to watch as part of his conditioning. The 'problem' with both *Amadeus* and *A Clockwork Orange* is that they represent apparent affronts to the histories of the composers or, to put it in more quotidian terms, to the composers' reputations. Kubrick's supposed crime is defaming Beethoven's cherished 'heroic artist' image and suggesting that, long after his death, he is running with a bad crowd. More distressing and much more important than the violence, however, is Kubrick's exposure of Beethoven's mutability, ambiguity, and outright flaws.[20]

Objections to new contexts for classical works, whatever they may be, seem to assume that the music has a stable identity, but reinvention and reappropriation have always been the name of music's game. Even contemporary attempts to reinvent a work in its 'original' form are best understood as exactly that: contemporary attempts. But when a new rendition or context seems to go against the spirit (if not the letter) of the work, hackles go up. Music's ontological slipperiness, on the other hand, is precisely what allows old works to live on through reinvention in new forms, and it is a large part of the logic behind the persistent production of recordings and performances of the same works again and again by different artists. Anyone who knows a musical work well is likely to have a strong reaction to each new concert rendition and to every multimedia form—contexts that differ much more in degree than in kind.

All of this is not to campaign for the widespread and wholesale use of classical music in multimedia (one would think objectors would find a work's falling into obscurity to be a far worse alternative). Rather, the point here is, first, to display some of the reasons why borrowed works can pack such a punch and access the audience in ways that seem personal and thus effective. Second, this discussion supports a concept of Kubrick as a kind of composer in his own right. Kubrick is not the only director to use classical music, but he knows how to put things together for optimum effect, and he succeeds remarkably in making the music seem to 'belong' to a film. Indeed, his own frequent comparisons of film and filmmaking to music suggest that music was at the heart of his approach to cinema.

Anyone can plunk an existing work into a piece of film and come up with something new and possibly compelling. The very fact of Kubrick's borrowing, and the fact that he seems to have done it so well and so strikingly, has distracted from the virtuosity and variety with which he does so. As the discussion of Beethoven in *A Clockwork Orange* shows, strategies of analyzing music in film depend upon the music in question. An analysis of art music in *A Clockwork Orange* or *Eyes Wide Shut* will likely attend to the music's status as diegetic or extra-diegetic, but that question doesn't apply to the art music in *The Shining*; this film calls for different tools, such as those David Code inventively offers.[21] While Kubrick's use of one movement of Bartók's *Music for Strings, Percussion and Celesta* has prompted its listeners to speculate about how the work's other movements might relate to the film, this same possibility lies unexplored, indeed unprompted, in relation to *A Clockwork Orange*. Such selective treatment of music is no accident; *The Shining* is designed musically and otherwise to reach beyond the frame in an almost supernatural manner, while *A Clockwork Orange* directly addresses and reframes our previous musical experiences and with great specificity bears upon our subsequent musical experiences.[22]

Kubrick makes ironic or unusual musical choices to open upon new areas and reach beyond the moment of seeing and hearing, beyond the initial perception of "unusual" and "ironic." But, as the array of detailed responses to the *Blue Danube Waltzes* in *2001* indicates, such combinations will soon leave any dichotomy in the dust. From each scene to the next, there are substantive differences between Kubrick's uses of music, and a wide variety of musical-dramatic techniques that transcend matters of origin and idiom. It is beyond the scope of this chapter to attempt a full exploration of how Kubrick manages to make the music in his dramas germane, as though it is both artifact and cause, even in cases when it defies expectation, or rubs against the affective grain. But the first steps in such an exploration would depend on those moments in which Kubrick reveals his hand in the design. Claudia Gorbman has made astute observations on the pitch relationships throughout *Eyes Wide Shut*; she points out the meaningful connections one can make by following Kubrick's clues, and looking and listening as closely as I believe Kubrick wants us to.[23] With similarly rigorous attention to detail, David Code offers an inventive interpretation of *The Shining* via the graphic bent of Penderecki's scores; his findings support an analysis of the film's dooming view of literacy in a capitalist world.[24] Such studies raise questions and open up new possibilities for reading and experiencing Kubrick's films.

Kubrick's efforts to get the most out of his music means making sure that the music's structures and shapes are detectable—something aided by editing that tailors the music more closely to the action, and in many cases tailors the visuals to the music. We might notice a synch point, and then another one. In this way, Kubrick fosters the sense that music *belongs*. He also calls our attention to the music by pairing narrative action with musical-expressive

qualities that seem somehow 'off'; these moments teasingly invite the attentive spectator to look for patterns that spring from the music, and they foster
spectator interest in the music both during the film and afterwards. Then
again, we might already know something about the music Kubrick borrows,
and as a result we understand the narrative in a new way. Making 'off' choices
in the soundtrack is Kubrick's way of telling us that what we get *isn't* just what
we see.

Kubrick's Legacy

Robert Marshall proposes that *Amadeus,* historical inaccuracies and all, was a
champion for the cause of classical music in general and to a certain extent
reinvented Mozart for contemporary audiences. In much the same way,
Kubrick reinvents his composers by orchestrating the encounters his audience
will have with them. Kubrick's ability to reach new and young audiences for
classical music, however, comes through his transformative interpretations. It
is as though Kubrick has set you up with his very attractive friend and then
comes along on your first date. And on your second date, as well. Kubrick's
methods of musical integration—and insinuation—give the music its sticking
power, and they make it unlikely that audiences will ever forget his role.

But Kubrick's greater achievement lies in the rearrangement and revision of
his chosen classical works—after *2001: A Space Odyssey,* the *Blue Danube
Waltzes* just didn't sound the same. When he employs lesser known works,
Kubrick benefits in a different way because of the absence of cultural memory
by which spectators might measure the experience; because for the unfamiliar
spectator the music lacks precedent, in such cases the music seems all the
more to *belong* to Kubrick. K.J. Donnelly wonders whether Richard Strauss's
Also sprach Zarathustra is an outstanding work in its own right, and he holds
that we may never know because we cannot divest it of its various contexts,
most of all its use in *2001.*[25] And Michel Chion observes that "it has become
difficult for many people, myself included, to hear the 'Blue Danube' Waltz
without thinking of spaceships."[26]

Kubrick achieves a nervy balance between fulfilling the promise of a subjective experience and offering something that is technically worked out
and artful. In developing the commonplace of incorporating existing music
into film in a conspicuous and finely nuanced game of mixing and matching,
Kubrick is a model, maybe even a patron saint, of remixes and multimedia mashups—the stuff that anyone can do, but few can do well. The play-
fulness of this description perhaps evokes the postmodern, but Kubrick
is ultimately in complete earnest, and what may seem to be the surface
whimsy of surprising musical choices gives way to bleak and difficult realities
underneath. Kubrick's surprises and juxtapositions are not disposable jokes;
they pose serious questions about the nature of film and art, and about their
relationship to spectatorship.

James Naremore's persuasive portrayal of Kubrick's cinema as modernist explores the interplay of aesthetic and conceptual opposites, and Kubrick's approach to music at least superficially belongs to this tradition.[27] Music is the main ingredient in Kubrick's signature 'off' quality, the disorientation that keeps us coming back for more in spite of the confrontations his films present, the disorientation that keeps his films open, alive, and always awaiting discovery.

Notes

1 Stanley Kubrick, interview with William Kloman (New York, April 1968), unpublished transcript. Stanley Kubrick Archive, University of the Arts, London.

2 K.J. Donnelly, *The Spectre of Sound: Music in Film and Television* (London: BFI, 2005), 8.

3 A.O. Scott, Critics' Picks: "Lolita," *New York Times*, July 26, 2010, available at: http://video.nytimes.com/video/2010/07/26/movies/1247468048570/critics-picks-lolita.html?ref=movies.

4 Stanley Kubrick, interview with Françoise Maupin, October 8, 1987, unpublished transcript. Stanley Kubrick Archive, University of the Arts, London.

5 Stanley Kubrick, interview with Danièle Heymann, "Un entretien avec le réalisateur de 'Full Metal Jacket'; Le Vietnam de Stanley Kubrick," October 20, 1987, unpublished transcript. Stanley Kubrick Archive, University of the Arts, London.

6 William Kloman, "In 2001, Will Love be a Seven-Letter Word?" *New York Times*, April 14, 1968, D-15.

7 Joseph Gelmis, "Interview with Stanley Kubrick," in *Perspectives on Stanley Kubrick*, ed. Mario Falsetto (New York: Macmillan, 1996 [orig. 1970]).

8 David Patterson, "Music, Structure and Metaphor in Stanley Kubrick's '2001: A Space Odyssey,'" *American Music* 22, no. 3 (Autumn 2004): 444.

9 Kloman, "In 2001, Will Love be a Seven-Letter Word?" D-15 (emphasis added).

10 Stanley Kubrick, telex to Dick Lederer, July 8, 1975. Stanley Kubrick Archive.

11 Stanley Kubrick, letter to the projectionist, December 8, 1975. Stanley Kubrick Archive.

12 Paul Merkley, "'Stanley Hates This But I Like It!': North vs. Kubrick on the Music for *2001: A Space Odyssey*," *Journal of Film Music* 2, no. 1 (Fall 2007): 1–34; Julia Heimerdinger, "'I am compromised. I now fight against it.' Ligeti vs. Kubrick and the Music for *2001: A Space Odyssey*," *Journal of Film Music*, 3, no. 2 (2011): 127–43; Kate McQuiston, "'An effort to decide': More Research into Kubrick's Music Choices for *2001: A Space Odyssey*," *Journal of Film Music*, 3, no. 2 (2011): 145–54.

13 A letter in the Kubrick Archive describes the wish to use the *Four Seasons* as produced by the Academy of St. Martin in the Fields. Jan Harlan to Mr. Hibbert of the Musicians' Union, September 10, 1975. Stanley Kubrick Archive.

14 Kubrick, interview by Danièle Heymann (translation from English transcript of the interview, 34, Stanley Kubrick Archive).

15 Anthony Burgess, "A Clockwork Orange," first screenplay draft, undated, 54. Stanley Kubrick Archive, University of the Arts, London.

16 Jan Harlan, Interview with the author. St. Albans, Hertfordshire, England, June 24, 2008.

17 It was well known that the Nazis were fans of Beethoven, and Scott Burnham and Robynn Stilwell are two scholars who have identified an original and continuing

concept of a violent Beethoven. See Scott Burnham, "Beethoven, Ludwig van," *New Grove Dictionary of Music and Musicians*, second edn, 114, and Robynn J. Stilwell, "Hysterical Beethoven," *Beethoven Forum* 10, no. 2 (2003): 162–82. See also the author's more detailed discussion of the history of violence in regard to Beethoven's Ninth Symphony and *A Clockwork Orange*: Kate McQuiston, "Value, Violence, and Music Recognized: *A Clockwork Orange* as Musicology," in *Stanley Kubrick: Essays on His Films and Legacy*, ed. Gary D. Rhodes (London: McFarland and Company, 2008), 105–22.

18 Robert L. Marshall, "Film as Musicology: *Amadeus*," *Musical Quarterly* 81, no. 2 (Summer 1997): 173–9. The screenplay for Forman's film is based on Peter Schaffer's 1979 play of the same title.

19 Marshall, "Film as Musicology: *Amadeus*," 174.

20 For a more developed discussion, see McQuiston, "Value, Violence, and Music Recognized: *A Clockwork Orange* as Musicology."

21 See David Code, "Rehearing *The Shining*: Musical Undercurrents in the Overlook Hotel," in *Music in the Horror Film: Listening to Fear*, ed. Neil Lerner (New York and London: Routledge, 2010), 133–51.

22 See Donnelly, *The Spectre of Sound: Music in Film and Television*, 37, 41–2.

23 Claudia Gorbman, "Ears Wide Open: Kubrick's Music," in *Changing Tunes: The Use of Pre-Existing Music in Film*, ed. Phil Powrie and Robynn J. Stilwell (Aldershot: Ashgate, 2006), 3–18.

24 Code, "Rehearing *The Shining*: Musical Undercurrents in the Overlook Hotel."

25 Donnelly, *The Spectre of Sound: Music in Film and Television*, 14.

26 Michel Chion, *Kubrick's Cinema Odyssey* (London: British Film Institute, 2001), 91.

27 James Naremore, *On Kubrick* (London: British Film Institute, 2007).

Chapter 11

The Filmmaker's Contract

Controlling Sonic Space in the Films of Peter Greenaway

Ian Sapiro

Peter Greenaway is a successful painter, and a leading writer and director of independent British films. His approach to filmmaking owes much to the influence of European films produced in the late 1950s and early 1960s, "probably focused most on Antonioni, Pasolini, Godard and Resnais," whose films he watched as soon as they opened in England.[1] His early experiences in the distribution department of the British Film Institute (BFI) and as an editor for the Central Office of Information (COI) were also significant in broadening his awareness of the possibilities of cinema,[2] although as Amy Lawrence states, some of his early short films were "virtual parodies of the kind of work done at the COI," owing to "a growing disillusionment with the concept of 'documentary truth.'"[3] Greenaway's first funded pictures, A Walk through H and Vertical Features Remake (both 1978, backed by the BFI and the Arts Council, respectively), were produced toward the end of his time at the COI, and they laid the foundations for what is probably his most prolific and popular period of filmmaking.

Between 1978 and 1991 Greenaway wrote and directed around a dozen films with scores by composer Michael Nyman. They are particularly distinctive for Greenaway's individual visual style, significant use of allegory (which is often of equal or greater importance than narrative), the strong influence of art, and Nyman's minimalist-influenced soundtracks. There are several publications which investigate Greenaway's narrative structuring and use of metaphor,[4] and the relationships between his films and art (through his painting and the work of other artists),[5] but music and sound are often largely overlooked or considered only in passing. Since it is during the years of his collaboration with Nyman that Greenaway established himself as a sound-conscious director, this chapter focuses on the films produced in this period, which demonstrate his authorial control over the sonic as well as the visual elements of his films.

The Greenaway/Nyman Collaboration

Alan Woods observes that "music is vitally important to Greenaway," and he emphasizes that Greenaway's use of music in film, like so much of what he does, contrasts with mainstream cinema.[6] Greenaway's unconventional approach to filmmaking, coupled with Nyman's relative inexperience as a film composer (his only experience of scoring for film prior to Greenaway's *Vertical Features Remake* was the 1976 British comedy *Keep It Up Downstairs*), meant that the two were not constrained by the normal practices or conventions of film scoring. Nyman's music "did not come after, or simply match, the action or images. It was introduced as a component in its own right, linked rather to the intellectual structures of the film … than to individual characters,"[7] and it was generally composed to a plot synopsis or structural outline before Greenaway had even shot the visual footage. Consequently, in the initial stages of a project both practitioners were able to operate with greater creative freedom than was usually found in the industry as they produced their part of the final film. Greenaway and Nyman shared an aesthetic perspective in which the aural space of a film was as important as the visual. As Greenaway noted:

> We are both concerned to find some equitable balance between music and the visual image. Traditionally in the filmmaking process, the visual image is decided on and the composer is brought along at a much later stage, which puts music in a secondary, even tertiary position, which I find unsatisfactory.[8]

So although the two creators worked in relative isolation, the intention was always that this would lead to greater unity between visual images and musical score since one would not be dependent on, or be present purely to support, the other. However, although Nyman appears to have been granted a level of freedom generally not afforded to most film composers, Greenaway actually maintained a strong authorial hand on the music for his pictures. He comments that on a typical film project "Michael Nyman and I, before a word of the script is written, discuss structures in terms of musical perception,"[9] implying that the musical frameworks for their films were constructed through a collaborative process. However, this does not always appear to have been the case; the schemes for *The Draughtsman's Contract* and *Drowning by Numbers* were both determined by Greenaway, and Nyman was told that his score for *1–100* should provide a suitable rhythm to which Greenaway could cut the film. In an extreme case, Greenaway wrote the screenplay for *Prospero's Books* while listening to an album of Nyman's music, without the composer even aware that a film project was in the offing.[10]

Accordingly, Nyman's musical expression was always contained within Greenaway's overarching concept of the film's sound. Furthermore, the absence of specific timings, hit points, and spotting notes (there were no spotting sessions for any of their films), and the nature of Nyman's music as long pieces rather than closely timed cues, allowed Greenaway not only to make decisions regarding the placement and duration of the music but also to construct a new musical scheme for a film once the score and visuals were both recorded.

Nyman has remarked that "at the point of synchronising the music with the picture then it's sort of taken out of [the composer's] hands,"[11] and Greenaway has admitted that "I'm not sure I always used [the music] in the way Michael Nyman intended" in his films.[12]

The University of Leeds holds the Michael Nyman Film Music Archive, a collection of materials donated to the institution by the composer on long-term loan for the purposes of scholarly study and research. The Greenaway films feature prominently, with a variety of materials including multi-track recordings and supporting documentation for *1–100* (1978), *The Draughtsman's Contract* (1982), *A Zed and Two Noughts* (1985), *Drowning by Numbers* (1988), *The Cook, the Thief, His Wife and Her Lover* (1989), and *Prospero's Books* (1991). Additionally, the resource contains a number of press cuttings relating to films for which Nyman provided scores, and those from the Greenaway collaboration are again prominent. The following case studies focus on three relatively high-profile films that span the Greenaway/Nyman collaboration (*The Draughtsman's Contract*, *Drowning by Numbers*, and *Prospero's Books*), combining the existing scholarship on Greenaway with information drawn from the Nyman Archive to demonstrate Greenaway's control over the sonic landscapes of his films.

The Composer's Contract

Greenaway's original proposal to the BFI for funding toward *The Draughtsman's Contract*, a period drama-cum-murder mystery set in England in 1694, included a sheet detailing the musical scheme for the film. "Appendix 4: Music" was accompanied by "a 45 rpm disc of a 'transfigured' Mozart theme by Michael Nyman,"[13] and Greenaway outlined how this music, and other, similarly adapted works, would form the sonic structure of the film.

The music scheme being considered was to take twelve such original music themes by Purcell, Handel (to keep it English—if naturalized English), Lully or (to cheat a little on dates) Bach and Mozart, and "transfigure" them for *The Draughtsman's Contract*, one theme for each drawing. The scheme was also to use this presently recorded "transfigured" Mozart (remixed perhaps to minimize the horn) as an overall signature—for titles and credits and as ironic accompaniment for the long montage sequence called "Reconaissance [*sic*]" in the plan of the film.[14]

It is unusual for a director to have such a clear idea of the music for a film before a project has even been commissioned or funded, and this example emphasizes that the sonic aspects of Greenaway's work feature heavily in his thinking from an extremely early stage in the creative process. The "transfigured" Mozart in the proposal is Nyman's *In Re Don Giovanni*, which "draws on the first section of Leporello's Act 1 'Catalogue' aria 'Madamina, il catalogo è questo' [from the opera *Don Giovanni*, and which had] obvious intertextual resonances with the draughtsman's sexual liaisons with mother and daughter."[15] Nyman reports that Greenaway heard *In Re Don Giovanni* at a concert in 1977 and as a result approached him to work on *The Draughtsman's Contract* and other films.[16] Greenaway's intention to include the piece in the film's score is important since it demonstrates his predilection for using both Mozart and pre-existing music within his films, themes which will be revisited below in the considerations of *Drowning by Numbers* and *Prospero's Books*.

The musical structure for *The Draughtsman's Contract* was adjusted between proposal and production, owing in part to the practicalities of film length, but the underlying premise remained intact. The transfigured Mozart was removed, and Nyman chose six ground basses by Purcell on which to base themes representing the six drawings which would feature in the film. His choices were in keeping with Greenaway's original intentions that the music should be both English and period-specific (which perhaps explains the removal of the Nyman/Mozart from the film), and he composed ever more complex variations on each ground bass to reflect the drawings as they progressed from sketches to completed drafts across a period of six days. The recorded cues are clearly labeled according to drawing and day numbers (e.g., "Drawing 1, Day 1"), but ultimately these tags bear little resemblance to their placement in the film. Once recording was complete, Nyman handed the multi-track mixes over to Greenaway, giving control of the film's sonic landscape back to the director to shape as he saw fit. Instead of trimming Nyman's music to fit the intended scenes, Greenaway instead matched music and images according to his own perception of "best fit," as Nyman explains:

> As the film starts, the first exterior that you see is the draughtsman's assistant pushing sheep around, so I thought for the music we'd have the most basic version of this ground bass .... But in the meantime Peter had listened to the music not as a dictator of structure but just as a punter. He listened to the piece that we know as "Chasing Sheep is Best Left to Shepherds", which is the most evolved of the six versions of this particular ground bass, and said, "This would be an amazing opening for a film." ... So structure goes completely out of the window in terms of the way the music is used.[17]

Despite devising the original musical framework for the film himself, Greenaway clearly felt that the structure had served its purpose once the score had been completed, and it was his desire to "find an equivalence of image and music ... a useful collaboration—not just a music-servicing relationship" that guided his placement of Nyman's cues in the film.[18] A strict matching of drawings to cues according to the original scheme, each growing in complexity through the film, may have worked against this ideal, since the score could then be seen merely as supporting ("servicing") the visual images.

Table 11.1 Cues used in *The Draughtsman's Contract*, in running order[19]

Cue	Name	Cue	Name
1	Queen of the Night	17	Drawing 5
2	*Drawing 1*	18	Drawing 6
3	*Drawing 2*	19	*Drawing 1*
4	*Drawing 3*	20	*Drawing 6*
5	Queen of the Night with Mistakes	21	Drawing 1
6	*Drawing 5*	22	Drawing 6
7	*Drawing 6*	23	Death of Neville Section B (sax)
8	Drawing 1	24	*Drawing 3*
9	Drawing 2	25	*Drawing 6*
10	Drawing 3	26	Death of Herbert Section A (twice)
11	Drawing 5	27	Death of Herbert Section C
12	Drawing 6	28	Death of Neville (sax)
13	*Drawing 1*	29	Return of Neville
14	*Drawing 2*	30	Death of Neville
15	*Drawing 3*	31	Drawing 1 (closing credits)
16	Drawing 1		

There are several cycles visible in Table 11.1, but what the table does not show is which of the variations are used in each cycle. As the above quote from Nyman details, the first appearance of the music for Drawing 1 (cue 2) is the most complex version of the theme, so despite Drawing 1 starting six cycles (plus the closing credits), it is not possible for the variations to be heard in the order originally intended by the composer. Greenaway took control of the aural environment, not only removing some cues (resulting in partial cycles) but also employing each theme's variations arbitrarily depending on the demands of the screen. Additionally, some of the cues heard in the film only partially represent the music recorded in the studio, with instrumental parts omitted from the film mixes despite being present on the multi-track recordings handed from Nyman to Greenaway.

By remixing the multi-track cues, Greenaway shows the remarkable attention to detail he pays to the sound of his films, and this emphasizes the degree to which he approaches sound with a strong authorial hand. He has remarked that "a lot of the information is contained on the soundtrack" for *The Draughtsman's Contract*,[20] calling it "an important binding element … between the sound and the images."[21] It is clear from the way in which the cues are used within the film that it is the director, not the composer, who has decided precisely what the soundtrack should communicate. Greenaway's fingerprints can be found all through the musical construction of the score, from the original ideas regarding sources and structures to the ordering, placement, and manipulation of individual cues; these are traits that are also found in later Greenaway/Nyman films.

Composing by Numbers

Drowning by Numbers focuses on three women named Cissie Colpitts—a grandmother, her daughter, and her niece—who drown their husbands and enlist the local coroner, Madgett, to help cover up their crimes.[22] Alongside this narrative, Greenaway places the numbers one to one hundred into the film, sometimes obviously, and sometimes more obscurely. This is a conscious reference to one of his earliest films, *1–100*. As noted above, Greenaway requested that the score for that film provide him with a cutting rhythm, and Nyman has stated that because of this referential link he considered a similar score for *Drowning by Numbers*:

> I was on the point of saying to Peter, "Yes, I can do another 1–100 score," when I thought, "Hold on a minute, I could spend a long time manufacturing this score and trying to write it in such a way that it can be integrated in all these numerical units, or the musical equivalent, [which] could be integrated into proper cues." And then I thought, "Don't go there, because the system will be corrupted and I'll just waste my time."[23]

But Greenaway's controlling instinct for all aspects of his films had already led him to another of his previous productions. In 1964 he had "bought a job-lot of 78 rpm gramophone-records [… and] in that collection was an old recording of Mozart's [Sinfonia] Concertante for Violin, Viola and Orchestra [K364]."[24] He had requested that Nyman's score for *The Falls* (1980) be based on a short passage from the slow second movement of the Sinfonia, and he returned to that piece as the source for all of the music in *Drowning by Numbers*. Nyman composed twenty-five cues to this brief, recording the music in mid-February and early March 1988; the recordings were then given to Greenaway, enabling him to exercise full authorial control over the sound of the film. As shown in Table 11.2, Greenaway appears to have adopted the same patchwork approach as in *The Draughtsman's Contract*, repeating and omitting cues, using some in full and some in part, and in one instance remixing the recording to change the sound. Accordingly, although the score was written by Nyman, it was originated, arranged, and structured by Greenaway.

For some cues, Nyman provided Greenaway with alternative mixes from which the director could choose, such as 3M1 ("Water tower" and "Bath" mixes) and 3M2 ("Thin" and "Full"),[25] although neither the gramophone mix of 4M4 nor the mix of 9M2 heard in the film were created by the composer. There are very few occasions where Greenaway used a cue in its entirety

Table 11.2 Musical cues heard in *Drowning by Numbers*

Cue number[26]	Cue name	Greenaway's use and manipulation of the cue
4M1	Trysting Fields	Starts 2.18 into cue, runs for 0.55, then cuts abruptly to the start and fades out after a further 2.38
–	Mozart Sinfonia	Runs for nearly 2.00 (twenty-eight bars) from start of the movement
1M2/2M1	Sheep and Tides	Stops abruptly after 0.17 as telephone stops ringing
1M2/2M1	Sheep and Tides	Stops abruptly after 0.38 as telephone stops ringing
2M4	Wheelbarrow Walk	Starts 1.20 into cue and runs to end of cue
1M2/2M1	Sheep and Tides	Whole cue (1.40)
1M2/2M1	Sheep and Tides	Starts 1.09 into cue and runs to end of cue
3M1 (Water tower)	Great Death Game	Stops abruptly after 1.00
3M2 (Full)	Dead Man's Catch	Runs for 1.14 then cuts abruptly back to start, running for a further 1.13
4M1B	(Part of) Endgame[27]	Whole cue (0.38)
4M1	Trysting Fields	Stops abruptly after 2.37
4M4	Bees in Trees	Remixed to sound as if it is being played diegetically on the gramophone. Stops abruptly after 1.32
3M1 (Water tower)	Great Death Game	First ten seconds repeated, then whole cue (1.08) heard
1M2/2M1	Sheep and Tides	Whole cue (1.40)
1M2/2M1	Sheep and Tides	Fades out after 1.22
4M1C	(Part of) Endgame	Whole cue (0.50)
6M4	Drowning by Number 2	Fades out after 1.56
–	Mozart Sinfonia	Runs for 1.30 (twenty-five bars) from start of the movement
5M1	Crematorium Conspiracy	Starts at 1.42 and runs to end of cue
3M1	Great Death Game	Fades out after 1.06
4M1	Trysting Fields	Fades out after 1.14. After a short break for dialogue fades back in at 1.21 and ends abruptly after 0.50
–	Mozart Sinfonia	Runs for 1.15 (twenty-three bars) from start of the movement
9M2	Fish Beech	Fades out after 2.15. Remixed to remove some sounds

Continued

Table 11.2 Cont'd

Cue number	Cue name	Greenaway's use and manipulation of the cue
4M1E	(Part of) Endgame	Whole cue (0.50)
4M1	Trysting Fields	Starts 1.14 into cue and fades out after a further 1.14
–	–	Starts abruptly and fades out. This music does not appear on any of the materials in the Nyman Archive, and is not on the soundtrack album. Its origins are unknown
–	Mozart Sinfonia	Runs for 6.13 (eighty-nine bars) from start of movement, omits forty-three bars, and runs for 1.18 (sixteen bars) to end of the movement
12M1, 4M1, 4M1C, 4M1E	(Part of) Endgame	Combination of several other cues from the film which does not exist in this form on any of the recordings: opening of 12M1, middle of 4M1, whole of 4M1C, returns to 4M1 having omitted a few bars, whole of 4M1E

without any form of alteration, and eight of Nyman's compositions, including the opening credits, were excised completely.

The original Mozart movement is heard following the drowning of each husband by his respective Cissie, and in the final scene it foreshadows Madgett's demise at the hands of all three Cissies. Greenaway uses the music as a narrative device, informing us that Madgett has served his purpose, is now surplus to the Cissies' requirements, and will be dispatched to a watery grave. Similarly, "Sheep and Tides" (cue 1M2/2M1) is heard under a number of voice-over explanations of Madgett's games given by his son, Smut.[28] In the first two instances Greenaway cuts the music abruptly as the telephone stops ringing, synchronizing the end of the music with the sound effect without concern for the integrity of the musical phrase. These false starts mirror Cissie #1's failed attempts to contact Madgett regarding the death/drowning of her husband, Jake, and the cue is eventually heard in full as she and Cissie #2 finally speak to him. However, other games are introduced by different cues, demonstrating Greenaway's penchant for selecting cues according to his perception of the required sonic accompaniment for each scene.

There are a number of cues in the film that do not exist in 'film form' on any of the session recordings made by Nyman, and the introduction of artificial repeats and the construction of the closing credits from four of the existing cues emphasizes the control Greenaway had over the sound of the film. Perhaps the most significant contribution the director made to the aural landscape of *Drowning by Numbers* in post-production was the insertion, near the end, of a cue that appears to have no sources at all in the Nyman Archive despite there being twenty-four reels containing multi-track or stereo recordings related to the film. It is possible that this is a piece of pre-existing music, like the Mozart Sinfonia, which also does not appear on any of the reels. If so, its stylistic congruence with the rest of the score perhaps indicates that Greenaway interpolated an existing Nyman composition into the film, setting a precedent for the Greenaway/Nyman collaboration *Prospero's Books*.

Prospero's Scores

In an interview with Andreas Kilb following the release of *The Cook, the Thief, His Wife and Her Lover* in 1989, Greenaway remarks that his next film will be based on Shakespeare's *The Tempest*, "a variation on that play, to which I have given the working title *Prospero's Books*."[29] The film has been described by Marlene Rodgers as "operatic in its use of music, song, [and] dance,"[30] so it is perhaps not surprising to find that music was a significant feature in the writing of the screenplay. As with his previous projects, Greenaway devised a musical structure for the film based on pre-existing material before meeting with Michael Nyman. In this case, however, the pre-existing music came from Nyman himself. Nyman explains:

> In 1989 I did a sequence of music, like a film score, for an exhibition in Paris to celebrate 200 years of the French Revolution [*La Traversée de Paris*]. ... There was a soundtrack album too, which I gave to Peter just to show him what I was up to, and he had written the whole of *Prospero's Books* listening to this music. He had already designated particular tracks to particular sequences.[31]

Jonathan Coe, in his review of the *Prospero's Books* soundtrack CD, observes that "at least six of the instrumental pieces are taken from *La Traversée de Paris*,"[32] and comparison of the two soundtracks (see Table 11.3) reveals that in fact seven tracks from *La Traversée* appear in Greenaway's film.[33] However, despite basing the musical scheme of the film around Nyman's music and constructing some of the scenes with particular pieces in mind, Greenaway once again exercised his artistic control over the sonic environment of *Prospero's Books* after receiving the completed tracks from the composer. Holly Rogers observes that "the director added loud and obtrusive sound effects to several of Nyman's pieces, clamorous noises that almost buried the completed instrumentation, and edited others to [remove] their instrumental accompaniment."[34] Nyman noted that his "beautifully crafted soundtrack was

Table 11.3 Tracks from *La Traversée de Paris* used in *Prospero's Books*

Track from La Traversée	Cue from Prospero's Books	Transformation
1. L'entrée	Prospero's Magic (opening titles)	Additional repetitions, layers of new music
3. Débarcadère	Reconciliation	No change
4. Le Labyrinthe	Come unto these Yellow Sands	Additional vocal line toward end of track
7. Le théâtre d'ombres chinoises	Miranda	Some sections omitted
9. Du faubourg à l'Assemblée	Prospero's Curse	No change
11. Passage de l'Égalité	Cornfield	No change
14. Cinéma d'actualités	History of Sycorax	No change

hedged around with some rather juvenile student electronics that no-one had warned [him] about."[35]

In addition to music and sound effects, the film's aural environment includes dialogue (spoken almost exclusively by Sir John Gielgud) and voice-over announcements describing each of Prospero's books. Thus the film's sound, like its visuals, comprises numerous overlaid elements that compete for space. Greenaway believes a viewer is able to understand and prioritize the multi-layered visual images, yet he asserts that similarly interpretative listening is not possible:

> Which takes precedence, the dialogue or the music? There's an inevitable battle. Unlike the eye, which has the ability to sort things out, the ear doesn't have that ability. So unless you organize things very well, you just get a whole cacophony of noise that is very difficult to sort. You have to be careful about mixing music [and] dialogue to make sure there's coherence and sympathy.[36]

Evelyn Tribble states that "Greenaway, [production sound supervisor Garth] Marshall and ... Nyman create a dense and unsettling cinematic soundscape through a sometimes uneasy collaboration,"[37] and the film's balance of speech, sound effects, and music bears out these tensions. Sonically, the film opens with sound effects—droplets of water—before Prospero's first words and the voice-over introduction to the Book of Water elevate speech to the top of the soundtrack hierarchy. The first musical cue is significantly delayed, the opening credits ("Prospero's Magic") only starting at 5:32, once the film has progressed to scene 13.2.[38] The music never truly rises to the top of the sonic pyramid: it is first overlaid with multiple voices, then competes with the sounds of fire and water before being overwhelmed (the music actually stops and fades back in later in the scene) by sound effects that include storm noises and some rhythmic and almost musical elements as Prospero's tempest builds. This sets the tone for the rest of the film, in which Greenaway generally relegates music to the lowest level of the soundscape so that the ear can easily detect the appropriate speech or sound effects.

Music is allowed to occupy the forefront of the aural space only toward the end of the film, during the almost ten-minute-long masque to which the union of Ferdinand and Miranda is choreographed. Although the opening is briefly obscured by sound effects and a voice-over for the Book of Mythologies, Greenaway quickly establishes music as the aural focus; the scene features three on-screen vocal soloists to emphasize the interlinking of song and narrative at this point. However, the presence of on-screen singers does not guarantee music's place in the sonic hierarchy, and Ariel's songs (mimed on-screen by a young boy, and sung by soprano Sarah Leonard) are not spared the director's treatment. There are moments when each of the five songs briefly inhabits the sonic foreground, but they all fade relatively rapidly to become background music beneath sound effects or dialogue that includes a number of voice-overs describing various of the books. Perhaps most tellingly, Prospero's controlling voice can be heard speaking the lyrics for each song, a metaphor for Greenaway's continued presence in—and ultimate power over— Nyman's music and the film's sound in general.

The Music, the Director, His Control, and its Impact

As these case studies have demonstrated, Greenaway's influence on and control over the sound of his films far exceeds what might normally be expected of a director. Evidence drawn from the materials in the Nyman Archive demonstrates that Greenaway was more heavily involved in the musical aspects of his films than is apparent simply from viewing the finished pictures, and that he took an active role in the creation of the music in both pre- and post-production. He devised the musical frameworks and, to some extent, specified the source materials to be used by Nyman in the composition of his scores, a procedure that reflects the parameters of their collaboration and the relative control exercised by each practitioner.

Paradoxically, Nyman's initial creative freedom to compose without the requirement to complement particular actions or fit specific timings resulted in him having less control over the finished product than might normally be the case, since Greenaway was similarly not constrained by predetermined synchronization points and as a result had significantly greater flexibility when combining sound and image. Comparison of the multi-track recordings and the film soundtracks shows that Greenaway took an active role in the post-production of his scores; far from simply sitting in the booth at recording sessions and balancing levels when dubbing, he rearranged, remixed, and reordered the recorded cues when matching music and image. Greenaway's control was so absolute that Nyman might not actually have heard the music within the context of the picture until the opening night of the film's release.

Greenaway has admitted that he "[has] been accused of wanting too much control—of having too much obsession for every detail."[39] As this investigation has shown, such detail includes the sound of his films. It is perhaps not surprising that the film in which Greenaway exerted the greatest influence as a 'sonic auteur'—*Prospero's Books*—brought about the end of his partnership with Nyman, who felt that his music had been compromised not by Greenaway's revision of the musical structure of the film in post-production (which he was expecting) but because "all the artistic agreements that we made had gone by the board" and because of the director's inclusion of electronic sounds that were "a lot closer to music than to sound effects."[40]

Since *Prospero's Books*, Greenaway has continued to write and direct independent British films, but he has not developed another long-term partnership with a composer. He considers himself to be "not, on the whole, a very good collaborator."[41] But this trait is perhaps a strength of his filmmaking, for it enables him to maintain authorial control of not just the visual but also the sonic aspects of his pictures.

Notes

1   Jonathan Hacker and David Price, *Take Ten: Contemporary British Film Directors* (Oxford: Clarendon Press, 1991), 208.
2   Hacker and Price, *Take Ten*, 208; Amy Lawrence, *The Films of Peter Greenaway* (Cambridge: Cambridge University Press, 1997), 9–10.
3   Lawrence, *The Films of Peter Greenaway*, 11.
4   See, for instance, Bridget Elliott and Anthony Purdy, *Peter Greenaway: Architecture and Allegory* (Chichester: Academy Editions, 1997); and Vernon Gras, "Dramatizing the Failure to Jump the Culture/Nature Gap: The Films of Peter Greenaway," *New Literary History* 26, no. 1 (Winter 1999): 125–43.
5   See David Pascoe, *Peter Greenaway: Museums and Moving Images* (London: Reaktion Books, 1997); and Alan Woods, *Being Naked, Playing Dead* (Manchester: Manchester University Press, 1996).
6   Woods, *Being Naked, Playing Dead*, 203.
7   Ibid., 203.
8   Karen Jaehne, "*The Draughtsman's Contract*: An Interview with Peter Greenaway," in *Peter Greenaway Interviews*, ed. Vernon Gras and Marguerite Gras (Jackson: University Press of Mississippi, 2000), 25.
9   Stephanie McBride, "Film: G Is for Greenaway," *Circa* 62 (Autumn 1992): 57.
10 David Cooper, Christopher Fox and Ian Sapiro, eds., "Keynote Interview with Michael Nyman," in *CineMusic? Constructing the Film Score*, ed. David Cooper, Christopher Fox, and Ian Sapiro (Newcastle upon Tyne: Cambridge Scholars Publishing, 2008), 174.
11 Ibid., 179.
12 Michel Ciment, "Interview with Peter Greenaway: *Zed and Two Noughts* (Z.O.O)," in *Peter Greenaway Interviews*, ed. Vernon Gras and Marguerite Gras (Jackson: University Press of Mississippi, 2000), 39.

13 Peter Greenaway, "Appendix 4: Music," from the original BFI proposal for *The Draughtsman's Contract* (n.d.), available at: www.bfi.org.uk/greenaway (accessed February 23, 2011).

14 Ibid. Greenaway has hand-written on the proposal that the "Reconaissance" scene (planning the drawings) is "an extended montage cut to music."

15 David Cooper and Ian Sapiro, "A Source-Studies Approach to Michael Nyman's Score for *The Draughtsman's Contract*," *Journal of Film Music* 3, no. 2 (2011), 144.

16 "*Guardian* Interview with Michael Nyman", on *The Draughtsman's Contract*, dir. Peter Greenaway. British Film Institute, 1982.

17 Cooper et al., "Keynote Interview," 171–3.

18 Woods, *Being Naked, Playing Dead*, 275.

19 Cooper and Sapiro, "A Source-Studies Approach," 149. Italics (original) show the various cycles or partial cycles of cues.

20 McBride, "G Is for Greenaway," 54.

21 Jaehne, "Interview with Peter Greenaway," 25.

22 Peter Greenaway, *Fear of Drowning* (Paris: Editions Dis Voir, 1988), 64.

23 Cooper et al., "Keynote Interview," 174.

24 Greenaway, *Fear of Drowning*, 130–2.

25 These titles are taken from the track sheets and reel boxes for the various recordings for *Drowning by Numbers*, Michael Nyman Archive, University of Leeds, 1988.

26 Musical cues are numbered so that they can be quickly identified in terms of their placement in a film. The first numeral denotes the reel of film, "M" indicates that it is a music cue, and the final number signifies its order within the reel of film. Hence 1M2 is the second music cue on the first reel of film. When cues run directly together across a change of reel, they are displayed in the format 1M2/2M1.

27 The final cue on the soundtrack CD is called "Endgame," and comprises a number of short cues from the film, though the track as heard on the CD does not appear in the film. Michael Nyman, *Drowning by Numbers*. Virgin Records (2004).

28 Greenaway provides descriptions of Madgett's unusual games (transcriptions of Smut's dialogue from the film) in *Fear of Drowning*. Examples range from the simple if unusual Reverse Strip Jump, which "is played from as high a jumping-point as a competitor will dare. After each successful jump, the competitor is allowed to put on an article of clothing" (96) through Bees in the Trees, a game based on musical chairs and "best played with funeral music and in the open air" (102) to more complex games such as Hangman's Cricket. Hangman's Cricket is based on French cricket, but "there is no limit to the number of players as long as each has an identity agreed by the two referees. Each identity has its own characteristic which must be obeyed." This direction is followed by a list of "more important identities" and specific rules for the adulterer, harlot, dunce, sailor, mother-in-law, gravedigger, maiden, twins, businessman, and red queen, most of which are matched visually onto characters from the film during Smut's voice-over description. The game "is best appreciated after [it] has been played for several hours. By then every player has a fair understanding of the many rules and knows which character he wants to play permanently. Finally an outright loser is found and is obliged to present himself to the Hangman … who is always merciless" (102–4).

29 Andreas Kilb, "I am the Cook: A Conversation with Peter Greenaway," in *Peter Greenaway Interviews*, ed. Vernon Gras and Marguerite Gras (Jackson: University Press of Mississippi, 2000), 63.

30 Marlene Rodgers, "*Prospero's Books*—Word and Spectacle: An Interview with Peter Greenaway," *Film Quarterly* 45, no. 2 (Winter 1991–2): 11.

31 Cooper et al., "Keynote Interview," 174.

32 Jonathan Coe, "Review of Michael Nyman: *Prospero's Books*, Decca 425 224 CD/MC," *The Wire* Issue 92 (October 1991). A cutting of the review is included in the Michael Nyman Archive, but the page number is not recorded.

33 I am indebted to Nigel Barr in Michael Nyman's office for providing me with a copy of the limited edition soundtrack for *La Traversée de Paris*.

34 Holly Rogers, "'Noises, Sounds and Sweet Airs': Singing the Film Space in *Prospero's Books*," in *CineMusic? Constructing the Film Score*, ed. David Cooper, Christopher Fox, and Ian Sapiro (Newcastle upon Tyne: Cambridge Scholars Publishing, 2008), 144.

35 Cooper et al., "Keynote Interview," 174.

36 Peter Greenaway, "Sound and Vision: An Open Discussion with Peter Greenaway," *The European Graduate School* (2002), available at: www.egs.edu/faculty/peter-greenaway/articles/sound-and-vision/.

37 Evelyn Tribble, "Listening to *Prospero's Books*," in *Shakespeare Survey Volume 61: Shakespeare, Sound and Screen*, ed. Peter Holland (Cambridge: Cambridge University Press, 2008), 165. Tribble incorrectly gives Marshall's first name as "Gareth."

38 In *Prospero's Books: A Film of Shakespeare's* The Tempest (London: Chatto & Windus, 1991), Greenaway breaks the two-hour film down into ninety-one scenes, several of which contain subsections. The timing for the first entry of the score has been taken from the PAL/Region 2 DVD version of the film released by Atlantic Film AB in 2010.

39 Hacker and Price, *Take Ten*, 217.

40 Cooper et al., "Keynote Interview," 174 and 175.

41 Howard A. Rodman, "Anatomy of a Wizard," in *Peter Greenaway Interviews*, ed. Vernon Gras and Marguerite Gras (Jackson: University Press of Mississippi, 2000), 122.

Chapter 12

The Attractions of Repetition
Tarantino's Sonic Style

Lisa Coulthard

In their introduction to *Lowering the Boom: Critical Studies in Film Sound*, Tony Grajeda and Jay Beck argue for a notion of acoustic auteurism that would reconsider and re-theorize auteurist principles by acknowledging the essentially collaborative nature of film sound. Arguing that sound is key to this new auteurist approach, they do not reject auteurism; rather, they rework the term to suggest that there are "genuine 'acoustic auteurs'" who can be analyzed in terms of their commitment to film sound and music.[1] Claudia Gorbman similarly recognizes the sonic obsessions of some directors when she coins the term "melomane" to describe those directors for whom sound and music are crucial, exciting, and innovative aspects of the medium. Put simply, melomanes are lovers of music whose films reveal this love: "More and more, music-loving directors treat music not as something to farm out to the composer or even to the music supervisor, but rather as a key thematic element and a marker of authorial style."[2] Not just another form of auteurism, the concept of the melomane takes into account the criticisms of auteurist methodology over the past few decades as well as the changes in the cinematic soundtrack and the shifts in music culture generally: it indicates a new kind of auteurism that considers a director's concentration on sound and music as proof of his or her authorial signature.

With a precise attention to sound and music that borders on the fanatical, Quentin Tarantino is easily classified as just such a melomane or acoustic auteur. Frequently commenting on his audiophilic as well as his cinephilic obsessions, Tarantino notes the importance of music in every phase of his creative process, from writing to production and post-production; he writes musical references into scripts, plays songs on set, works intimately with his sound team to provide appropriate versions of songs, and compiles and releases soundtrack albums and CDs after a film's release. This obsession with music carries over into his filmworlds, in which musical scores and songs figure prominently both for the film viewers and for the characters themselves, who discuss, select, play, sing, and dance to diegetic music.

This centrality of music as experience, topic, and obsession in Tarantino's films is key to understanding his auteurism as well as his postmodernism and popular appeal. Primarily formed from pre-existing song and score, Tarantino's soundtracks highlight the reflexive, parodic, and ironic aspects of his work and suggest the extent to which his films require that music be taken seriously as a structuring element, thematic subject, affective experience, and sincere homage. That is to say, more than mere pastiche, musical reference in Tarantino indicates an affective, emotional attachment to, and investment in, the music being (re)played. This is where Gorbman's term "melomane" becomes essential and interesting; it is not merely a recognition of the importance of music in film, but a mania for it, that characterizes these sonic auteurs.

A love for music certainly comes to the fore in Tarantino's films; it is both a character and a feeling that seduces, interprets, and communicates. But music in Tarantino is also part of a larger sonic obsession that stresses the acoustic impact of dialogue, noise, atmosphere, and effects—Tarantino is an audio-mane as much as a melomane. Whether it be the tendency of human bodies to make artificial, inorganic sounds (for example, the hollow thump of Mia Wallace's chest in the overdose scene *Pulp Fiction* [1994] or the metallic ting of The Bride's head in *Kill Bill: Vol. 1* [2003]), the foregrounding of the regular meter of footsteps either in rapid pursuit or slow advance (the frenetic drum beat footsteps of the Crazy 88s versus the measured leisurely pace of Bill in *Kill Bill: Vol. 1*), the communication of character through the sounds of clothing (the leather creaks of Hans Landa's SS coat at the beginning of *Inglourious Basterds* [2009]) or the roars and clicks of machines throughout his films, sound effects and noise are central to what we interpret as Tarantino's acoustic mania.

Moreover, sound effects and noise work in conjunction with dialogue and music to create multivalent soundscapes that make it difficult to determine whether any sound can be classified only as an effect or a musical cue. These crossovers make connections between sonic elements and indicate the extent to which the soundtrack as a whole (rather than just music cues alone) takes on an identifiable character and style, a style that in Tarantino is most easily described as one of repetition and rhythm. Stressing rhythmically regular, repetitive, and percussive popular music, Tarantino's sonic style also emphasizes the equally rhythmic qualities of vocal and sound effects: rock and pop beats interact with rapid-fire dialogue and the noise of car engines, sword hits, punches, or gun shots. Put simply, Tarantino's films create an acoustic universe dominated by precise rhythms, tones, and textures that reverberate across the soundscapes. Words and music echo and rhyme in Tarantino's films their repetitions reflected in the reiterations of homage and referential borrowing that constitute his visual and audio style.

Despite this complex sonic interplay, the determining rhythm of any Tarantino film begins with music. Given Tarantino's emphasis on pastiche and reflexive borrowing, it is no surprise that music in his films forms a compendium of cinematic references. But his melomania is more than a collection of cultural icons or an expert pastiching of pre-existing songs and score materials, as it constructs acoustic contours and internal rhythms within and across films. Music in Tarantino is characterization, narrative, theme, and—first and foremost—sound. Thinking of melomania in this way, we can begin to appreciate the extent to which sound plays a role in determining the overall structure of Tarantino's films.

Origins and Openings: Music and the Title Sequence

Tarantino has often noted that his creative process begins with choosing the music that will open the film: once this music is determined, he knows the direction, tone, and texture of the piece he is writing. This piece of music might not always make it to the soundtrack of the final product, let alone to the opening credit sequence, but its character will be reflected in both. Looking at the opening credit music of his films, we can see the way in which the tone of each film is set by this choice: 1970s pop rock in *Reservoir Dogs*, surf music in *Pulp Fiction*, soul in *Jackie Brown* (1997), the ballad in *Kill Bill*, 1960s exploitation film music in *Death Proof* (2007), and the scores of classic Westerns in *Inglourious Basterds* (2009). The opening music creates a musical dominant that sets the tone, rather than strictly determines the songs and score (there are numerous cues in *Basterds*, for example, that have nothing to do with Westerns); but in each case the tonal determination of the opening is significant and carries beyond the credits and even beyond music to establish and define the overall flow and rhythm of each film.

For instance, after the Dick Dale opening of *Pulp Fiction*, surf music appears in four other key scenes: the rape of Marsellus, the piercing discussion between Jody and Trudi, the scenes of Vince shooting heroin and driving to Mia's place, and the departure of Vince and Jules from the diner at the end. In some ways these are central moments in the narrative, or at least the central moments for Vince. Moreover, if we remember that the opening music is in fact split between "Misirlou" and "Jungle Boogie" (Kool & the Gang), the surf music is further contextualized as belonging to Vince, while soul is associated with his partner Jules. This early musical split between Vince and Jules sets the tone for the two musical dominants of the film: surf music (Dick Dale, The Tornados, The Centurians, The Revels, The Lively Ones) and soul (The Brothers Johnson, Al Green, and Dusty Springfield's 'white' soul). With its California gangsters and petty criminals, *Pulp Fiction* is a mix of the exploitation cinemas suggested by both surf and soul (blaxploitation, surfer, and biker films), and these acoustic and narrational contours are evident in the musical mixing of the film's opening moments.

In similar ways, the mood of each of Tarantino's films is set by the opening music: *Kill Bill*'s opening ballad—Nancy Sinatra's "Bang Bang"—sets the tone for the strong presence of haunting, melancholic film scores in the film; *Jackie Brown*'s soul/funk opening is repeated throughout that film's musical choices;

Death Proof's use of Jack Nitzsche's "The Last Race" paves the way for the centrality of Eddie Beram's "Riot in Thunder Alley" in the climactic scene; the classical-style film score that opens *Inglourious Basterds* makes clear the film's sonic indebtedness to the Western. More than merely setting the musical character of a film, these opening selections establish overall sonic contours that apply to effects, voice, and rhythms of editing. For example, if we think of *Jackie Brown*'s soulful opening that pairs Bobby Womack's "Across 110th Street" with the image of fluid and continuous movement, we note the ways in which these opening rhythms are reflected across the film as a whole. The meandering dialogue sequences, the dialogue that talks around issues without ever confronting them directly, the use of silence and pauses—these elements follow from the melodic, soulful opening music. In terms of narrative, the lyrics of "Across 110th Street" suggest the constant struggle of the downtrodden and the impossibility of escape; these are themes that recur throughout the film, not just in Jackie's struggle but also in the fated movement of characters within confined spaces, in the emphasis on circular life patterns, and in the recurrent sense of survival. There is little speed in *Jackie Brown*; there are no car chases, no revving engines, no extended fight scenes or fast and furious dialogue, and this languor is reflected and determined by the soundtrack's emphasis on soul. In contrast, if we think of the speed associated with both Jack Nitzsche's "The Last Race" and the surf rhythms of "Misirlou," we can see that musical kineticism is reflected in the speed and vivacity of dialogue, effects, and action in *Death Proof* and *Pulp Fiction*, respectively.

A film like *Kill Bill* would seem to contradict this argument insofar as the opening credit song is a slow and mournful ballad that is at odds with the intense energy of the film. Yet the crucial point to remember is that "Bang Bang" is the opening song for the film as a whole, and not merely its first installment. In fact, this opening piece corresponds quite explicitly to the mournful tone and melodramatic rhythms of *Kill Bill: Vol. 2* (2004), a detail that makes sense when we think of the film's original incarnation as a single work. Moreover, the song lyrics speak directly to the film's central thematic issues (male violence, female victimhood, love, loyalty, revenge, history, memory) that dominate both installments. While the musical tone of "Bang Bang" might seem at rhythmic odds with *Vol. 1*'s kineticism, the lyrics parallel the story in poignant and affectively significant ways that give it center stage in both films, even though it is featured only as the opening music of the first installment.

It is important that all of Tarantino's musical openings utilize popular score and song. Popular song's symmetrical form, repeated phrase patterns, regular rhythmic pulses, and easily understood structures have been widely noted by scholars of popular music in film: Jeff Smith notes that "the riff is suited to popular music's economy of means,"[3] and he discusses the role of syncopation, repetition, and the hook within the symmetrical pattern of the verse–bridge–chorus structure; Kevin Donnelly similarly stresses pop music's highly formalized nature, noting in particular its tendencies toward a four-beat pattern with machine-like accents on the second and fourth beats;[4] Ian Inglis argues that "technicity, repetition and iteration"[5] have replaced more traditional concepts of melody, progression, and narrative in contemporary popular music; Phil Powrie discusses how the strophic nature of popular song anchors and structures the listening frame through repeated forms.[6] As these comments suggest, repetition operates as a formal, cognitive, and affective strategy in the structure of popular music. Detached from any of its negative connotations, repetition is here used in a strictly adjectival way to describe a musical form aimed at eliciting a direct, emotional response through rapid comprehension, memorization, and engagement. Repetition is an efficient device, reliant upon short bursts of information that are easily absorbed through such easily identifiable recurring and predictive structural elements as the riff, hook, verse, bridge, and chorus.

Because of audience familiarity, the use of pre-existing popular song has the potential to make these aspects of repetition, easy cognition, and emotional engagement all the more palpable and prominent. Indeed, a preference for the familiar—what cognitive scientists call the "exposure effect"[7]—is in ample evidence in popular music, which relies upon familiarity to breed and intensify desire. As Ronald Rodman notes in his analysis of music in Tarantino, this familiarity can extend beyond specific songs to apply to an entire genre or style of music; even if one is not familiar with "Misirlou," for example, one can still respond with a knowledge of Dick Dale, surf music, or even rock 'n' roll in general.[8] Moreover, if a listener does not recognize "Misirlou" either specifically or generically, familiarity still functions through the song's powerful internal repetitions.

In his "'Would You Like to Hear Some Music?': Music in-and-out-of-Control in the Films of Quentin Tarantino," Ken Garner emphasizes Tarantino's preference for repetitive structures and precise rhythms when he comments on the "musematic repetition" in the opening credit songs of Tarantino's early films.[9] Developed by Richard Middleton, who is in turn indebted to the work of Philip Tagg, the term 'musematic' here refers to the brevity of repeated units: Middleton divides repetition in popular song into musematic and discursive repetition, where 'discursive' describes longer units of expression and 'musematic' refers to short rhythmic units such as riffs.[10] As a musical analogue for the linguistic morpheme, the museme is a minimal unit of identifiable, meaningful sound and 'musematic' suggests the repetition of these units in a prolonged, unvaried structure that tends toward an "epic-recursive," "one-levelled structural effect."[11] Applying this idea to the opening credit music of *Reservoir Dogs*, *Jackie Brown*, and *Pulp Fiction*, Garner emphasizes the "sheer 'epic' energy of the credit themes,"[12] something that is particularly prominent in what is clearly the most musematic of the three songs: Dick Dale and the Del-Tones' version of the traditional "Misirlou." Dale's version of the song takes repetition to a new level through the technique of double picking (in which a single note is played repeatedly in quick succession) and through the fact that the song uses only the guitar's E string (the opening riff is played on the top E string and then repeated at a higher octave on the bottom E string).

While Dick Dale and "Misirlou" are perhaps extreme examples, musematic repetition is common in surf music and much of rock music generally. It is a feature that Garner ties to the ability of these musical forms to excite through tempo, volume, and melodic recursiveness; as Garner notes, this kind of music eschews lyricism, narration, commentary, and development in favor of an abstract emotional intensity that can be easily connected to Tarantino's usage of musematic music for moments of heightened arousal.[13] But we must also consider the pleasures of repetitive and recursive musical forms that cannot be easily dismissed as pure arousal. While Garner's analysis is persuasive, it tends to simplify the musicological complexity of Middleton's discussion of musematic and discursive repetition. In so doing, it downplays the variations in musical form and genre (1970s lyric-based bubblegum rock, instrumental surf music, blaxploitation funk/soul) across the opening credit music in the three Tarantino films he analyzes, and, significantly, delimits the cognitive, situational, and affective pleasures associated with repetitive (and repeatedly heard) popular music. Cognitive scientists studying music have long recognized the role of repetition in the pleasure of popular music, suggesting that this operates both within the songs themselves (internal repetition) and in terms of the listening environment (the repeated listening to a song). What these studies suggest is that familiarity has its own rewards that frequently outweigh the impact of experimentation, originality, or innovation. In other words, the more we hear a song and the more we understand and are familiar with a certain kind of repetitive song structure (one that allows us to predict what is coming next), the more we tend to like it: familiarity breeds desire.

While this provides justification for the annoyingly repetitive radio play of popular hit songs, it also prompts us to question the pleasures of popular songs when they appear in cinema soundtracks. When the song heard on a film soundtrack is one well known to the audience, there is an added layer to the comfortable pleasures of repetition. But this comforting pleasure in the familiar can work in interestingly disruptive ways, as when the musical attractions of Stealers Wheels' "Stuck in the Middle with You" are so clearly at odds with the violent action portrayed onscreen in *Reservoir Dogs*.

Lyricism and Lyrics: Musematic Words

This discrepancy of "Stuck in the Middle with You" is based on musical structure, but it is also a function of the role of the song's lyrics and their uncomfortable relation to the spoken lines of dialogue. As Middleton notes, words in lyric-based musematic songs can disrupt or intensify the already repetitive song form.[14] Each of Tarantino's films features a dominant lyric-based popular song that plays a central role in the film by telling the story or offering a commentary on the action; along with the already mentioned "Stuck in the Middle with You" in *Reservoir Dogs*, examples include "Girl, You'll Be a Woman Soon" in *Pulp Fiction*, "Didn't I Blow Your Mind" in *Jackie Brown*, "Hold Tight" (and arguably "Baby It's You") in *Death Proof*, and "Putting out the Fire (with Gasoline)" in *Inglourious Basterds*.

In each case, the song defines a musical moment that acts as a sonic dominant, both suspending and furthering the film's action. Each song is a lyric-based popular song, and the lyrics stress the songs' connections to the stories. This is most obvious when the songs are used diegetically (when, for example, Mia Wallace in *Pulp Fiction* sings along to a song she has chosen), but it is arguably just as evident in the intimate connection between song and character established with "Putting out the Fire" and Shoshanna in *Inglourious Basterds*. More than a literal comment on the action, each song sets the emotional center of the film in which it appears, operating as an affective map for reading the action and determining the rhythm and emotional variances and range. The tight, repetitive, musematic structure of *Death Proof*'s "Hold Tight" not only tells us to hold on for the film's wild kinetic ride; it also creates an upbeat, energetic tonal center and creates an interpretive meta-textual resonance by pairing one forgotten, devalued cultural object (the band called Dave Dee, Dozy, Beaky, Mick & Tich, whose recording of "Hold Tight" plays on the car radio and is discussed by the characters) with another (Grindhouse cinema).

Tarantino's preference for lyric-based pop songs over score (a predilection that he moves away from in *Kill Bill* and *Inglourious Basterds*) cannot be separated from the vocal rhythms of his dialogue, which tend toward the structures and forms of popular lyric-based song insofar as regular meters, repetitions, and refrains dominate. Names in Tarantino are usually single-syllable and consonant-heavy (for example, Budd, Bill, Joe), clever homophones (B.B., Elle, Jules), catchy descriptors (Nice Guy Eddie, the Bear Jew), or alliterative and/or rhyming two-word phrases (Marsellus Wallace, Jungle Julia, Honey Bunny, Hattori Hanzo, Shoshanna Mimieux, Vincent Vega, Winston Wolf). Names are important in Tarantino films (as the famous naming scene in *Reservoir Dogs* indicates), and the sounds of names are as important for characterization as the names themselves.

In addition to catchy names, short and memorable phrases pervade Tarantino's films—something that is particularly noticeable in the films' two-word titles: *Reservoir Dogs*, *Pulp Fiction*, *Jackie Brown*, *Kill Bill*, *Death Proof*, *Inglourious Basterds* (even *True Romance*). The brevity and consonance of characters' names and film titles suggest an echoing structure that parallels the musematic repetition discussed earlier; aimed at easy recognition and infectiousness, these linguistic riffs demand audience attention through the use of alliteration, consonance, and assonance as well as through their defining metrical beats. These same qualities are also in ample evidence in Tarantino's lines of repetitive and rhyming dialogue that tend toward the aphoristic: "My name's Paul and this is between y'all" (English Bob in *Pulp Fiction*); "To my brother Budd, the only man I ever loved" (Elle in *Kill Bill*); "Zed's dead, baby, Zed's dead" (Butch in *Pulp Fiction*); "Alright ramblers, let's get rambling" (Joe in *Reservoir Dogs*); "whatever with your however" (Kim in *Death Proof*); "Facts can be so misleading, where rumors, true or false, are often revealing" (Landa in *Inglourious Basterds*).

These phrases operate as musematic riffs—memorable, catchy, and best described as single-level structures designed for immediate cognition. But they also work in conjunction with longer phrases that are equally characterized by echoing, rhyming, repetition, and the use of regular metrical rhythms, usually iambic or anapestic. Consider this example from *Kill Bill: Vol. 2*:

> Before that strip turned blue, I was a woman. I was your woman. I was a killer who killed for you. Before that strip turned blue, I would have jumped a motorcycle onto a speeding train … for you. But once that strip turned blue, I could no longer do any of those things. Not anymore.

Or this example from *Inglourious Basterds*:

> And the Germans will be sickened by us. And the Germans will talk about us. And the Germans will fear us. And when the Germans close their eyes at night and their subconscious tortures them for the evil they've done, it will be thoughts of us that it tortures them with.

Consider also of the discussion of tipping in *Reservoir Dogs*, the argument about playing ship's mast in *Death Proof*, the debate over foot massages in *Pulp Fiction*, the poetry quotation of Robert Frost's "Stopping by Woods on a Snowy Evening" for the Arlene/Butterfly scenes in *Death Proof*, and the rehearsal of the story in *Reservoir Dogs*. Dialogue in Tarantino stresses repetition of words and phrases in a manner that emphasizes rhyming (including alliteration, consonance, and assonance), prosody (regular metrical patterns), and versification. Dialogue and song echo and merge in a way that amplifies a sense of repetition and metrical precision.

In his analysis of Jean Vigo's *L'Atalante*, Michel Chion comments on the "psittacism or echolalia" in Vigo's films that "lends a certain musicality to the dialogue and discreetly removes it from naturalism."[15] The parallel to Tarantino is instructive when Chion goes on to cite examples that closely resemble the repetition of words that characterizes much of Tarantino's dialogue: compare Vigo's "I'm going to get the missus"—"You're going to get the missus?"[16] with Tarantino's "He don't tip"—"He don't tip?"—"You don't tip?" (*Reservoir Dogs*). Psittacism here is a kind of parroting echo that does not mock, undermine, or empty the words of meaning (as is often implied in the derogatory usage of the term) but, rather, refocuses attention on the words as sound. The patterns are those of an almost ritualistic call and response, and we see it at work throughout Tarantino's dialogue, which many rate as among the best in contemporary Hollywood cinema.

Indeed, this kind of rhythmic repetition is central to the pleasures of Tarantino's films, and it is an integral part of their reception. With writing that stresses brevity, rhythmic regularity, and metrical precision, it is no surprise that lines of Tarantino's dialogue seem to quickly and efficiently lodge themselves into the public consciousness. As scholars of cognition, memory, poetry, and oral history have noted, rhyme schemes and regular meter make sounds more predictable and therefore easier to process and memorize. Indeed, fan pages, blogs, reviews, and books quote fervently and extensively from Tarantino's films; there is an obsessiveness in this quoting that aligns it easily with the memorable pop tune lyrics that are heard within Tarantino's films. In his short but brilliant book on *Pulp Fiction*, Dana Polan offers an astute commentary on the tendency in Tarantino fandom and (amateur) scholarship toward overinvested discussions that focus on minutiae, quotation, and forced intimacy. Referring to the director as "QT" or "Quentin," these web pages, books, and articles claim a personal relationship to the films, and by extension to the director himself, through a compulsively detailed knowledge of the films. Dialogue and music in the films are not only hospitable to this kind of fanaticism; they actively cultivate it. Taking banal dialogue and rendering it memorable through the acoustic impact of poetic conceits and techniques, dialogue in Tarantino easily filters into the everyday lives of fans and allows them to enter film worlds through quotation and repetition.

But the soundtracks and songs also have a cult following, and it is not insignificant that one of the key characteristics of Tarantino's soundtrack albums is the inclusion of dialogue between the music tracks. With the *Kill Bill* CD Tarantino takes this even further by including sword hits and other sound effects. If we consider these extra-filmic aspects to be a part of Tarantino's auteurism, his melomania comes into even sharper focus. Unlike most directors, Tarantino exercises a degree of control over these CD releases, and as a result his soundtrack albums are highly anticipated by fans and usually prove to be extremely popular: his fans tend to think of them as 'mixed tapes' of the sort mentioned in *Death Proof*—as signs of intimacy through the sharing of musical tastes.

In both dialogue and music, we note the ways in which Tarantino's acoustic auteurism creates memorable and impactful listening moments. The quoting of dialogue on his soundtrack albums makes this point concrete: Tarantino's cinema highlights film as a sonic medium and experience. An intensely audiophilic director, Tarantino fills his films with eminently quotable music and dialogue; he foregrounds music as subject, as both theme and experience, and he transforms dialogue exchanges into acoustic events as memorable and pleasurable as any song lyric or rock riff.

Notes

1 Jay Beck and Tony Grajeda, "Introduction: The Future of Film Sound Studies," in *Lowering the Boom: Critical Studies in Film Sound*, ed. Jay Beck and Tony Grajeda (Urbana: University of Illinois Press, 2008), 13.

2 Claudia Gorbman, "Auteur Music," in *Beyond the Soundtrack: Representing Music in Cinema*, ed. Daniel Goldmark, Lawrence Kramer, and Richard Leppert (Berkeley: University of California Press, 2007), 149.

3 Jeff Smith, *The Sounds of Commerce: Marketing Popular Film Music* (New York: Columbia University Press, 1998), 8.

4 K.J. Donnelly, *The Spectre of Sound: Music in Film and Television* (London: BFI, 2005), 28.

5 Ian Inglis, "Introduction: Popular Music and Film," in *Popular Music and Film*, ed. Ian Inglis (London: Wallflower Press, 2003), 5.

6 Phil Powrie, "Blonde Abjection: Spectatorship and the Abject Anal Space In-between," in *Pop Fiction: The Song in Cinema*, ed. Steve Lannin and Matthew Caley (Bristol: Intellect Books, 2005), 105.

7 David Huron, *Sweet Anticipation: Music and the Psychology of Expectation* (Cambridge, MA: MIT Press, 2006), 134.

8 Ronald Rodman, "The Popular Song as Leitmotif in 1990s Film," in *Changing Tunes: The Use of Pre-existing Music in Film*, ed. Phil Powrie and Robynn J. Stilwell (Aldershot: Ashgate, 2006), 121, 126.

9 Ken Garner, "'Would You Like to Hear Some Music?': Music in-and-out-of-Control in the Films of Quentin Tarantino," in *Film Music: Critical Approaches*, ed. K.J. Donnelly (New York: Continuum, 2001), 191.

10 Richard Middleton, "'Play It again Sam': Some Notes on the Productivity of Repetition in Popular Music," *Popular Music* 3 (1983): 235–70; and Philip Tagg, "Analysing Popular Music: Theory, Method, and Practice," *Popular Music* 2 (1982): 37–67.

11 Middleton, "'Play It again Sam,'" 238.

12 Garner, "'Would You Like to Hear Some Music?,'" 192.

13 Ibid., 198.

14 Middleton, "'Play It again Sam,'" 236.

15 Michel Chion, *Film, A Sound Art*, trans. Claudia Gorbman (New York: Columbia University Press, 2009), 61.

16 Quoted in ibid., 61.

Chapter 13

Dream Timbre

Notes on Lynchian Sound Design

Isabella van Elferen

So many rooms in his films, all of them more ghastly than the last, and all of them sounding like the resonating chambers of multiple nightmares.[1]

There are few film directors whose sonic style seems easier to characterize than David Lynch. Sound and music are as prominent a part of his movies as color, light, and camerawork. Audio and visual media cooperate to build the surreal universes of nonlinear narratives and overlapping realities of his dreamscapes, and the combination is typically evaluated as extremely disconcerting. Even though the validity of a cinematographic, let alone audiovisual-cinematographic, auteur as an analytic concept remains highly debatable, in the case of David Lynch a consistent personal sonic style is overwhelmingly evident. This style, moreover, is deemed so innovative that it has been said to "renew the cinema by way of sound."[2]

The name David Lynch has come to connote a dreamy but uncanny audio-visuality. An online review of Lynch's 2006 film *Inland Empire* emphasizes the role that the director's "signature ominous sound design" plays in the spatio-temporal and psychological destabilizations of the movie, but it does not proceed to describe further characteristics of this signature sound.[3] In a similarly inexact way Former Ghosts front man Freddy Rupert mentions Lynch's disquieting soundtracks as a major influence for the band's 2011 album *New Love*: "That you can use something so sweet and nostalgic-sounding to illustrate something that is utterly disturbing."[4] A final example comes from personal experience. When I told a colleague early in 2011 in which London hotel I was going to be staying, he commented that that particular hotel was "such a David Lynch place," a qualification upon which he elaborated with a description of endless linoleum corridors in which the only sign of life appears to be the intermittent buzz of a broken lamp.

Nostalgic and even sweet, yet empty, disturbing, and ominous … vague as these characterizations are, they are all unmistakably Lynch. It is remarkable that while David Lynch's sonic style is so singular and so recognizable—while this style itself has become part of the David Lynch brand—this style itself has only been described in the most general of terms. The artist himself remains characteristically elusive when describing music's contribution to his films. He comments only on its potential to cross borders: "[M]usic opens up doors, because even one little sound or a sequence of notes can give you an idea for a story."[5] Sound, Lynch says, is "almost like a drug. ... [I]t instantly does something to you."[6]

This chapter aims to pass through the mist surrounding Lynchian sound design. Observing and defining its characteristics beyond hazy metaphors, it addresses the unsettling feelings the Lynch sound design so universally evokes, and it investigates how this sound design "opens up doors." A key question is: doors to *what or where?*

The Lynchian Universe: "We Live *Inside* a Dream"[7]

Lynch's films are famous for their complexity. With densely accumulated, seemingly unrelated but simultaneous narrative lines, his film plots are notoriously difficult to understand. The overarching theme in Lynch's films is the blurring of lines between what is real and what is dreamed, imagined, narrated, fantasized, or mediated. Sometimes with a mystery template as a starting point, Lynch's characters and their viewers wander through labyrinths of reality and fiction that evolve into kaleidoscopes of time and space. These journeys rarely come to a clear end, and the mysteries seldom get solved. Frustrating as this is for conventional audiences, the films do not so much revolve around answers as around the big questions of life and being.

Lynch's works explore the limits of cinematic and medial signification.[8] In his films representation and performativity always go together. Stressing the fact that cinema never merely tells a story but rather embodies and effects it, Lynch employs mediation as part of the performativity of his movies. With the help of nonconventional camera use (angles, zooms, fast edits, jump cuts) and alienating extra-diegetic inserts on the one hand, and the reversal and doubling of cinematic motifs on the other, his films foreground the medium of film as an active agent in the blurring of boundaries between reality, fiction, memory, and the unconscious. This part of his cinematic style becomes most bewilderingly evident in *Inland Empire*, in which such boundary blurrings are represented as well as invoked through the use of a great variety of cameras, films, and filming styles. The result is a pastiche of mediation and perception that climaxes with an ambiguously fictional/real death taking place in a street which itself represents the utmost conflation of desire and fantasy, reality and mediation: Hollywood Boulevard.[9]

Another possible reading of Lynch's work focuses on his tiptoeing on the boundaries between the Lacanian Symbolic and Imaginary, setting in motion cinematic experiments that may reveal a glimpse of the impossible Real.[10] Media theory and psychoanalysis, in this case, lead to very similar conclusions. A veil as well as a window, an illusion as well as a gateway, a simulacrum as well as an experienced reality, the film medium in Lynch's work simultaneously functions as the Symbolic and as the Imaginary, a function that irregularly also gives way to a hinting at the unrepresentable Real. Lynch's work discloses a nagging doubt that remains occluded in traditional Hollywood cinema: the possibility that such notions as signification and reality, or truth and self, might ultimately turn out to be irrelevant. Eric G. Wilson has argued that the comprehensive ambivalence of Lynch's films engender an ontological self-reflexivity: "Lynch … throws viewers into irreducible ambiguity, or a relentless interpretive limbo; however, this limbo is not a meaningless stasis but a rich abyss that approaches the no-thing that is being itself."[11]

This theme is expressed in a number of recurrent motifs. Dreams and hallucinations make up important parts of Lynch's films. Carefully screened with the help of alienating camera and editing techniques, they reveal the fears and desires living in the interior world of the unconscious. Dreams are not deceptions in Lynch; they present alternate realities and overlapping or distorted temporalities. These dream worlds often contain secrets that emphasize their importance for the reality of the day-to-day. They are represented directly in dream scenes and sequences, and they are talked about in dialogues. Dreams are also used more generally as confusing narrative structures, as in *Mulholland Drive* (2001) or *Lost Highway* (1997). Lynch also claims that some of his ideas are based on his own dreams, the Red Room of *Twin Peaks* (1990–1) being one of the most disturbing examples of this procedure. He has often described the importance of dreams and their relation to cinema:

> Waking dreams are the ones that are important, the ones that come when I'm quietly sitting in a chair, gently letting my mind wander. When you sleep, you don't control your dream. I like to dive into a dream world that I have made or discovered; a world I chose. … That right there is the power of cinema. … The dream was played just for them. It's so unique and wonderful to that person. But with sounds and situations in time you could get much closer to putting that together for somebody else with the film.[12]

Kelly Bulkeley argues that dreams in Lynch's works have overlapping functions. They visualize the blurring of reality and illusion, and by doing so they emphasize the power of the unconscious over perception and experience.[13] The nightmarish reality of *Eraserhead* (1977) is driven by these principles. The frequent blurring of day- and night-time in Lynch's films—reflected in the recurrent motif of curtains—also emphasizes the importance of dreams: the night is a mysterious time during which people dream and during which secret things may happen.

Related to the dream motif is the inside/outside trope. This visual and narrative pattern reflects the possible conflict between the inner and outer side of each individual: "You have an interior and an exterior and sometimes they're in contradiction—everybody, every human."[14] Lynch acknowledges that the two sides of every human are of major importance to his worldview and his films: "The inside/outside thing is ... sort of what life and movies are all about to me."[15] This trope occurs in all of Lynch's works, from the confined spaces whose claustrophobic inside-ness govern narrative and personae in *Eraserhead* and *The Elephant Man* (1980) through the character inversions in *Twin Peaks*, *Lost Highway*, and *Mulholland Drive* to the complete confusion between various internal and external realms in *Inland Empire*. The recurrent visual motif of empty corridors can be considered in this light: do they lead somewhere, into, out of, or through something?

The internal and external twilight zones depicted in Lynchian dreams and hallucinations are classic examples of what Freud calls *das Unheimliche*: the home, the safe area of the familiar, is made unhomely, uncanny, when once familiar but now repressed fear or desire acquires an absent presence within it.[16] Lynch's films ostentatiously push the uncanny into the audience's faces, demanding that viewers confront their own represseds, the ghosts from their own pasts. They enforce the mirror images that one would rather not see, revealing the inevitable presence of pasts, others, fears within the here, the now, the self. More specifically, the Lynchian uncanny unveils the repressed of traditional cinema: the unspeakable possibility of unstable signification and reality leading to the destabilization of truth and self.

As in Gothic fiction, uncanny revenants in Lynch's films often take the shape of supernatural beings; examples are *Twin Peaks*'s Bob, *Lost Highway*'s Mystery Man, and *Inland Empire*'s Phantom. The returning trope of the Doppelgänger, of doubling and mirroring, is a manifestation of the uncanny that reflects another main characteristic of the Freudian uncanny: that of the self becoming "duplicated, divided and interchanged."[17] The return of the repressed can be conceptualized in the figure of the Möbius strip, with its gradual turning from one to the other side. The uncanny spatio-temporality of this figure is a governing concept in many of Lynch's works. It drives the transition from White Lodge to Black Lodge in *Twin Peaks*, from Fred to Pete in *Lost Highway*, from Betty to Diane in *Mulholland Drive*, from then to now, from inside to outside.[18] Finally, the Lynchian uncanny performatively extends over the borders of cinematic representation into the experiential sphere of the viewer. Helen Wheatly has described *Twin Peaks* as Gothic television that gradually destabilizes both the family home in the series narrative and the domestic viewing sphere. By inviting the repressed into the living room, the show literally makes the home unhomely.[19]

In Lynch's films, in summary, "we can never know ... if we are awake or asleep, real or recorded."[20] This uncanny ambiguity is represented through a convergence of over- and under-determination on the levels of narration as well as mediation creating a cinematic form of *sfumato*.

Lynch, Sound, and Music: "No Hay Banda"[21]

David Lynch has a keen interest in music, which shows in his filming habits. Music is played during rehearsals in order to get the actors in a certain mood as they immerse themselves in their roles, and he himself has music on his headphones while shooting to help him concentrate on the project.[22] Lynch was in charge of the sound design on all his films and composed additional music for most of them. Composing music has become increasingly important in his career, with three albums not related to films and a small number of singles coming out in recent years.[23] It is not for nothing that the start of *Blue Velvet* (1986) revolves around a character finding a severed *ear*. "People call me a director," Lynch has said, "but I really think of myself as a sound man."[24]

Music and sound play an important role in engaging audiences in the Lynchian universe. If Lynch's complex, destabilizing use of cinematic narration and mediation create ambiguity and uncanniness, his soundtracks intensify that effect to a degree that sometimes verges on the unbearable. As with the visual design of his films, the distinction between and conflation of various levels of auditory perception is crucial. Before addressing the ways in which Lynchian sound design enables an overlap of diegetic, extra-diegetic, and meta-diegetic sound and music, this chapter will discuss Lynch's treatment of these different perceptual levels of film music.

Diegetic sound in Lynch's films is hard to ignore. It is pushed into the foreground of the sound design, emphatically suggesting presence. In spite of that it often sounds empty, void. Doors are slammed too loudly, cigarettes are lit at deafening volumes, fires blaze and waterfalls roar as if they are personally communicating a message to the viewer—but the message, invariably, is one whose only content is its own non-signification. Sometimes things do *not* make sounds when they normally would, and in this they become significant; Nadine Hurley's silent drape runners in *Twin Peaks*, for example, enable her to close her curtains unnoticeably, thus erasing the difference between day and night. Human sounds that are not necessarily part of the dialogue—such as laughing, crying, and screaming—are presented elaborately and at high volume levels. When this same technique is used for such more intimate sounds as chewing and swallowing, kissing and lovemaking, it creates the uneasy feeling of involuntarily listening in. This becomes especially evident when the sound of human breathing—with difficulty in *The Elephant Man*, through an inhaler in *Blue Velvet*—becomes all-too-audible.

The reverse effect is achieved through Lynch's sonic treatment of dialogue. While over-emphasizing diegetic sounds that would be virtually inaudible in conventional Hollywood cinema, Lynch at the same time undermines the narrative importance of dialogue through the insertion of long silences that create the "sonic discomfort" of thwarted viewer expectations.[25] The sound of people talking is interspersed with what Lynch calls "room tone," an uncomfortable buzz of white noise that represents "the sound that you hear when there's silence, in between words or sentences."[26] When people do speak, they often say nothing at all, confirming the idea that in Lynchian sound design dialogue tends to be of sonic rather than narrative value. As Lynch has said, "You could see dialogue as a kind of sound effect or a musical effect."[27]

One consequence of this treatment of diegetic sound is that silence in a Lynch movie never automatically connotes absence, just as sound is not to be confused with presence. This is epitomized by the scene in *Mulholland Drive* in which sounds representing absence are theatrically staged in the club named for silence, Club Silencio:

> No hay banda. Il n'est pas d'orchestre [sic]. There is no band. It is all a recording. *No hay banda, yet there is a band.*[28]

Lynch's approach to diegetic sound thus reveals two important inversions of cinematic convention. One of these is a challenge to the assumption that foregrounded sound is a signifier of narratively important events or cues; an increase in volume does not necessarily equal an increase in signification, and what it does mean often remains emphatically unclear. The second reversal of film sound principles is based on what R. Murray Schafer calls *schizophonia*, that is, the separation of sound from its origin by means of recording technology.[29] Because sound is assumed to proceed from a physical source, listeners automatically search for the material body that generates the sounds they hear; this is a natural reflex that governs sonic perception, but Lynch undermines it when in effect "there is no band." The obfuscation of causal relationships between source, sound, and signification engenders cognitive dissonance in audiences, a dissonance that operates in 'the danger zone' of the Lynchian uncanny.

A form of diegetic sound that regularly occurs in Lynch's films involves people singing or playing an instrument; examples include Isabella Rossellini's rendering of "Blue Velvet" in the same-titled film, Nicolas Cage's performance of Elvis's "Love Me" in *Wild at Heart* (1990), and Bill Pullman's wild saxophone improvisation in *Lost Highway*. Such scenes often end in someone crying, a motif that represents the Lynchian inside/outside trope. Music enters listeners through their ears; having passed into listeners' innermost cores, it 'messes around' with them and stirs unconscious emotions; in crying, this internal turmoil spills back over into the outside. The medium of music thus literally follows the Möbius strip trajectory from one side to the other and back. Music that has this effect is simultaneously very present—as an obviously embodied part of the diegesis—and very intangible, since the tears seem to well up from nowhere. This paradoxical conflation of foregrounded presence and hidden origin contributes to the Lynchian ambiguities regarding reality and signification. Here, too, Club Silencio is a prime example. Betty and Rita break down in tears as Rebekah Del Rio performs Roy Orbison's "Crying," and their emotions only increase when the singer falls to the floor and is carried off stage as her now disembodied voice continues to sing. Scenes like these illustrate that Lynch's interest in music goes far beyond cinematic conventions of musical signification. In Lynch's films, music interferes with people's insides; as a result, music can also change the outside world.

Similar challenges to film-musical traditions can be found in the extra-diegetic music in Lynch's films. Since *Blue Velvet* Lynch has most often worked with composer Angelo Badalamenti, whose mark on Lynchian sound design has been so lasting that he is almost as responsible as Lynch himself for its eerily nostalgic reputation. Badalamenti's scores usually contain a small number of traditional elements, such as the occasional stinger for scare effects or leitmotifs tied to certain persons or situations. These well-known techniques are employed so unconventionally, however, that instead of being inattentively heard signifiers that pertain to on-screen events, as in traditional films, they draw attention to their own floating evasiveness.

This is partly due to Badalamenti's ability to capture in music the frightening yet enticing dreaminess of Lynch's films. By means of references to the music hall (*Eraserhead*), to classical Hollywood film music (*Blue Velvet*), or to popular music of the 1950s (*Twin Peaks*, *Wild at Heart*), Badalamenti creates moods of nostalgia for times that lie eternally locked in the past. Within this sentimental framework, the simultaneous presence of long, sustained synthesizer chords and endlessly looped, nonlinear drones provides continual warnings that tranquillity can be deceptive. The ambiguity of Badalamenti's extra-diegetic music is increased by the ways it is used within the context of film narrative and visual imagery. By letting leitmotifs migrate among different characters and situations,[30] by underscoring scenes with foreboding drones, and by avoiding an over-use of stinger effects, Badalamenti's scores for Lynch films undermine and gradually dismantle the unwritten rules of film-musical signification.

Twin Peaks is the most elaborate product of the Lynch–Badalamenti collaboration, and it marks the birth of this scoring style. The jazzy but eerie saxophone tune to which the little man in the Red Room dances in Dale Cooper's dream, for instance, returns from time to time and never fails to create confusion. Does the leitmotif mean that the little man is present, or that Cooper is dreaming again, or that the Black Lodge is near? Or does it mean none of the above? *Twin Peaks* is the reason why Badalamenti has come to be known as the "master of the suspended chord";[31] the continuous presence of his sustained synthesizer chords haunted the show's plotline—and viewers—possibly even more than did the character of Bob.

Diegetic and extra-diegetic music in Lynch's work follow procedures similar to those that govern his visual and narrative techniques. Turning up the volume on seemingly meaningless diegetic sounds, questioning ideas of musical embodiment, ignoring the traditional signifying functions of extra-diegetic music—all of these add a sonic dimension to the uncanny *sfumato* of over- and under-signification that determines Lynch's cinematic style.

Trans-diegetic Music: "There's Always Music in the Air"

Besides challenging cinematic rules regarding musical signification, Lynch's soundtracks also contribute to the overlap of realities in his films. The alienating effect of many scenes is achieved by a music-induced conflation and blurring of representational and experiential levels.

This musical boundary blurring becomes most explicitly evident in scenes that have to do with dreams. Like Roy Orbison's "In Dreams" as sung by Ben in *Blue Velvet*, diegetic music in Lynch's films often refers to dreams. But much of the diegetic singing—like "In Heaven" as performed by the Lady in the Radiator in *Eraserhead*—*happens* in dreams. These links between music and dreams are indicative of the reality-altering qualities that they share in Lynch's films: having a dream and listening to music, each in their own way, evoke a highly immersive alternate reality.

In other dream scenes music is more literally presented as a different view on reality. During Cooper's dream in *Twin Peaks*, the Man from Another Place announces that "where we are from the birds sing a pretty song and there's always music in the air." Suddenly music emerges, literally in the air, and the Man starts dancing. When Cooper wakes up, the quiet synthesizer chords of the Laura Palmer theme are heard, but as he smiles sardonically and snaps his fingers the dream's dance tune returns. If this is diegetic music, where does it come from? If this schizophonic music is extra-diegetic, how can the Man dance to it? When, and how, does Cooper hear this music? The scene destabilizes the notion that diegetic and extra-diegetic levels can be separated at all, and it replaces the conventional dichotomy with the idea that the only reality at hand involves music that is somehow "in the air."

An even more disturbing example can be found in the soundtrack to *Eraserhead*, a film in which reality and nightmare, desire and fear, are indistinguishable. The film's extra-diegetic score consists of white noise that slowly moves from buzzing to hissing to whirring and back. The noise is continuously present, and is ruthlessly negligent of the difference between dream and reality—perhaps it exists only in Henry's head. The constant noise is extremely unnerving, not least because its volume is so high it almost makes deafness desirable. Are dreams that *loud*? Is reality that noisy? Why can't these be sonically distinguished?

A similar musical confusion of diegetic levels occurs in Lynch's hallucination scenes. In these scenes all diegetic sound is faded out and replaced with foregrounded extra-diegetic music—often recognizable pre-existing music with strong connotations—that provides a musical comment on the events on screen. If the hallucination is a lovely vision the visual footage is played in slowmotion, accompanied by lingering synthesizers and an airy female voice. The blissful confusion after Nikki's shooting of the Phantom in *Inland Empire*, for instance, is overlaid with Lynch's ethereal "Polish Poem" (containing the telling lyrics "on the other side I see") performed by Chrysta Bell. In more unpleasant hallucinations, such as Fred/Pete's transformation in *Lost Highway*, the underscore is quite different. As alienating and gruesome shots follow one another in rapid editing, white noise and industrial sounds accumulate over a low bass drone and build up in a crescendo. When pre-existing music is used for such nightmarish hallucinations, it is often up-tempo industrial music with aggressive connotations, like the music of Nine Inch Nails and Rammstein music in *Lost Highway*. Who hears these sounds? Fred, Pete, the movie spectator? All of these, or no one? Is it all real?

Cinematic sound designed in this way collapses traditional diegetic classifications. Claudia Gorbman has argued that such "meta-diegetic" film music is neither diegetic nor extra-diegetic but, rather, functions as the expression of the subjective experience of film characters.[32] Lynchian sound design deliberately blurs the distinction between diegetic, extra-diegetic, and meta-diegetic music. Extra-diegetic music or white noise often suddenly appears to be diegetic when a shot of a jukebox, radiator, or lamp explains the source of the sound, but when this alleged source suddenly gets turned off, or the film proceeds to another scene, the sound is still there, and the viewer is left wondering whether it was extra-diegetic after all.

The dream and hallucination scenes present similar but more complex mashups of diegetic layers. Musical and visual elements are mixed into an estranging audiovisual whirlpool that erases the distance between various levels of diegesis. Boundaries between reality and imagination are crossed at high speed, borders between extra-diegetic distance and diegetic intimacy are rendered irrelevant note by note. In some cases the difference between extra-diegetic and meta-diegetic music becomes virtually indistinguishable. The music for Fred's hallucinations in *Lost Highway*, for example, seems to be meta-diegetic and extra-diegetic at the same time; while reflecting Fred's inner rumblings, it also sutures the cuts to other scenes, and this suggests that all the music in the film could be meta-diegetic.

The folding into each other of diegetic, extra-diegetic, and meta-diegetic film-music levels in Lynch's films can be read as another sonic reflection on the inside/outside trope. It articulates the movements between interior and exterior spaces even more powerfully than do the cinematic visuals. In addition to dream or hallucination scenes, the audiovisual inside/outside trope plays out in sex scenes, in which a similar dialectic between unconscious and external surroundings is explored; an example is Alice's and Pete's lovemaking in *Lost Highway*, which is overlaid with This Mortal Coil's "To the Siren." The same meta-diegetic technique occurs in more metaphysical reflections on inside and outside, such as the Black Lodge sequence in Episode 29 of *Twin Peaks*, which questions the inner and outer limits of Being itself. These and countless similar scenes show a comparable cinematic formula of fast edits or slowmotion, stroboscopic light and starkly contrasting colors (often red and blue). In all these cases extra-diegetic music is played at such a high volume that it mutes all diegetic sound and becomes a direct communication of the on-screen overflowing of the unconscious.[33] In the audiovisual design of these scenes, the narratological and psychological complexity of Lynch's dreamlike topology culminates.

The musical blurring of perceptual levels in Lynch films clearly does not stop at extra-diegesis. Robynn Stilwell redefines meta-diegetic music as "musical 'direct address,' threatening to break the fourth wall that is the screen."[34] The transgression it causes may be embedded in a movie plot (one that features, say, dreams or hallucinations), but it spills over its boundaries into the extra-diegetic space of the spectator. The "direct address" of meta-diegetic music causes a direct involvement of cinema audiences in fictional space, which Stilwell likens to "walking through Alice's mirror."[35] In the case of David Lynch, this metaphor is doubly appropriate: not only is his work full of references to *Alice in Wonderland/Through the Looking Glass*, but his unconventional and challenging use of audiovisual media enables viewers' involvement in the movies' events. In this sense it is not surprising that the leitmotifs in Lynch's films are not tied to single characters or situations; they are designed to haunt diegetic, meta-diegetic, and extra-diegetic spaces alike, thereby loosening the boundaries between them. His soundtracks traverse the boundaries between these levels of narration, perception, and experience, and they can most accurately be described as *trans-diegetic*.

It is because of music's potential to facilitate the boundary-crossings addressed in Lynch's work that sound design is key to his cinematic expression. Music is neither simply representational nor purely performative; because it expresses as well as effects emotions, memories, and connotations, it is both a medium and a message. Music undermines the Lacanian knot of Symbolic, Imaginary, and Real; defying signification and yet producing it, and generating desire with which it has no originary connection, it leaves the Real not impossible but irrelevant. Music moves from outside to inside and back, affecting listeners' subjectivity as well as their relation to their surroundings. Like dreams, music destabilizes linear temporality; immersion in listening can dilate, compress, or even eliminate the experience of time. For this reason Michel Chion notes that music can move cinema audiences between times and spaces, working as what he calls a "spatiotemporal turntable."[36] Music is also an ideal vehicle for the uncanny, because its irrepressible evoking of affect and memory allows the past to haunt the present. Kevin Donnelly has argued that musical connotations in movie soundtracks have a ghostly dimension, serving as a "repository of reminders, half-memories and outbursts of emotion and the illogical … [,] these 'ghosts' and 'memories' that can haunt a film."[37]

Melodies and motifs unexpectedly turn up, posit their commentary on the on-screen events, and then vanish into the air just as suddenly as they appeared.

In this light, it is no wonder that Lynch describes music as a "drug" or a "door"; music can provide a passageway beyond mediation, signification, reality, time, and space, and this is exactly what his trans-diegetic use of film music effects. Roaming all the layers of diegesis and extra-diegesis, Lynchian soundtracks take film characters and viewers alike into the twilight zone that lies "*inside* a dream." Or, as Simon Frith has put it, "we are only where the music takes us."[38]

Dream Timbre

Sonic *sfumato*, schizophonic, trans-diegetic—the three main characteristics of Lynch's sonic style are epitomized in his approach to timbre. Timbre is the one musical parameter that cannot be caught in words or even in musical scores. It is the most dreamlike of all musical qualities; the moment you try to describe it, it fades away. It refuses description, allowing only the vague approach of adjectives: dark, light, raw, angelic. Interestingly, it is precisely the indescribable "grain of the voice"[39] (whether this voice is human or instrumental) that expresses the themes in Lynch's work most poignantly.

Since it lacks rhythm, melody, and harmonic progression, timbre is the only actual quality of the white noise that is Lynch's foremost sonic trademark. His soundtracks are conceived as thick textures in which acoustic sounds are mixed into the background and made fuzzy by an overlay of white noise. The timbre of this white noise can best be described by metaphors of air blowing through metal pipes, or the whirring of electrical cables, or the sound of wind in trees. It travels through all the diegetic, extra-diegetic, and meta-diegetic timespaces of his films. It is heard in room tone, all through *Eraserhead*, under the fan in *Twin Peaks*, at the trailer park in *Fire Walk with Me* (1992), in Fred Madison's flat in *Lost Highway*, in the taxi to Club Silencio in *Mulholland Drive*, in the rooms behind the door marked "Axxon N" in *Inland Empire*. The same sound accompanies the title menu of most of Lynch DVDs, and it is used on Lynch's website. The sound is sometimes gentle and sometimes aggressive, but it is always foreboding in its indeterminacy.

The white noise finds its vocal counterpart in ethereal females singing in extremely slow tempos, such as Julee Cruise in *Twin Peaks* and Chrysta Bell in *Inland Empire*. The same vocal preferences are notable in spoken voices: the characters played by Patricia Arquette (*Lost Highway*), Laura Dern (*Blue Velvet, Wild at Heart, Inland Empire*), and Kimmy Robertson (*Twin Peaks*) share low-volume, high-pitched voices with a lot of false air and little breath support. The synthesizer timbre of which Lynch and Badalamenti are so fond has similar qualities, forming an instrumental counterpoint to the white noise and female voices; the fact that Badalamenti slows down his tracks after recording them doubtlessly adds to their effect. The male vocal timbres in Lynch's films are more varied, although they show a slight preference for grimy timbres, slurred articulation, and unusual intonation. Jack Nance's voice (*Eraserhead, Blue Velvet, Twin Peaks, Wild at Heart, Lost Highway*) is a noteworthy example of this characteristic and memorable timbre, which incidentally sounds much like the timbre of Lynch's own voice.

There is a curious logic to the fact that in David Lynch's oeuvre the indescribable musical parameter of timbre speaks the unspeakable. When discussing the way sound and image in his films come together to create something new, Lynch hints at the abstract quality of his work that this timbre expresses:

> The thing that I'm after is when the whole becomes greater than the sum of the parts. It's so beautifully abstract. The great thing is that it can't be picked to death and talked about to death, because it's so fantastically complicated.[40]

David Lynch's sonic style is as clearly identifiable as it is "fantastically complicated." Obsessively dismantling signification, schizophonically challenging origin, and trans-diegetically erasing the limits of perception, it discloses the Lynchian uncanny of uncertain realities, truths, and selves. Timbre—the most important constituent factor of Lynch's sonic style—serves as the vocalization of this unfathomable possibility.

Notes

1 David Toop, *Sinister Resonance: The Mediumship of the Listener* (New York and London: Continuum, 2010), 115.
2 Michel Chion, *David Lynch* (London: British Film Institute, 2006), 42.
3 Zoran Samardzija, "DavidLynch.com: Auteurship in the Age of the Internet and Digital Cinema," *Scope: An Online Journal for Film & TV Studies* 16 (2010), available at: www.scope.nottingham.ac.uk/article.php?issue=16&id=1171.
4 Freddy Ruppert, "The Spirit of Former Ghosts," *Subbacultcha! Unruly Music Magazine* (February 2011), 23.
5 Chris Rodley, *Lynch on Lynch* (London: Faber & Faber, 1997), 133.
6 Andy Klein, "Like a Drug ...," *The Hollywood Reporter. Film & TV Music Special Issue* (1990), available at: www.thecityofabsurdity.com/intmusic.html.
7 Script line spoken by FBI agent Jeffries (played by David Bowie) in *Twin Peaks: Fire Walk with Me.*
8 Cf. Isabella van Elferen, "Haunted by a Melody: Ghosts, Transgression, and Music in *Twin Peaks*," in *Popular Ghosts: The Haunted Spaces of Everyday Culture*, ed. María del Pilar Blanco and Esther Peeren (New York and London: Continuum, 2010), 282–95.
9 In *Mulholland Drive* Hollywood is similarly referenced as a place that is able to blur the limits of reality: "I just came here from Deep River, Ontario, and now I'm in this dream place!"
10 Bernd Herzogenrath, "On the *Lost Highway*: Lynch and Lacan, Cinema and Cultural Pathology," *Other Voices: The (e)Journal of Cultural Criticism* 1, no. 3

(1999), available at: www.othervoices.org/1.3/bh/highway.html; and Todd McGowan, *The Impossible David Lynch* (New York: Columbia University Press, 2007).

11 Eric G. Wilson, *The Strange World of David Lynch: Transcendental Irony from Eraserhead to Mulholland Dr.* (New York and London: Continuum, 2007), viii.

12 Rodley, *Lynch on Lynch*, 15.

13 Kelly Bulkeley, "Dreaming and the Cinema of David Lynch," *Dreaming* 13, no. 1 (2003): 56.

14 Rodley, *Lynch on Lynch*, 25.

15 Ibid., 169. Cf. Chion, *David Lynch*, 169–70.

16 Sigmund Freud, "The Uncanny" (1919), in *Sigmund Freud: The Uncanny*, trans. David McLintock with an introduction by Hugh Haughton (New York: Penguin, 2003).

17 Ibid., 142.

18 Herzogenrath, "On the *Lost Highway*: Lynch and Lacan, Cinema and Cultural Pathology."

19 Helen Wheatly, *Gothic Television* (Manchester: Manchester University Press, 2006), 162–71, 180.

20 Wilson, *The Strange World of David Lynch*, 160.

21 Script line spoken by Club Silencio host Bondar (played by Richard Green) in *Mulholland Drive*.

22 Cf. Kevin J. Donnelly, *The Spectre of Sound: Music in Film and Television* (London: British Film Institute, 2005), 25; Rodley, *Lynch on Lynch*, 133.

23 *Dozen* (2007); *Good Wood* (2008); *I Can See Sound* (2010); "Good Day Today/I Know" (2011). Lynch appeared as guest singer on Danger Mouse and Sparklehorse's *Dark Night of the Soul* (2010).

24 Quoted in Chion, *David Lynch*, 159.

25 Philip Halsall, *50 Percent Sound*, Chapter 1. The British Film Resource, 2002, available at: www.britishfilm.org.uk/lynch/Schap1.html.

26 Rodley, *Lynch on Lynch*, 72–73.

27 Ibid., 72.

28 Emphasis added. A Lacanian reading of Club Silencio is given in Robert Miklitsch, "Real Fantasies: Connie Stevens, *Silencio*, and Other Sonic Phenomena in *Mulholland Drive*" in Jay Beck and Tony Grajeda, *Lowering the Boom: Critical Studies in Film Sound* (Urbana and Chicago: University of Illinois Press, 2008), 233–47.

29 R. Murray Schafer, *The Soundscape: Our Sonic Environment and the Tuning of the World* (Rochester: Destiny, 1994), 90–1.

30 Cf. Kathryn Kalinak, "'Disturbing the Guests with This Racket': Music and Twin Peaks," in *Full of Secrets: Critical Approaches to* Twin Peaks, ed. David Lavery (Detroit: Wayne State University Press, 1995), 82–92; Ron Rodman, *Tuning in: American Narrative Television Music* (Oxford: Oxford University Press, 2010), 280–7.

31 For instance, by *Guardian* interviewer Mark Kermode in the 2007 *Guardian* interview with David Lynch at the British Film Institute, available at: www. guardian.co.uk/film/2007/feb/08/davidlynch.

32 Claudia Gorbman, *Unheard Melodies: Narrative Film Music* (Bloomington and Indianapolis: Indiana University Press, 1987), 22–6, 144–50.

33 Cf. Kevin Donnelly's reading of the lovemaking scene in *Lost Highway* in *The Spectre of Sound*, 24–30.

34 Robynn J. Stilwell, "The Fantastical Gap between Diegetic and Nondiegetic," in *Beyond the Soundtrack: Representing Music in Cinema*, ed. Daniel Goldmark, Lawrence Kramer, and Richard Leppert (Berkeley: University of California Press, 2007), 197.

35 Stilwell, "The Fantastical Gap," 186.
36 Michel Chion, *Audio-Vision: Sound on Screen* (New York: Columbia University Press, 1994), 81.
37 Donnelly, *The Spectre of Sound*, 21.
38 Simon Frith, "Music and Identity," in *Questions of Cultural Identity*, ed. Stuart Hall and Paul du Gay (Los Angeles and London: Sage, 1996), 125.
39 The phrase is the title of Roland Barthes's famous essay "The Grain of the Voice," in *Image Music Text: Essays Selected and Translated by Stephen Heath* (London: Fontana Press, 1977), 179–89.
40 Andy Klein, "Like a Drug …"

Contributors

Per F. Broman is an associate professor of music theory and Associate Dean at Bowling Green State University. He was co-editor of *What Kind of Theory Is Music Theory?* (2008) and has just finished a biography of composer Sven-David Sandström (2012).

Lisa Coulthard is an associate professor of film studies at the University of British Columbia in Vancouver, Canada. She has published widely on contemporary cinema and is currently completing a book on music and sound in the films of Quentin Tarantino.

Elizabeth Fairweather is a Ph.D. candidate and lecturer in the Department of Music at the University of Huddersfield in the UK. Her research focuses primarily on music in science-fiction and fantasy films, especially the work of Jerry Goldsmith.

Joseph G. Kickasola is an associate professor of film and digital media at Baylor University and Director of the Baylor Communication in New York program. He is the author of *The Films of Krzysztof Kieślowski: The Liminal Image* (2004).

Danijela Kulezic-Wilson teaches film music and comparative arts at University College Cork, Ireland. Her research interests include approaches to film that emphasize film's inherent musicality, the musical use of silence in film, and the musicality of sound design.

Michael Lee is a professor of musicology at the University of Oklahoma and editor of the journal *Horror Studies*. His current research focuses on the music of the RKO Studios.

Matthew McDonald is an assistant professor of music at Northeastern University in Boston, where he teaches courses in music theory, music history, and film music. His book on the music of Charles Ives will be published by Indiana University Press.

Kate McQuiston is an assistant professor of musicology at the University of Hawai'i at Mānoa. Her article "'An Effort to Decide': More Research into Kubrick's Music Choices for *2001: A Space Odyssey*" appeared recently in the *Journal of Film Music*.

Nathan Platte is an assistant professor of musicology at the University of Iowa. He has contributed articles on film music to *19th-Century Music* and *The Journal of Musicology*, and he is co-author of *Franz Waxman's* Rebecca: *A Film Score Guide*.

Ian Sapiro is a postdoctoral research assistant in the School of Music at the University of Leeds, working principally in film music and orchestration. He is currently writing a volume for Scarecrow Press on Ilan Eshkeri's score for *Stardust*.

Isabella van Elferen is an assistant professor of music and media at Utrecht University. She has published widely on baroque music, musical subcultures, and music in film, television, and videogames. She specializes in Gothic genres, and her new book *Gothic Music: The Sounds of the Uncanny* will appear in 2012.

James Wierzbicki is a senior lecturer in musicology at the University of Sydney who deals with film music, electronic music, and questions of modernism and the postmodern. He is the author of *Film Music: A History* (2009) and co-editor of the *Routledge Film Music Sourcebook* (2011).

Ben Winters is a lecturer in music at The Open University in the UK. He is the author of *Erich Wolfgang Korngold's* The Adventures of Robin Hood: *A Film Score Guide* (2007), and he also has research interests in Viennese modernism and film music theory.

Bibliography

Abbate, Carolyn. "Music—Drastic or Gnostic?" *Critical Inquiry* 30, no. 2 (Spring 2004): 505–36.

Adorno, Theodor, and Hanns Eisler. *Composing for the Films*. London: Continuum, 1947; republished 2005.

Altman, Rick, with McGraw Jones and Sonia Tatroe. "Inventing the Cinema Soundtrack: Hollywood's Multiplane Sound System." In *Music and Cinema*, 339–59. Edited by James Buhler, Caryl Flinn, and David Neumeyer. Hanover and London: Wesleyan University Press, 2000.

Arnheim, Rudolf. *Film as Art*. Berkeley: University of California Press, 1957.

Balázs, Bela. *Theory of the Film: Character and Growth of a New Art*. New York: Dover, 1970.

Bansak, Edmund G. *Fearing the Dark: The Val Lewton Career*. Jefferson: McFarland Publishers, 1995.

Barnes, Randall. "Collaboration and Integration: A Method of Advancing Film Sound Based on The Coen Brothers' Use of Sound and Their Mode of Production." Ph.D. dissertation. Bournemouth University, 2005.

Barthes, Roland. "The Grain of the Voice." In *Image Music Text: Essays Selected and Translated by Stephen Heath*, 179–89. London: Fontana Press, 1977.

Bazin, André. *What Is Cinema?* Translated by Hugh Gray. Berkeley: University of California Press, 1967.

Beck, Jay, and Tony Grajeda, eds. *Lowering the Boom: Critical Studies in Film Sound*. Urbana: University of Illinois Press, 2008.

Behlmer, Rudy, and Roger Ebert, eds. *Memo from David O. Selznick: The Creation of "Gone with the Wind" and Other Motion Picture Classics, As Revealed in the Producer's Private Letters, Telegrams, Memorandums and Autobiographical Remarks*. New York: Modern Library, 1972.

Bellour, Raymond. "The Unattainable Text." *Screen* 16, no. 3 (Autumn 1975): 19–27.

Belton, John. "Technology and Aesthetics of Film Sound." In *Film Sound: Theory and Practice*, 63–72. Edited by Elisabeth Weis and John Belton. New York: Columbia University Press, 1985.

Benjamin, Arthur. "Film Music." *The Musical Times* 78, no. 1133 (July 1937): 595–7.

Bergman, Ingmar. *Laterna Magica*. Stockholm: Norstedt, 1987.

Bergman, Ingmar. *Bilder*. Stockholm: Norstedt, 1990.

Bernstein, Matthew. "The Producer as Auteur." In *Auteurs and Authorship: A Film Reader*, 180–9. Edited by Barry Grant. Malden: Blackwell Publishing, 2008.

Bird, Robert. *Andrei Tarkovsky: Elements of Cinema*. London: Reaktion Books, 2008.

Bodeen, DeWitt. "Val Lewton Proved that Even Low-Budgeted Films Can Have Artistic Integrity." *Films in Review* (Fall 1963): 210–25.

Bordwell, David. *The Way Hollywood Tells It*. Berkeley, Los Angeles, and London: University of California Press, 2006.

Bordwell, David, Janet Staiger, and Kristin Thompson. *The Classical Hollywood Cinema: Film Style and Production to 1960*. London: Routledge & Kegan Paul, 1985.

Boschi, Elena. "'Please, Give Me Second Grace': A Study of Five Songs in Wes Anderson's *The Royal Tenenbaums*." In *CineMusic? Constructing the Film Score*, 97–110. Edited by David Cooper, Christopher Fox, and Ian Sapiro. Newcastle upon Tyne: Cambridge Scholars Publishing, 2008.

Bowman, Laura, and LeRoy Antoine. *The Voice of Haiti*. New York City: Clarence Williams Music, 1938.

Brooke, Michael. "The Weight of the World." *Sight and Sound* 19, no. 1 (2009): 54–5.

Brophy, Philip. "Carter Burwell in Conversation: Music for the Films of Joel and Ethan Coen." In *The Coen Brothers' Fargo*, 128–36. Edited by William G. Luhr. Cambridge: Cambridge University Press, 2004.

Brown, Royal S. "Herrmann, Hitchcock, and the Music of the Irrational." *Cinema Journal* 21, no. 2 (Spring 1982): 14–49.

Brown, Royal S. *Overtones and Undertones: Reading Film Music*. Berkeley: University of California Press, 1994.

Brownlow, Kevin. *The Parade's Gone By*. New York: Alfred A. Knopf, 1968.

Bulkeley, Kelly. "Dreaming and the Cinema of David Lynch." *Dreaming* 13, no. 1 (2003): 49–60.

Burnand, David, and Miguel Mera. "Fast and Cheap? The Film Music of John Carpenter." In *The Cinema of John Carpenter: The Technique of Terror*, 49–65. Edited by Ian Conrich and David Woods. London: Wallflower Press, 2005.

Burns, Ellen. "Ingmar Bergman's Projected Self: From W.A. Mozart's *Die Zauberflöte* to *Vargtimmen*." *Analecta Husserliana* 94 (2007): 459–68.

Burwell, Carter. "Composing for the Coen Brothers." In *Soundscape: The School of Sound Lectures 1998–2001*, 195–208. Edited by Larry Sider, Diane Freeman, and Jerry Sider. London and New York: Wallflower Press, 2003.

Burwell, Carter. "Carter's Notes." Available at: www.carterburwell.com/projects/A_Serious_Man.html.

Caballero, Carlo. "Silence, Echo: A Response to 'What the Sorcerer Said.'" *19th-Century Music* 28, no. 2 (Fall 2004): 160–82.

Cage, John. *Silence: Lectures and Writings by John Cage*. Middletown: Wesleyan University Press, 1961.

Calhoun, Dave. "The Coen Brothers Discuss 'A Serious Man'." Available at: www.timeout.com/film/features/show-feature/9032/The_Coen_brothers_discuss-A_Serious_Man-.html.

Chatwin, Bruce. *The Songlines*. London: Jonathan Cape Ltd., 1987.

Chion, Michel. *Audio-Vision: Sound on Screen*. Edited and translated by Claudia Gorbman. New York: Columbia University Press, 1994.

Chion, Michel. *Kubrick's Cinema Odyssey*. London: British Film Institute, 2001.

Chion, Michel. *David Lynch*. London: British Film Institute, 2006.

Chion, Michel. *Film, A Sound Art*. Translated by Claudia Gorbman. New York: Columbia University Press, 2009.

Chugunova, Maria. Interview with Andrey Tarkovsky, published as an appendix in Andrey Tarkovsky, *Time Within Time: The Diaries 1970–1986*, 356–58. Translated by Kitty Hunter-Blair. Calcutta: Faber, 1991.

Ciment, Michel. "Interview with Peter Greenaway: *Zed and Two Noughts (Z.O.O)*," In *Peter Greenaway Interviews*, 28–41. Edited by Vernon Gras and Marguerite Gras. Jackson: University Press of Mississippi, 2000.

Citron, Marcia J. *When Opera Meets Film*. Cambridge: Cambridge University Press, 2010.

Clair, René. "The Art of Sound." Translated by Vera Traill. In *Film Sound: Theory and Practice*, 92–5. Edited by Elisabeth Weis and John Belton. New York: Columbia University Press, 1985.

Code, David. "Rehearing *The Shining*: Musical Undercurrents in the Overlook Hotel." In *Music in the Horror Film: Listening to Fear*, 133–51. Edited by Neil Lerner. New York and London: Routledge, 2010.

Cook, Pam. "Authorship and Cinema." In *The Cinema Book*, 114–206. Edited by Pam Cook and Mieke Bernink. London: British Film Institute, 2007.

Cooper, David, and Ian Sapiro. "A Source-Studies Approach to Michael Nyman's Score for *The Draughtsman's Contract*." *Journal of Film Music* 3, no. 2 (2011): 137–51.

Cooper, David, Christopher Fox, and Ian Sapiro, eds. "Keynote Interview with Michael Nyman." In *CineMusic? Constructing the Film Score*, 165–79. Edited by David Cooper, Christopher Fox, and Ian Sapiro. Newcastle upon Tyne: Cambridge Scholars Publishing, 2008.

Cormack, Mike. "The Pleasures of Ambiguity: Using Classical Music in Film." In *Changing Tunes: The Use of Pre-existing Music in Film*, 19–30. Edited by Phil Powrie and Robynn J. Stilwell. Aldershot: Ashgate, 2006.

Counts, Kyle B. "The Making of Alfred Hitchcock's *The Birds*: The Complete Story behind the Precursor of Modern Horror Films." *Cinefantastique* 12, no. 2 (Fall 1980): 15–35.

Coursodon, Jean-Pierre. "A Hat Blown By the Wind." In *The Coen Brothers: Interviews*, 41–5. Edited by William Rodney Allen. Jackson: University Press of Mississippi, 2006.

Deleuze, Gilles. *Cinema 2: The Time-Image*. Minneapolis: University of Minnesota Press, 1989.

DeMary, Thomas. "The Mystery of Herrmann's Music for Selznick's *Portrait of Jennie*." nos. 2–3 *Journal of Film Music* 1, (2003): 153–82.

Denby, David. "The Real Rhett Butler." *The New Yorker* 85, no. 15 (25 May 2009): 72–8.

de Nora, Tia. *Music in Everyday Life*. Cambridge: Cambridge University Press, 2000.

d'Escriván, Julio. "Sound Art (?) on/in Film." *Organised Sound* 14, no. 1 (2009): 65–73.

Donnelly, Kevin J. "Hitchcock's Music Lesson." *Film International* 122, no. 4 (2002): 1–7.

Donnelly, Kevin J. *The Spectre of Sound: Music in Film and Television*. London: British Film Institute, 2005.

Dorter, Kenneth. "Conceptual Truth and Aesthetic Truth." *Journal of Aesthetics and Art Criticism* 48, no. 1 (Winter 1990): 37–51.

Duncan, Paul, and Bengt Wanselius, eds. *The Ingmar Bergman Archives*. Hong Kong and Los Angeles: Taschen, 2008.

Dyer, Richard. *Stars*. London: British Film Institute, 1998.

Dyer, Richard. "Introduction to Film Studies." In *The Oxford Guide to Film Studies*, 3–10. Edited by John Hill and Pamela Church Gibson. Oxford: Oxford University Press, 1998.

Egorova, Tatiana. *Soviet Film Music: An Historical Survey*. New York and London: Routledge, 1997.

Eisenstein, Sergei. *Film Form: Essays in Film Theory*. San Diego: Harcourt Brace and Co., 1949.

Eisenstein, Sergei, Vsevolod Pudovkin, and Grigori Alexandrov. "A Statement." In *Film Sound: Theory and Practice*, 83–5. Edited by Elisabeth Weis and John Belton. New York: Columbia University Press, 1985.

Elliott, Bridget, and Anthony Purdy. *Peter Greenaway: Architecture and Allegory*. Chichester: Academy Editions, 1997.

Falsetto, Mario, ed. *Perspectives on Stanley Kubrick*. New York: Macmillan, 1996 (orig. 1970).

Fink, Nathan. "The Sound of Suspense: An Analysis of Music in Alfred Hitchcock's Films." Paper presented at 9th International Conference on Music Perception and Cognition, August 22–6, 2006. Barcelona: International Society for Music Perception and Cognition, 2006: 193–8.

Franklin, Peter. "Movies as Opera (Behind the Great Divide)." In *A Night in at the Opera: Media Representations of Opera*, 77–110. Edited by Jeremy Tambling. London: John Libbey & Co, 1994.

Freud, Sigmund. "The Uncanny." In *Sigmund Freud: The Uncanny*, 121–62. Translated by David McLintock with an introduction by Hugh Haughton. New York: Penguin, 2003.

Frith, Simon. "Music and Identity." In *Questions of Cultural Identity*, 108–27. Edited by Stuart Hall and Paul du Gay. Los Angeles and London: Sage, 1996.

Garner, Ken. "'Would You Like to Hear Some Music?': Music in-and-out-of-Control in the Films of Quentin Tarantino." In *Film Music: Critical Approaches*, 188–205. Edited by K.J. Donnelly. Edinburgh: Edinburgh University Press, 2001.

Gelmis, Joseph. "Interview with Stanley Kubrick." In *Perspectives on Stanley Kubrick*, 26–30. Edited by Mario Falsetto. New York: Macmillan, 1996 (orig. 1970).

Gerstner, David A., and Janet Staiger, eds. *Authorship and Film*. New York and London: Routledge, 2003.

Goldmark, Daniel. *Tunes for 'Toons: Music and the Hollywood Cartoon*. Berkeley, Los Angeles, and London: University of California Press, 2005.

Goldmark, Daniel, Lawrence Kramer, and Richard Leppert, eds. *Beyond the Soundtrack: Representing Music in Cinema*. Berkeley: University of California Press, 2007.

Gonzales, ed. "Gerrymandering: An Interview with Gus Van Sant." *Slant Magazine* (2003). Available at: www.slantmagazine.com/film/features/gusvansant.asp.

Gorbman, Claudia. *Unheard Melodies: Narrative Film Music*. Bloomington and Indianapolis: Indiana University Press, 1987.

Gorbman, Claudia. "Ears Wide Open: Kubrick's Music." In *Changing Tunes: The Use of Pre-Existing Music in Film*, 3–18. Edited by Phil Powrie and Robynn J. Stilwell. Aldershot: Ashgate, 2006.

Gorbman, Claudia. "Auteur Music." In *Beyond the Soundtrack: Representing Music in Cinema*, 149–62. Edited by Daniel Goldmark, Lawrence Kramer, and Richard Leppert. Berkeley: University of California Press, 2007.

Grant, Barry Keith, ed. *Auteurs and Authorship: A Film Reader*. Oxford: Wiley-Blackwell, 2008.

Gras, Vernon. "Dramatizing the Failure to Jump the Culture/Nature Gap: The Films of Peter Greenaway." *New Literary History* 26, no. 1 ("Narratives of Literature, the Arts, and Memory") (Winter 1999): 125–43.

Greenaway, Peter. *Fear of Drowning*. Paris: Editions Dis Voir, 1988.

Greenaway, Peter. *Prospero's Books: A Film of Shakespeare's* The Tempest. London: Chatto & Windus, 1991.

Greenaway, Peter. "Sound and Vision: An Open Discussion with Peter Greenaway." The European Graduate School (2002). Available at: www.egs.edu/faculty/peter-greenaway/articles/sound-and-vision/.

Grievson, Lee, and Haidee Wasson, eds. *Inventing Film Studies*. Durham, NC and London: Duke University Press, 2008.

Hacker, Jonathan, and David Price. *Take Ten: Contemporary British Film Directors*. Oxford: Clarendon Press, 1991.

Halsall, Philip. *50 Percent Sound*. The British Film Resource, 2002. Available at: www.britishfilm.org.uk/lynch/Schap1.html.

Harvey, Sylvia. "What is Cinema? The Sensuous, the Abstract and the Political." In *Cinema: The Beginnings and the Future*, 228–52. Edited by Christopher Williams. London: University of Westminster Press, 1996.

Hayward, Susan. *Cinema Studies: The Key Concepts*. London: Routledge, 2000.

Heimerdinger, Julia. "'I am compromised. I now fight against it.' Ligeti vs. Kubrick and the music for *2001: A Space Odyssey*." *Journal of Film Music* 3, no. 2 (2011): 127–43.

Herzogenrath, Bernd. "On the *Lost Highway*: Lynch and Lacan, Cinema and Cultural Pathology." *Other Voices: The (e)Journal of Cultural Criticism* 1, no. 3 (1999). Available at: www.othervoices.org/1.3/bh/highway.html.

Higham, Charles, and Joel Greenberg. *The Celluloid Muse: Hollywood Directors Speak*. London: Angus and Robertson, 1969.

Hitchcock, Alfred. "My Own Methods." *Sight and Sound* 6, no. 22 (Summer 1937).

Huron, David. *Sweet Anticipation: Music and the Psychology of Expectation*. Cambridge, MA: MIT Press, 2006.

Husserl, Edmund. *Ideas*. New York: Collier Books, 1962.

Inglis, Ian, ed. *Popular Music and Film*. London: Wallflower Press, 2003.

Insdorf, Annette. *Double Lives, Second Chances: The Cinema of Kieślowski*. New York: Hyperion, 1999.

Jaehne, Karen. "*The Draughtsman's Contract*: An Interview with Peter Greenaway." In *Peter Greenaway Interviews*, 21–7. Edited by Vernon Gras and Marguerite Gras. Jackson: University Press of Mississippi, 2000.

Jönsson, Sofia Lilly. "Ljudestetik i spelfilm: Om sju minuter i Bergmans *Fanny och Alexander*." Master's thesis. Department of Musicology and Theater, Stockholm University, 2011.

Jordan, Randolph. "The Work of Hildegard Westerkamp in the Films of Gus Van Sant: An Interview with the Soundscape Composer." *Offscreen* 11, nos. 8–9 (2007). Available at: www.offscreen.com/index.php/pages/essays/jordan_westerkamp/.

Kael, Pauline. "Circles and Squares." *Film Quarterly* 16, no. 3 (Spring 1963): 12–26.

Kalinak, Kathryn. *Settling the Score: Music and the Classical Hollywood Film.* Madison: University of Wisconsin Press, 1992.

Kalinak, Kathryn. "'Disturbing the Guests with This Racket': Music and Twin Peaks." In *Full of Secrets: Critical Approaches to* Twin Peaks, 82–92. Edited by David Lavery. Detroit: Wayne State University Press, 1995.

Kalinak, Kathryn. *How the West Was Sung: Music in the Westerns of John Ford.* Berkeley: University of California Press, 2007.

Kassabian, Anahid. *Hearing Film: Tracking Identifications in Contemporary Hollywood Film Music.* New York and London: Routledge, 2001.

Kickasola, Joseph G. *The Films of Krzysztof Kieślowski: The Liminal Image.* New York: Continuum, 2004.

Kieślowski, Krzysztof. *Kieślowski on Kieślowski.* Edited by Danusia Stok. London: Faber & Faber, 1995.

Kilb, Andreas. "I Am the Cook: A Conversation with Peter Greenaway." In *Peter Greenaway Interviews*, 60–5. Edited by Vernon Gras and Marguerite Gras. Jackson: University Press of Mississippi, 2000.

Klein, Andy. "Like a Drug … ." *The Hollywood Reporter. Film & TV Music Special Issue* (1990). Available at: www.thecityofabsurdity.com/intmusic.html.

Klinger, Gabe. "Interview with Leslie Shatz: Sound Auteur." *Fipresci* ("Undercurrent 1") (2006). Available at: www.fipresci.org/undercurrent/issue_0106/shatz_klinger.htm.

Knowlson, James. *Damned to Fame: The Life of Samuel Beckett.* New York: Simon & Schuster, 1997.

Koskinen, Maaret. *Ingmar Bergman's The Silence: Pictures in the Typewriter, Writings on the Screen.* Seattle: University of Washington Press, 2010.

Kramer, Jonathan D. *The Time of Music: New Meanings, New Temporalities, New Listening Strategies.* New York: Schirmer Books; London: Collier Macmillan Publisher, 1988.

Kubernik, Harvey. *Hollywood Shack Job: Rock Music in Film and on Your Screen.* Albuquerque: University of New Mexico Press, 2006.

Kulezic-Wilson, Danijela. "Sound Design Is the New Score." *Music, Sound and the Moving Image* 2, no. 2 (Autumn 2009): 127–31.

Laretei, Käbi. *Såsom i en översättning: teman med variationer.* Stockholm: Bonnier, 2004.

LoBrutto, Vincent. *Gus Van Sant: His Own Private Cinema.* Santa Barbara, Denver, and Oxford: Praeger, 2010.

London, Kurt. *Film Music: A Summary of the Characteristic Features of Its History, Aesthetics, Technique; and Possible Developments.* Translated by Eric S. Bensinger. London: Faber & Faber, 1936.

Long, Michael. *Beautiful Monsters: Imagining the Classic in Musical Media.* Berkeley: University of California Press, 2008.

Manvell, Roger, and John Huntley. *The Technique of Film Music.* London: Focal Press, 1975.

Marshall, Robert L. "Film as Musicology: *Amadeus*." *Musical Quarterly* 81, no. 2 (Summer 1997): 173–9.

Mazullo, Mark. "Remembering Pop: David Lynch and the Sound of the '60s." *American Music* 23, no. 4 (Winter 2005): 493–513.

McBride, Stephanie. "Film: G Is for Greenaway." *Circa* 62 (Autumn 1992): 52–7.

McGowan, Todd. *The Impossible David Lynch*. New York: Columbia University Press, 2007.

McQuiston, Kate. "Value, Violence, and Music Recognized: *A Clockwork Orange* as Musicology." In *Stanley Kubrick: Essays on His Films and Legacy*, 105–22. Edited by Gary D. Rhodes. London: McFarland and Company, 2008.

McQuiston, Kate. "'An effort to decide': More Research into Kubrick's Music Choices for *2001: An Space Odyssey*." *Journal of Film Music*, 3, no. 2 (2011) 145–54.

Merkley, Paul. "'Stanley Hates This But I Like It!': North vs. Kubrick on the Music for *2001: A Space Odyssey*." *Journal of Film Music* 2, no. 1 (Fall 2007): 1–34.

Middleton, Richard. "'Play It again Sam': Some Notes on the Productivity of Repetition in Popular Music." *Popular Music* 3 (1983): 235–70.

Miklitsch, Robert. "Real Fantasies: Connie Stevens, *Silencio*, and Other Sonic Phenomena in *Mulholland Drive*." In *Lowering the Boom: Critical Studies in Film Sound*, 233–47. Edited by Jay Beck and Tony Grajeda. Urbana and Chicago: University of Illinois Press, 2008.

Miller, John Matthew. "David O. Selznick and His *Portrait of Jennie*." Master's thesis. University of Texas, 1987.

Mitchell, Tony. "Tarkovsky in Italy." *Sight and Sound* 52, no. 1 (Winter 1982): 54–6.

Morton, Lawrence. "The Music of *Objective Burma!*" *Hollywood Quarterly* 1, no. 4 (July 1946): 378–95.

Mottram, James. *The Sundance Kids: How the Mavericks Took Back Hollywood*. New York: Faber & Faber, 2006.

Naremore, James. "Authorship." In *A Companion to Film Theory*, 9–24. Edited by Toby Miller and Robert Stam. Oxford: Wiley-Blackwell, 1999.

Naremore, James. *On Kubrick*. London: British Film Institute, 2007.

Nemerov, Alexander. *Icons of Grief: Val Lewton's Home Front Pictures*. Berkeley: University of California Press, 2005.

Newman, Kim. *Cat People*. London: British Film Institute, 1999.

Orgeron, Devin. "La Camera-Crayola: Authorship Comes of Age in the Cinema of Wes Anderson." *Cinema Journal* 46, no. 2 (Winter 2007): 40–65.

Pascoe, David. *Peter Greenaway: Museums and Moving Images*. London: Reaktion Books, 1997.

Patterson, David. "Music, Structure and Metaphor in Stanley Kubrick's '2001: A Space Odyssey.'" *American Music* 22, no. 3 (Autumn 2004): 444–74.

Paul, William. "What Does Dr. Judd Want? Transformation, Transference, and Divided Selves in *Cat People*." In *Horror Films and Psychoanalysis*, 159–75. Edited by Steven Jay Schneider. Cambridge: Cambridge University Press, 2004.

Polan, Dana. *Scenes of Instruction: The Beginnings of the U.S. Study of Film*. Berkeley: University of California Press, 2007.

Powrie, Phil. "Blonde Abjection: Spectatorship and the Abject Anal Space In-between." In *Pop Fiction: The Song in Cinema*, 100–20. Edited by Steve Lannin and Matthew Caley. Bristol: Intellect Books, 2005.

Powrie, Phil, and Robynn J. Stilwell, eds. *Changing Tunes: The Use of Pre-existing Music in Film*. Aldershot: Ashgate, 2006.

Prieto, Eric. *Listening In: Music, Mind, and the Modernist Narrative*. Lincoln and London: University of Nebraska Press, 2002.

Raykoff, Ivan. "Hollywood's Embattled Icon." In *Piano Roles: 300 Years of Life with the Piano*, 329–57. New Haven: Yale University Press, 2000.

Reichardt, Sarah. "Commodity vs. Artwork: Timelessness and Temporality in the Music for *Portrait of Jennie*." Paper presented at the The Hollywood Musical and Music in Hollywood conference, Boulder, Colorado, 2001.

Renaud, Charlotte. "La citation musicale dans les films d'Ingmar Bergman." Ph.D. dissertation. Université de La Sorbonne Paris III-Censier, 2007.

Roberts, John Storm. *The Latin Tinge: The Impact of Latin American Music on the United States*, second edition. New York and Oxford: Oxford University Press, 1999.

Rodgers, Marlene. "*Prospero's Books*—Word and Spectacle: An Interview with Peter Greenaway." *Film Quarterly* 45, no. 2 (Winter 1991–2): 11–19.

Rodley, Chris. *Lynch on Lynch*. London: Faber & Faber, 1997.

Rodman, Howard A., "Anatomy of a Wizard." In *Peter Greenaway Interviews*, 120–8. Edited by Vernon Gras and Marguerite Gras. Jackson: University Press of Mississippi, 2000.

Rodman, Ronald. "The Popular Song as Leitmotif in 1990s Film." In *Changing Tunes: The Use of Pre-existing Music in Film*, 119–36. Edited by Phil Powrie and Robynn J. Stilwell. Aldershot: Ashgate, 2006.

Rodman, Ronald. *Tuning in: American Narrative Television Music*. Oxford: Oxford University Press, 2010.

Rogers, Holly. "'Noises, Sounds and Sweet Airs': Singing the Film Space in *Prospero's Books*." In *CineMusic? Constructing the Film Score*, 141–64. Edited by David Cooper, Christopher Fox, and Ian Sapiro. Newcastle upon Tyne: Cambridge Scholars Publishing, 2008.

Rowell, Erica. *The Brothers Grim: The Films of Ethan and Joel Coen*. Lanham: Scarecrow Press, 2007.

Rózsa, Miklós. *A Double Life*. New York: Wynwood Press, 1982, 1989.

Ruppert, Freddy. "The Spirit of Former Ghosts." *Subbacultcha! Unruly Music Magazine* (February 2011).

Russell, Mark, and James Young, eds. *Film Music*. Boston: Focal Press, 2000.

Samardzija, Zoran. "DavidLynch.com: Auteurship in the Age of the Internet and Digital Cinema." *Scope: An Online Journal for Film & TV Studies* 16 (2010). Available at: www.scope.nottingham.ac.uk/article.php?issue=16&id=1171.

Samson, Jim. "Chopin Reception: Theory, History, Analysis." In *Chopin Studies 2*, 1–17. Edited by John Rink and Jim Samson. Cambridge: Cambridge University Press, 2006.

Sarkar, Bhaskar. "Threnody for Modernity." In *Tarkovsky*, 235–57. Edited by Nathan Dunne. London: Black Dog Publishing, 2008.

Sarris, Andrew. "Notes on the Auteur Theory in 1962." *Film Culture* 27 (Winter 1962–3): 1–18.

Sarris, Andrew. "The Auteur Theory and the Perils of Pauline." *Film Quarterly* 16, no. 4 (Summer 1963): 26–33.

Sarris, Andrew. *The American Cinema: Directors and Directions 1928–1968*. New York: E. P. Dutton, 1968.

Schaeffer, Pierre. "Acousmatics." In *Audio Culture: Readings in Modern Music*, 76–81. Edited by Christoph Cox and Daniel Warner. New York: Continuum, 2004.

Schafer, R. Murray. *The Soundscape: Our Sonic Environment and the Tuning of the World*. Rochester: Destiny, 1994.

Schrader, Paul. *Transcendental Style in Film: Ozu, Bresson, Dreyer*. Cambridge and New York: Da Capo Press, 1972.

Schwartz, Elliott, and Daniel Godfrey. *Music Since 1945: Issues, Materials, and Literature*. Belmont: Wadsworth, 1993.

Shklovsky, Viktor. "Art as Technique." In *Russian Formalist Criticism: Four Essays*, 3–24. Edited and translated by Lee T. Lemon and Marion J. Reis. Lincoln: University of Nebraska Press, 1965.

Shpinitskaya, Julia. "*Solaris* by A. Tarkovsky: Music-Visual Troping, Paradigmatism, Cognitive Stereoscopy." *Transcultural Music Review* 10 (December 2006). Available at: www.sibetrans.com/trans/index.htm.

Siegel, Joel E. *Val Lewton: The Reality of Terror*. New York: The Viking Press, 1973.

Sjöman, Vilgot. *L 136: dagbok med Ingmar Bergman*. Stockholm: Norstedt, 1963.

Slide, Anthony, ed. *Selected Film Criticism, 1941–1950*. Metuchen: Scarecrow Press, 1983.

Slobin, Mark, ed. "The Steiner Superculture." In *Global Soundtracks: Worlds of Film Music*, 3–35. Middletown: Wesleyan University Press, 2008.

Smith, Jeff. *The Sounds of Commerce: Marketing Popular Film Music*. New York: Columbia University Press.

Spring, Katherine. "Chance Encounters of the Musical Kind: Electronica and Audiovisual Synchronization in Three Films Directed by Tom Tykwer." *Music and the Moving Image* 3, no. 3 (Fall 2010). Available at: www.jstor.org/pss/10.5406/musimoviimag.3.3.0001.

Staiger, Janet. "Authorship Approaches." In *Authorship and Film*, 27–57. Edited by David A. Gestner and Janet Staiger. New York and London: Routledge, 2003.

Staples, Donald E. "The Auteur Theory Reexamined." *Cinema Journal* 6 (1966–7): 1–7.

Steene, Birgitta. *Ingmar Bergman: A Reference Guide*. Amsterdam: Amsterdam University Press, 2006.

Stilwell, Robynn J. "Hysterical Beethoven." *Beethoven Forum* 10, no. 2 (2003): 162–82.

Stilwell, Robynn J. "The Fantastical Gap between Diegetic and Nondiegetic." In *Beyond the Soundtrack: Representing Music in Cinema*, 184–202. Edited by Daniel Goldmark, Lawrence Kramer, and Richard Lepper. Berkeley: University of California Press, 2007.

Stothart, Herbert. "Film Music." In *Behind the Screen: How Films Are Made*, 139–44. Edited by Stephen Watts. London: Arthur Baker Ltd., 1938.

Strick, Philip. "Hour of the Wolf." *Sight and Sound* 37, no. 4 (Autumn 1968): 203–4.

Sullivan, Jack. *Hitchcock's Music*. New Haven: Yale University Press, 2006.

Tagg, Philip. "Analysing Popular Music: Theory, Method, and Practice." *Popular Music* 2 (1982): 37–67.

Tarkovsky, Andrey. *Sculpting in Time: Reflections on the Cinema*. Translated by Kitty Hunter-Blair. Austin: University of Texas Press, 1986.

Telotte, J.P. *Dreams of Darkness: Fantasy and the Films of Val Lewton*. Urbana: University of Illinois Press, 1985.

Thomson, David. *Showman: The Life of David O. Selznick*. New York: Alfred A. Knopf.

Tiomkin, Dimitri, and Prosper Buranelli. *Please Don't Hate Me*. Garden City: Doubleday & Company, Inc., 1959.

Toop, David. *Sinister Resonance: The Mediumship of the Listener*. New York and London: Continuum, 2010.

Totaro, Donato. "Nature as 'Comfort Zone' in the Films of Andrei Tarkovsky." *Offscreen* 14, no. 12 (December 2010). Available at: www.offscreen.com/index.php/pages/essays/nature_as_comfort_zone/.

Tribble, Evelyn. "Listening to Prospero's Books." In *Shakespeare Survey Volume 61: Shakespeare, Sound and Screen*, 161–9. Edited by Peter Holland. Cambridge: Cambridge University Press, 2008.

Truffaut, François. *Hitchcock*. New York: Simon & Schuster, 1984.

Truppin, Andrea. "And Then There Was Sound: The Films of Andrei Tarkovsky." In *Sound Theory, Sound Practice*, 234–48. Edited by Rick Altman. New York and London: Routledge, 1992.

Turner, George. "A Retrospective of the 'Original' Val Lewton's *Cat People*." *Cinefantastique* (May–June 1982): 22–7.

Van Elferen, Isabella. "Haunted by a Melody: Ghosts, Transgression, and Music in *Twin Peaks*." In *Popular Ghosts: The Haunted Spaces of Everyday Culture*, 282–95. Edited by María del Pilar Blanco and Esther Peeren. New York and London: Continuum, 2010.

Watts, Stephen. "On Music in Films." In *Hitchcock on Hitchcock: Selected Writings and Interviews*, 241–5. Edited by Sidney Gottlieb. Berkeley: University of California Press, 1995.

Weis, Elisabeth. *The Silent Scream: Alfred Hitchcock's Sound Track*. Rutherford: Farleigh Dickinson University Press, 1982.

Weis, Elisabeth, and John Belton, eds. *Film Sound: Theory and Practice*. New York: Columbia University Press, 1985.

Wexman, Virginia Wright, ed. *Film and Authorship*. New York: Rutgers University Press, 2002.

Wheatly, Helen. *Gothic Television*. Manchester: Manchester University Press, 2006.

Wierzbicki, James. "Sound as Music in the Films of Terrence Malick." In *Poetic Visions of America: The Cinema of Terrence Malick*, 110–22. Edited by Hannah Patterson. London: Wallflower Press, 2003.

Wierzbicki, James. "Grand Illusion: Arthur Benjamin's 'Storm Cloud' Music and *The Man Who Knew Too Much*." *Journal of Film Music* 1, nos. 2–3 (Fall–Winter 2004): 217–38.

Wierzbicki, James. "Shrieks, Flutters, and Vocal Curtains: Electronic Sound/Electronic Music in Hitchcock's *The Birds*." *Music and the Moving Image* 1, no. 2 (Summer 2008). Available at: http://mmi.press.uiuc,edu/1.2/wierbicki.html.

Wierzbicki, James. *Film Music: A History*. New York and London: Routledge, 2009.

Wilson, Eric G. *The Strange World of David Lynch: Transcendental Irony from* Eraserhead *to* Mulholland Dr. New York and London: Continuum, 2007.

Winters, Ben. "The Non-diegetic Fallacy: Film, Music, and Narrative Space." *Music & Letters* 91, no. 2 (May 2010): 224–44.

Woods, Alan. *Being Naked, Playing Dead.* Manchester: Manchester University Press, 1996.

Index